SHAKESPEARE
AND THE MYSTERY OF
GOD'S JUDGMENTS

Shakespeare
and the Mystery of
God's Judgments

ROBERT G. HUNTER

N/PD

THE UNIVERSITY OF GEORGIA PRESS
ATHENS

Library of Congress Catalog Card Number: 75–11449
International Standard Book Number: 0–8203–0388–7

The University of Georgia Press, Athens 30602

Set in 11 on 13 pt. Intertype Garamond type
Printed in the United States of America

Contents

Acknowledgments

I would like to thank Dartmouth College, Vanderbilt University, and the Kenan Foundation for the funds and free time that made writing this book possible. Those who have read and commented helpfully on what I have to say include Martin Meisel, Scott Colley, R. Chris Hassel, Peter Saccio, and my wife, Anne. I am grateful to them all, and especially to the first and the last. A very large debt is owed to Suzzanne Macksond Wooten, who typed a manuscript that even I sometimes could not read. Marty Marina typed the subsequent versions, Lance Lyday checked the references, and Barbara B. Reitt compiled the index. Larry Crist corrected my translations from medieval French and Paul Hardacre found a reference I had thought lost for good. Finally, the staff of the University of Georgia Press has been most helpful and efficient.

Introduction

THIS BOOK presents a hypothesis which it does not try to prove. It assumes that a necessary (though far from sufficient) cause for the ability of the Elizabethans to write great tragedy was the impact on their minds of some of the more striking ideas of the Protestant Reformation. Luther and Calvin believe that our wills are not free. They also believe that the majority of us will spend our eternities in hell. This combination of beliefs leads to a concept of the human condition and the divine nature that, to say the least, takes some thinking about, and such thinking by both playwright and audience helped, I suggest, to make tragedy a possible form in Shakespeare's time. The divine justice which punishes a man who has no freedom of choice must be called mysterious if it is not to be called monstrous and the spectacle of the destruction even of a Richard III or a Macbeth in the context of a Calvinist universe must evoke some pity along with a great deal of terror. The most pious Christian's "Thy will be done" sounds a bit grim under the circumstances, and all the more so the ordinary sinner's: "The words of heaven; on whom it will, it will, / On whom it will not (soe) yet still 'tis just" (*Measure for Measure* 1.3.7–8).

Claudio is reminding us of the ninth chapter of Saint Paul's Epistle to the Romans, a passage which, with its image of God as a creator and destroyer of the vessels of his wrath, is a primary source for what I shall call the mystery of God's judgments. But this allusion to Paul raises an obvious question about my hypothesis: if the mystery of God's judgments has been a part of Christian theology since its inception, why should it have contributed to the ability of Christian writers to create tragedy only after almost sixteen hundred years? Anything like a complete answer to that question is far beyond my powers but I shall attempt a partial one.

The theology of Luther and Calvin causes us to ask how God can be just if man is not free. The reformers, of course, saw themselves as the inheritors and restorers of true Augustinianism, but orthodox Catholic theology, as defined by Saint Augustine, avoids the Protestant version of the mystery by insisting that man is free. Augustine, however, in his fight against the Pelagian heresy, maintains that man must receive divine grace before he can make those choices that will lead to his salvation. Thus the mystery of God's judgments remains a mystery for the Catholic, though his formulation of it is rather different: how can man be said to be free and God consequently just if man requires God's grace in order to make a right choice? This question, though just as difficult to answer as the Protestant one, is somehow less urgent, more easily disregarded, and the didactic Christian dramatists of the Middle Ages disregard it. By analyzing two medieval miracle plays I hope to show what Shakespeare's tragic art is not, and how some part of the difference is the result of his regarding of the mystery from which his predecessors turned away.

My primary purpose in this study is not, however, to test a literary-historical hypothesis. I am interested in what happened to the drama as a result of Protestantism mainly because I think that four or five of Shakespeare's greatest plays were a part of what happened, and I hope that an analysis of them from this perspective will help in understanding them. But I should warn or reassure my reader at this point. What I have written is not, it seems to me, a study of Shakespeare's Christianity or of the Christianity of Shakespeare's art. What it has turned out to be is a study of Shakespeare's negative capability. The mysteries which Shakespeare confronts in these plays remain mysteries when the plays are over and are, if anything, more profoundly disquieting than they were before his imaginative considerations of them. The tragedies seem to me consistently to provide us with questions rather than answers and what they inspire in their beholders is, I think more likely to be doubt than faith.[1]

CHAPTER 1

Robert le Dyable

SOMETIME DURING 1375, the Goldsmith's guild of Paris had produced for it a play called *Robert le Dyable*. It was the thirty-third in a series of such plays—called *Miracles de Nostre Dame par personnages*—which *le puy des orfevres* sponsored at annual intervals throughout a good part of the fourteenth century.[1] Fortunately for our understanding of the medieval theater, forty of these plays were collected in a nicely illuminated manuscript which has survived to the present. These *miracles*—piously didactic in intention, satisfyingly theatrical in execution—are all examples of how the playwrights of the fourteenth century embodied dramatically a coherent, Christian view of the universe and man's place in it. *Robert le Dyable*, which turns an extremely popular legend into theater, does the embodying with even more theatrical flair than most of the others.

Robert le Dyable opens with a quarrel between the generations.[2] Robert's father, the duke of Normandy, wants his son to be "courtois et debonnaire" as a knight should be, protecting the good and persecuting the bad, but Robert will have none of it:

> Ne cuidez point que je me paine
> De bien faire: n'en ay talent.
>
> (Ll. 18–19)

(Don't get the idea that I'll do good: I don't feel like it.)

He goes off resolving to annoy monks and priests and rob them of their treasure. Left alone, the duke prays God to give his son the grace to repent, but Robert joins his low companions and they proceed to rob a rich peasant and to steal the treasure of an abbey. The barons complain to the duke, revealing that Robert has become a rapist as well as a thief ("il viole les nonnains.") The duke sends two of his servants to Robert with orders for him to return to his father at once, but he puts out the right eye of each messenger and sends them back to his father, who

3

proclaims Robert an outlaw and banishes him from the duchy. But Robert refuses to leave, withdraws to his fortress in the woods, and murders seven hermits. He then hears that his mother is visiting the nearby *Chateau d'Arques* and that his father will not be there, so he decides to pay the duchess a visit. When they hear that he is coming, the duchess and her servants scatter in all directions. This gives Robert pause:

> Chascun me fuit, chascun m' eslongne.
>
> . . . .
>
> Nis ma mére me fuit, de quoy
> J'ai dueil.   (Ll. 701–706)

(Everyone runs away from me, everyone leaves me. Even my mother runs away, which makes me sad.)

He stops his mother, tells her he does not understand why he is unable to refrain from doing evil and reveals his suspicion that she or his father may have been guilty of some unusually heinous sin at the time of his conception. The duchess admits that he is right. She and the duke had been married for many years, but despite their prayers and labors, they had been unable to conceive a child. One day, wanting to be alone, she took to her bed and there dwelt upon the injustice of her sterility. Finally, in her anger, she said a terrible thing:

> "Puis que Dieu mettre
> "Ne veult enfant dedans mon corps
> "Sy l'i mette le dyable."
>   (Ll. 734–736)

("Since God doesn't want to put a baby in my body, let the devil put it there.")

At this point her husband returned from the hunt and, noticing that his wife had been crying, he kissed and comforted her and they made love. Following his usual custom on these occasions, the good man prayed that his wife might conceive a child who would please and serve God. The duchess, however, repeated her appeal to the devil, and at that moment, Robert was conceived.

4

This knowledge of the special circumstances surrounding his origin has an intense effect upon Robert. He prays to God for grace and announces his determination to save his soul from the devil. He will reform his wicked life, and to demonstrate his sincerity, he returns to his fellow outlaws and reveals his intentions. They are incredulous ("Renart, je croy, devient hermittes") and when he sees that he will be unable to convert them, Robert kills the lot. Then he locks up the treasure he has stolen and turns the key over to one of the abbots he had robbed, instructing him to make restitution to Robert's victims and to inform his parents that he has gone to Rome to confess his sins to the pope. The duke has already expressed doubts as to the efficacy of such measures:

> Voir, s'il aloit de ci en Arle
> A coudes nuz et a genouz,
> N'aroit il pas amendé touz
> Ses meffaiz, non pas la moitié.
>
> (Ll. 816–819)

(Look, if he went from here to Arles on naked elbows and knees, he wouldn't have made up for his misdeeds, not by half.)

But Robert perseveres and the pope grants him an audience. When he has heard his story, the Holy Father advises him to seek out a particularly austere hermit—the pope's own confessor—and abide by his advice. This Robert does and having heard his confession, the hermit goes into his chapel to pray for the repentant sinner. While there he falls asleep and God, the Virgin Mary, Gabriel, Michael, and John, accompanied by two angels who sing a "rondel" in praise of the Virgin, visit the hermit and God tells him what Robert must do in penance for his crimes: he will disguise himself as an idiot, pretend to be unable to speak, and eat only such food as he is able to snatch from dogs.

Robert carries out his instructions to the letter. We next see him dressed in rags, grinning foolishly, and looking longingly at the basket of a cheese-seller. He is set upon by two "compaignons" who mock and kick him, blacken his face with charcoal, crown him with an old sock and tease him until he weeps. Luckily for his tormentors, the former terror of Normandy manages to control his temper and he soon arrives at the banquet hall of the emperor, who notices him and gives his servants instructions to feed the poor idiot. Robert refuses what he is offered however. Then the emperor tosses a bone to his favorite hound ("Louvet, Louvet, tien, Louvet, tien: /Runge cela"). Robert immediately disputes possession of the bone with Louvet and wins. From then on he is allowed to share the dog's food and to sleep with Louvet in the straw below the stairs.

At this point the empire is invaded by Saracens. God sends Gabriel to Robert with instructions to disguise himself and join the battle. He must go to a meadow with a fountain in the middle of it, and there he will find a suit of white armor and, wearing this, he will save the day for the Christians—and so he does, not once but twice. After the first battle the emperor wants to discover who his champion is. The emperor's dumb daughter, who has watched Robert arm himself, tries to reveal with gestures that the idiot is the hero in question but the only result of her efforts is that her father scolds her *maîtresse* for turning her into a fool. At the end of the second battle, one of the Christians wounds the White Knight in the thigh and breaks off his lance in the wound. The emperor then announces that whoever can show him the proper wound and the lance's head may have his daughter in marriage. The emperor's seneschal, who has long admired the princess, has an armorer run up a copy of Robert's white suit of arms, wounds himself in the thigh, and claims the girl. God, in the meantime, tells the hermit to instruct Robert that his penance is over. The pope arrives to perform the marriage ceremony, but when the bride-to-be is presented with the seneschal, she discovers that her speech has been miraculously restored and reveals the truth in no uncertain terms. Robert continues to play the fool until the hermit arrives with God's instructions, whereupon he agrees to conform to divine will, give up his aspirations to a contemplative life, marry the princess, and found a line in which all heaven will take delight. Thereupon the company leaves the stage to the sound of a final hymn in praise of the Blessed Virgin.

Robert le Dyable is a first-rate piece of theater. The protagonist's role combines cruelty, violence, penitence, and pathos with a low-comedy mime part that ends in a burst of chivalric heroism. The most exigent of leading actors could not ask for more. But in addition, these highly colored dramatic treats are presented with a High Gothic elegance and sophistication which are not surprising if one remembers that 1375 is approximately the period of Chaucer's *Troilus and Creseyde* and that the play was originally performed for an audience of Gothic goldsmiths which must have included artists of a very high order. To be sure the art of this play is of a deliberately limited kind. The strong contrasts of emotional response potential in the action are, in fact, carefully controlled, kept within the bounds of charm, in part by a traditional verbal form (rhyming octosyllabic couplets) that would not permit expressions of great intensity even if the authors were capable of them.

The charm of this High Gothic artifact, and our association of it with pretty illuminations and elegantly attenuated statuary, suggests that we are dealing with art whose interest is limited to surfaces, but this is not the case. In fact, the "miracle" has a meaningful structure and plays with our emotions in a coherent way and to a specific end. The whole work is informed with a view of the nature of things that is clear to the writer of the piece and that he has carefully and with admirable clarity projected through his drama. He presents his audience with a traditional Christian vision of the world that makes human life comprehensible and bearable without seriously cheating—without, that is, excluding sin, cruelty, and evil from the elements that go to make the artifact.

Basic to this vision is the stage on which it is presented. The theater for which *Robert le Dyable* was written was, in an unusually literal sense, the representation of a little world. This microcosm, unlike its Elizabethan version, was not projected through the convention that made of the stage an unlocalized place, an everywhere that became for the moment whatever the playwright wished it to be. The miracle plays were staged with *décor simultané*,[3] on a long, comparatively narrow stage which contained, usually in the form of little houses, all the places which make up the play's microcosm. Simultaneously present and visible during the action of *Robert le Dyable* were the pope's palace and the emperor's, at least one hermitage, an abbey, the duke of Normandy's castle, and Robert's outlaw den. One has the sense, though this is more difficult to demonstrate, that the characters of the play were almost equally present, that the actors retire rather than exit when their part in a scene is played, and that they stand ready to step forward again

7

when their presence is required. Thus when the emperor sends a chevalier to invite the pope to officiate at the princess's wedding, we can imagine the messenger taking the few steps needed to get to Rome and there finding the pope and his two *sergents d'armes* ready to receive him.

The effect of these conventions is to intensify one's sense that the dramatic artifact presented to us by the playwright is, in fact, a miniature universe which resembles our own but whose workings have been made admirably clear. The medieval mystery cycles did this in terms of time as well as space. (The spatial effect was lost, of course, when the mysteries were presented on pageant wagons rather than through *décor simultané*.) They narrate a universal history which begins with the Creation and ends with the Last Judgment. In both mystery and miracle the most important omnipresence in terms of character and place stood at far stage right. Heaven, containing God, the Virgin, and their attendant angels, is constantly in view of the audience at a miracle play, and the world of that play is for its God a theater of his own creation in which he is both spectator and participant. He watches the action unfold and he intervenes in it when he wishes to insure that his will is done by making that will unmistakably clear to his creatures.

"Will" indeed—the various forms of *vouloir*—is the most important word in *Robert le Dyable* and the conflict of wills—human against human, of course, but more importantly human against divine—is the basic conflict of the play. The clash of wills between father and son which opens the action is soon referred by the father to the divine will in a prayer which is eventually answered:

> E! biau sire Diex, s'il vous plaist,
> Si vostre grace li donnez
> Qu'a repentance l'amenez
> Des maux qu'a faiz, et de cuer fin
> Mercy vous requier, ains sa fin,
> > Biaux sires Diex.   (Ll. 50–55)

(Ah, good lord God, if you please give him the grace that will lead him to repentance for the evils he has done and, with a pure heart, I ask you to show him mercy before his end, good lord God.)

8

But the efficacious working of God's sufficient grace waits upon the inner and apparently free movement of Robert's own will, and the unregenerate Robert's reason for being is the assertion of his own will in opposition to that of his fellow humans. His followers pander to that will and his victims are afraid to oppose it. "Maistre, par foy, j'en sui d'accort, / Puis que c'est vostre voulenté," says one of his outlaws, Boute en Couraie. The peasant he robs is equally sycophantic:

> Sire, ne doubtez que ne face
> Ce que voulrez, sanz contredire.
>
> (Ll. 176–177)

(Lord, have no doubt that I'll do what you want, without contradiction.)

The abbot comes nearest to a verbal equation of Robert's will with God's: "Vostre voulenté sera faitte." His will unchecked from within and unopposed from without, Robert becomes a little god of the fallen world, ignoring any possibility of a divine pleasure that might conflict with his own and undeterred by the opposition of humanity to the fulfillment of his desires:

> Je scé bien et ne doubte pas
> Que les seigneurs de Normandie
> Nous héent a mort, quoy c'on die;
> Mais cuer ay ainsi obstiné
> Que ne craing homme qui soit né;
> Et si vous jur par le Dieu pis
> S'ay fait mal, encor feray pis;
> Ne ne verray dame tant belle,
> Soit mariée ou soit pucelle,
> De qui n'aie, vueille ou ne vueille,
> Ma voulenté, qui que s'en dueille.
>
> (Ll. 340–350)

(I know well and don't doubt that the lords of Normandy hate us to the death, whatever may be said; but I have a heart so stubborn that I don't fear any man born; and I swear to you by God's chest if I've done evil, I'll do even worse; every beautiful woman I see, be she married or maid, I'll have my will of her, whether she will or no, no matter who may be pained by it.)

God is a handy source for oaths—one can swear by his *poitrine*—but Robert's consciousness of him does not extend beyond blasphemy for the first third of the play. This insensitivity to the divine dimension of his world changes at the moment when Robert sees his old mother take flight at the sight of him. Her fear brings home to him the fact that he has created around himself an all-hating world and that the God of this world may hate him too, and for good reason:

> Certes, or voy je sanz doubter
> Que le monde me het a mort,
> Et si fait Diex, il n'a pas tort.
>
> (Ll. 698–700)

(Surely, I see without doubt that the men of this world hate me to the death and so does God and he's not wrong.)

In his determination to discover the reasons for the instinctive evil of his nature, Robert learns not only that his mother bears a major responsibility for the wickedness from which she has tried to run away, but also that the unconscious opposition to God's will which has been the theme of his life began at the moment of his conception. At that moment his mother's opposition to the will of God was total, conscious, and stated: "Puis que Dieu mettre / Ne veult enfant dedans mon corps / Sy l'i mette le dyable." The duchess thus repeats the original sin of Eve by defying the will of God. By dedicating her son to the diabolical embodiment of opposition to God's will, she turns Robert into a human version of that embodiment.

Robert remains human, however. "Le Dyable" is a name, given him after painful experience by "les enfanz noz voisins." It designates his actions and not his essence, or rather it designates only half his essence. Two prayers were spoken at the time of his conception and both of them are answered in the course of the play. Robert is potentially what his father prayed for too, the loving servant of God, and in being a combination of servant and enemy Robert is merely a human being, though self-divided to an extraordinary degree. Insofar as he is cursed, it is with an especially virulent form of our common curse: Robert has a very severe case of original sin.

From his mother's confession Robert gains conscious knowledge of the true meaning of what he has been and done. He has not willed the existence of the evil in his nature though he has freely willed his acquiescence to the promptings of that nature. But his will is free and his nature double, and the access of knowledge strengthens his will in his determination to follow the guidance of the good within himself. To be sure, he needs help, but he knows where to turn and for what: "Ha! sire Dieu, grace me faictes." As it does with most of unsaintly mankind, the desire to do good arises first out of a fear of the consequences of evil:

> Se je ne met reméde en moy,
> En grant aventure me voy
> D'estre dampné sanz finement.
> (Ll. 763–765)

(If I don't take some remedy, there's a good chance that I'll see myself damned eternally.)

God's grace is the first requisite if one is to escape God's just wrath. But Robert also hopes that he is capable of putting "remedy" within himself. The devil, he knows, aims only at gaining his soul. But, if he can, Robert will see to it that the devil fails:

> L'anemi ne tent nullement
> Qu'a ce que m'ame puist avoir;
> Mais, se puis, il y fauldra, voir.
> (Ll. 766–768)

(The enemy aims only at getting my soul, but, if I can, he'll fail to get it.)

"Se puis"—the problem of "pouvoir" is added to that of "vouloir."

Robert now wills the identity of his will with God's. But in order to be able to confirm and sustain that identity, he must turn to the Church, to the sacramental aspects of sanctifying grace. This means turning to the holy men whom he has taken special delight in persecuting, but he does so willingly, confident that they can direct him in the proper use of his will and determined to do penance enough to expiate his sins.

The form his penance takes is a literalization, in some detail, of Paul's description of the Apostles in 1 Corinthians 4, for Robert, too, is "made a spectacle unto the world:"

> 10. We are fools for Christ's sake, but ye are wise in Christ; we are weak, but ye are strong; ye are honorable, but we are despised.
>
> 11. Even unto this present hour we both hunger, and thirst, and are naked, and are buffeted, and have no certain dwelling place;
>
> 12. And labor, working with our own hands: being reviled, we bless; being persecuted, we suffer it:
>
> 13. Being defamed, we intreat: we are made as the filth of the world, and are the offscouring of all things unto this day.

By voluntarily subjecting himself to such degradation, by patiently suffering mockery and "buffeting" at the hands of the *"compaignons"* (a parallel with Christ's passion that must have been clear to an original audience thanks to the frequent dramatizations of Christ's "Buffeting"), the fool of Christ becomes a type of Christ and is finally rewarded by being made the champion of Christ, the savior and the prince of Christendom. Robert's rewards are of this world as well as the next.

Robert is a fool for Christ's sake, but he is also a fool for our sake and the delight we take in his idiocies is psychically related to the delight we have previously taken in his violence. We assume nowadays that such theatrical violence as we are treated to in the first, unregenerate half of Robert's story has for the source of its power the universality of the human impulses that it dramatizes and that it serves its audiences therapeutically by making it possible for us to release our destructive drives in harmless, vicarious acts of imagined villainy.[4] One of the primary jobs of civilization is to develop tactics for coping with such impulses by satisfying them harmlessly. The art of the first half of *Robert le Dyable* is an example of one such tactic and so is the art of the second.

The buffoonery of Robert's pseudoidiocy is wit in a rudimentary form, to be sure, but its aggressive component is all the more obvious as a result. Not that black humor is missing from the scenes of cruelty. When his father's messengers complain at losing an eye apiece Robert silences them with "Taisiez: vous en dormirez miex," while his serial murder of seven hermits in quick succession provides a nice example of that "infléchissement de la vie dans la direction de la mécanique" which Bergson saw as a primary source of laughter.[5] But the "humor" that serves as an emotionally disinfecting accompaniment to the violence of the play's opening half becomes a socially acceptable substitute for it in the scenes of Robert's penance. This is clearest, perhaps, in the moment at the end of the play where the pope and the emperor, before the hermit has entered to reveal the will of God, plead with Robert to speak to them and show them his wounded thigh. Robert's "reply" is given in two stage directions: "Ici fait Robert au pape la figue, et le seigne d'un os" (here Robert makes the fig at the pope and blesses him with a bone) and "Ici jeue Robert de l'escremie d'un festu à l'emperiére" (here Robert pretends to fence with the emperor, using a straw). A fig for the pope and "Touché" for the emperor. Robert mocks the pope's high function by making the sign of the cross over him with a bone recently snatched from Louvet, and we can remember the time when the straw with which Robert runs the emperor through was the real thing. Mockery has taken the place of violence.

Solutions in sublimation, in the violent and comic art of the theater, do not exhaust the play's presentation of the means of dealing with man's inherent destructiveness. Finally, according to the view embodied by the play, one can transform the moral nature of the instinctual drive by placing it in the service of God. Robert uses the power of his own will, aided of course by grace, to repress his desire to subjugate all other wills to his. Once Robert has successfully done so, God rewards him by allowing him to exercise his talent for destruction in order to achieve the destruction of God's enemies. Killing pagans (offensively invading pagans, to be fair) becomes the final expiation for killing hermits. In his moral and spiritual progress Robert recapitulates the whole epic theme of God's providence. The special evil of his conception results in the special violence of his fallen nature but this in turn, thanks to divine grace and human will, is transformed into the courage of God's champion.

In something of the same way the reformed rapist is transformed into a proper husband for a princess and the founder of a line of holy kings. The necessity for playing this final role inspires the last and gentlest clash of wills between Robert and his God. When the emperor insists on presenting him with "la pucelle" along with half the empire, Robert at first demurs. He wants to retreat from the world in order to complete the payment of his debt to God:

> Certes, afin qu'a Dieu m'aquitte,
> Dès ores mais vie d'ermitte
> Voulray mener.
>
> (Ll. 2245–2247)

(Certainly, in order that God may pardon me, I will, from now on, lead a hermit's life.)

But the will of God, as transmitted through the hermit, is otherwise.

> Robert, sachiez Diex ordener
> Autrement a voulu de toy;
> Entens, il te mande par moy
> Et m'en a bien fait mencion
> Que prengnes sans dilacion
> La fille et ne le laisses mie;
> Car de vous deux istra lignie
> Tele, ce dit, bien vueil c'on m'oie,
> Dont tout paradis ara joie
> Ça en arrière.   (Ll. 2248–2257)

(Robert, know that God wants to ordain otherwise for you; understand that he commands you through me and he has made it clear to me that you should take the girl without delay and not leave her. For of the two of you will be born a line—listen carefully to what I say—at which all heaven will rejoice in time to come.)

Robert's reply concludes the theme of divine and human will in conflict:

Puis qu'il est en telle maniére,
Le contraire ne doy vouloir.

(Ll. 2258–2259)

(Since it is thus I must not wish it otherwise.)

This is the climax of the play's didacticism. The cooperation of man's will with God's is the first and final lesson. *Robert le Dyable*'s instructions are delightful, however. A beautiful princess and half an empire are crosses that most of us could find the strength to bear. To be sure, the hero has earned them by voluntarily becoming a fool for Christ's sake, by making himself as the filth of the world. But there is nothing mysterious about these rather amusing sufferings. They are undergone for a set of comprehensible reasons—self-hatred for evil done, love of God and above all a desire to earn salvation in exchange for penance. They occur—the whole play occurs—in a comprehensible world, a version of our world that has been made to make sense. The significance of the play's action is admirably clear but the clarity is of that sort that is achieved by concealing difficulties.

Concealment may be the wrong word. It is probably illogical to accuse a work of art of concealing what it does not include. What *Robert le Dyable* chooses not to include is, however, one of the major difficulties in the orthodox Catholic theology it is dramatizing. The play, we have seen, is concerned with the interaction of God's will and man's and its story is designed to reveal how a man's will can come to subject itself to God's. But the story it tells is not quite the whole story, though a major part of the whole story is told through the dramatization of Robert's penance, his attainment of habitual, sanctifying grace through the sacramental processes of confession and satisfaction. The concealment or omission occurs before those processes take place, at what I have called the turning point of the action—the moment at which Robert is brought to desire grace.

Here again the story has been cleverly designed to embody orthodox doctrine. Robert is impelled toward God by what his mother tells him about his sinful origin. We have seen that the story she tells makes Robert a particularly striking example of fallen man. Her telling of it serves in turn as an example of the way grace begins the work of raising man from his fallen condition. The ultimate origin of grace—what is called uncreated grace—is that will of God which derives from a just and benevolent divine nature. Uncreated grace takes created form in a multiplicity of aspects and functions, most of which we can (I hope) safely disregard here. In the case we are considering we see dramatized a moment of actual (as opposed to habitual) grace[6] in which a man is moved by God to take an action which leads to his salvation. The grace which we see operating is external (as opposed to internal.)[7] God, employing the duchess of Normandy as his instrument, presents Robert with a revelation of the truth about himself. Again the highly particular truth is universalized by analogy. What Robert learns about the moment of his conception is what we should all know about our conceptions— that we are conceived in sin, the enemies of God. It is in what happens next that the mystery is concealed or overlooked. Robert's will responds to revealed truth with contrition, with a heartfelt desire for grace. (We know it is heartfelt because it is granted.)

It is quite possible for the unaided human intellect to be convinced by the divine revelation of supernatural truth. It is not possible for the human will to move unaided from that conviction to any sanctifying action, such as that of true contrition. According to orthodox theology as developed by Augustine in his fight against Pelagian heresy, man has an absolute need for internal grace in order to perform any action that can lead to his justification.[8] The heartfelt desire for God's grace must be preceded by God's grace. What we must receive, says Augustine, referring to John 1:16, is "grace for grace,"[9] and he insists that our ability to turn to God is itself the gift of God.[10]

This necessity for prevenient grace is left out of the dramatization of Robert's conversion. At first it might seem that theatrical limitations make dramatizing so arcane an internal happening impossible but this is not the case, I think. With God in your cast, most, if not all, things are possible. God could be shown expressing his will that Robert desire grace and Robert could be shown responding to that divine will by desiring what he is told to desire. Such a spectacle would, however, quite change our sense of what we were seeing. We would find ourselves no longer present at the theater of God's judgments, but spectators at a cosmic puppet show in which the human actors were rewarded for responding to a jerk of their strings. In other words the theatrical affimation of prevenient grace is necessarily a theatrical denial of the freedom of man's will.

In this case at least the limits of the theater and the limits of human reason appear to me to coincide. It is not given to most of us to understand how the human will can be said to be free when it cannot act for its own good unless impelled to do so by a supernatural force. We have here arrived at the first aspect of the mystery of God's judgments whose consideration in the drama is the subject of this study. One way of solving that mystery is through the heresy, or semiheresy, called semi-Pelagianism. This is an attempt to escape from the rigors of Augustinianism by finding in human will and nature more health and strength than the Doctor of Grace could discover. The semi-Pelagian holds that our wills are free and strong enough to initiate that movement toward God which is rewarded by grace.[11] The other solution entails a movement in the opposite direction, beyond Augustine to a denial of the freedom of the will. This is Luther's way and Calvin's way, but this solution in what is called voluntarism—the exaltation of divine will—is a solution which reveals or creates another mystery: how can God be just if he punishes throughout eternity creatures who are without free will? This is the mystery, I will maintain, whose presence contributes something to the emotional and intellectual power of certain Shakespearean tragedies.

These mysteries are ignored by the medieval miracle plays and the result is a species of semi-Pelagianism by default, but the ignoring of mystery is itself the result of the play's Christian didacticism. The authors of plays like *Robert le Dyable* are eager to entertain us and they succeed, but they are also bent on instructing us and what they want to teach is the necessity of repentance—necessity, and, of course, possibility. They urge us, by dramatic example, to exercise our wills in the practice of contrition and the theology which guides them assures us that such freely willed contrition is absolutely necessary for our salvation. That theology also teaches us that we must be impelled to such contrition by God, but to dramatize *that* necessity would be to cloud the human issue that the medieval playwright is trying to make clear. To achieve its didactic purposes the miracle play must confine its attention to the free human will.

This aspect of the content of the "miracles" determines their form. The spectacle of the free human will exercising itself to the achievement of its salvation is necessarily, in the broadest and deepest sense, comic. In no medieval play of which I am aware is the opposite spectacle presented. Never, before the sixteenth century, so far as I know, are we shown a dramatic protagonist being hauled off to hell, like Dr. Faustus, or Don Juan, because he has not achieved repentance for his sins. Sinners are, of course, hauled off to hell, especially in the mystery cycles. But these are generalized sinners and we are not shown the process—particularly the psychological process—by which such lost souls arrive at their damnation. At first glance this seems rather odd. What better admonition to repentance could there be than the horrible example of those who fail to repent? And yet on consideration it is clear that the contemplation of such an example would lead at once to the problem of why the failure occurred. Why should any believing sinner fail to say what Robert le Dyable succeeds in saying: "Grace me faictes?" To consider that problem leads to the consideration of yet another mystery, that of election and reprobation—the theological subject of the next chapter.

Elizabethan tragedy, I shall theorize, is in part the result of a desire to embody in art the mysteries that were forced upon the consciousness of intelligent artists and their audiences by the controversies of the Reformation. I think, however, that there is another result for drama in addition to this formal or generic one. The theology of grace which forms a part of the potentially tragic Christian mystery, carries a psychology along with it. Augustine's sense of grace is not derived simply by ratiocination. It is based on his experience of his own mind in the process of conversion and it conveys the sense that mind consists of more than consciousness—that consciousness coexists with other dimensions. The theologian defines those dimensions as supernatural. What our minds contain that is not of our conscious minds may be the voice of internal grace or the temptings which God permits the powers of evil to visit us with. Whether the secular playwright accepts such definitions is less important than his acceptance of what prompts the feeling that such definitions are necessary—the sense of forces at work within the mind but outside the consciousness of man. It is only with a sense of such dimensions that the subtle imitation of psychological states becomes possible.

With *Robert le Dyable* we are far from tragedy and far from the subtle imitation of psychological states. And yet both, I would maintain, are potentially present in the theology that these plays embody. But the comic vision and the comparatively simple psychology of the miracle play are there too and these are the aspects of the vision of orthodox theology which the writers of the miracles, for highly creditable didactic reasons, chose to dramatize. Yet these plays do not deny or overlook original sin and human depravity. On the contrary, they emphasize our weaknesses in order to reassure us about the possibility of our amendment. Their purpose is to transmit to us the glad tidings of great joy: though we have fallen into filth as the result of Adam's sin, God, through the incarnation of Christ, has saved us from the hell which we deserve, and so a play like *Robert le Dyable* can end with a hymn of praise.

On vous doit bien, vierge, loer,
Quant pour nous d'enfer desvoier
Dieu se fist en vous homme,
Pour nous de l'ort lieu desbouer
Ou Adam nous fist emboer
Par le mors de la pomme.

(We should truly praise you, Virgin, since, in order to turn us from hell, God made himself man in you, in order to cleanse us from the filth of that place where we were mired by Adam's eating of the apple.)

CHAPTER 2

The Conflict of Conscience

GOD'S REJECTION of man is not a subject for the miracle plays of the Middle Ages. Man's rejection of God is. Robert the Devil can of course be said to reject God, in his unregenerate days, by refusing to conform to the sort of conduct called for by the ten commandments. But Robert sins out of passion. He is prompted to his rapes and murders not by a conscious desire to defy God but by the diabolical forces that are a part of his fallen human nature. But there exists a distinctly different kind of rejection—the kind later exemplified by Dr. Faustus—which is also dramatized in the miracle plays. This is man's rejection of God through malice, the deliberate, willed choice of the forces of evil over the forces of good. Apostasy—conversion to Islam for example—is sometimes dramatized in the miracle plays, but the most effective theatrical form of the sin is, again, Faustian—the pact with the Devil.

The great pre-Faustian pact-maker was Theophilus of Adana and his story has survived in at least five medieval dramatizations—one French, one Italian, and three German. The French version, Rutebeuf's *Théophile*,[1] written around 1270, is the earliest surviving miracle play of the Virgin and precedes *Robert le Dyable* by a hundred years. Theatrically much simpler than the later versions of the form, Rutebeuf's play makes a very similar point and does so with the same sort of calculated charm that characterizes *Robert le Dyable*. Verbally, in fact, Rutebeuf's verse surpasses, in combining intricate artificiality with amusing colloquial realism, anything the later anonymous author is capable of. Rutebeuf like Marlowe opens his play at the moment of his protagonist's defection from God. Théophile's rebellion has its beginning in worldly discontent. He has lost his job. Formerly the administrative assistant to a bishop in Asia Minor, he has himself, we learn later, refused elevation to the episcopate, but now the new bishop has fired him despite the exemplary fashion in which he has performed his duties. This is the way of the world, but Théophile, in his anger, assigns ultimate blame for the injustice not to human nature, but to God's apparent lack of concern for suffering humanity: "Diex? Oïl! qu'en a il a fere?" (l. 13) (God? Yes! What does he care about it?)

The idea of God sitting so high and mighty and not caring a bit infuriates Théophile:

> Se or pooie a lui tancier,
> Et combatre et escremir,
> La char li feroie fremir!
> Or est lasus en son solaz;
> Laz, chetis! et je sui es laz
> De povreté et de soufrete.
>
> (Ll. 30–35)

(If I could tell him what I think of him and fight him and beat him up, I'd make his flesh quake. But he's up there surrounded by his delights and here I am, poor me, trapped in poverty and suffering.)

At this point a certain Salatin enters and, when he understands the situation, sympathizes deeply with Théophile, who wonders how he could possibly regain his former position. Salatin reassures him. Nothing could be easier. All Théophile has to do is renounce God and all the saints and worship an unnamed party who will see to it that Théophile's worldly honors are soon returned to him. Théophile agrees and Salatin tells him to come back the next morning. Théophile has strong misgivings which he expresses in soliloquy. Unlike Faustus, he knows perfectly well that so far as hell is concerned "ce n'est pas fable" (l. 113). But Théophile keeps his appointment. Salatin calls up the devil and Théophile agrees to worship him. The Devil, having been taken in before, insists that the agreement be put in writing and then instructs Théophile how he is to behave in the future—wickedly, of course. Théophile agrees and the bishop immediately decides to give him back his job. The new Théophile is briefly characterized in a scene in which he lords it over a pair of fellow priests—former friends, one of whom assumes he must be drunk.

At this point (in fact, seven years pass, but we are only told this later) a stage direction makes the announcement "Ici se repent Theophiles." The event occurs in a chapel dedicated to the Virgin and is dramatized by forty-eight lines of self-reproach and near despair. These conclude with a determination to appeal to the Virgin for a hearing. Théophile's prayer (nine twelve-line stanzas rhyming aabaab bbabba) is so elaborate and so long that the monosyllabic reply the Virgin finally makes to it ("Qui es tu, va, qui vas par ci?") seems lacking in grace. In fact the "pucele debonere . . . Flors d'aiglentier et lis et rose" (l. 555) is characterized as a strong-minded woman, blunt in her speech. When Théophile has explained who he is, she wants nothing more to do with him:

> Je n'ai cure de ta favele.
> Va t'en, is fors de ma chapele.
> (Ll. 552–553)

(I'm not interested in your chatter. Go on, get out of my chapel.)

He persists, however, and she soon relents, remembering his former devotion to her. Once she has made up her mind to help, she wastes no time in rescuing her repentant worshiper by the most direct method possible. She goes off to Hellgate, summons the devil imperiously, and demands the return of the pact:

> Rent la chartre que du clerc as,
> Quar tu as fet trop vilain cas.
> (Ll. 577–578)

(Give back the charter that you got from the clerk, for you've behaved too vilely in this case.)

Satan is horrified by the injustice of heaven:

> Je la vous rande!
> J'aim miex assez que l'en me pende!
> Ja li rendi je sa provande,
> Et il me fist de lui offrande
> Sanz demorance,
> De cors et d'ame et de sustance.
> (Ll. 579–584)

(Give it back? I'd rather be hung! I already gave him back his prebend and he made me an offering of himself without hesitation, of body, soul and substance.)

One cannot help feeling that the devil has a case, but the Virgin is merely rude: "Et je te foulerai la pance!" (l. 585) (And I will stamp on your belly.) So Théophile gets back his charter and shows it to the bishop, telling him the story of its miraculous recovery. The bishop decides that the miracle must be made public and ends the play with a sentiment with which one can only agree: "Disons: Te Deum laudamus!"

Here again is the universe of *Robert le Dyable* and, if anything, it is even closer to semi-Pelagianism than the orthodox optimism of the later play. Human will again is presented as the essential factor in the relationship between God and man.[2] Théophile freely wills his rejection of his creator and only after the rejection does the instrument of Satan tempt him to ratify his new allegiance to evil in exchange for worldly glory. Then Théophile freely repents, and only after his repentance does divine grace, embodied in the Virgin, make possible his triumph over evil. The availability of grace to the repentant sinner is, if anything, more strongly emphasized here than it is in *Robert le Dyable*, for Théophile's sin, if I interpret it correctly, is far more heinous than Robert's rapes and murders. What Théophile does, I think, is to commit a light-hearted and light-headed version of the most terrible of all Christian sins, the sin against the Holy Ghost.

The exact nature of this sin is something of a theological puzzle. Christ refers to it in three of the gospels, the fullest definition appearing in Matthew 12 : 31–32:

All manner of sin and blasphemy shall be forgiven unto men: but the blasphemy against the Holy Ghost shall not be forgiven unto men. And whosoever speaketh a word against the Son of man, it shall be forgiven him: but whosoever speaketh against the Holy Ghost, it shall not be forgiven him, neither in this world, neither in the world to come.

Aquinas, at about the time Rutebeuf wrote his play, investigates the nature of this sin:

Three meanings have been given to the sin against the Holy Ghost.
For the earlier doctors . . . say that the sin against the Holy Ghost
is literally to utter a blasphemy against the Holy Spirit. . . . Augustine, however (*De Verb. Dom.* xi), says that blasphemy or the sin
against the Holy Ghost, is final impenitence, when, namely, a man
perseveres in mortal sin until death. . . . But others understand it
differently, and say that the sin of blasphemy against the Holy
Ghost, is a sin committed against that good which is appropriated
to the Holy Ghost: because goodness is appropriated to the Holy
Ghost, just as power is appropriated to the Father, and wisdom to
the Son. Hence they say that when a man sins through weakness,
it is a sin *against the Father*; that when he sins through ignorance,
it is a sin *against the Son* and that when he sins through certain
malice, i.e. through the very choosing of evil . . . it is a sin *against
the Holy Ghost*.[3]

Théophile certainly sins through weakness and both he and the Virgin
claim rather feebly that he sins through ignorance (see ll. 400–401 and
570–571). But above all he sins "through the very choosing of evil."
And yet he is forgiven, which appears to prove that he has not, in fact,
committed the sin against the Holy Ghost. It would seem, indeed, that
given God's infinite mercy and man's free will the only possible orthodox definition of such sin would have to be Augustine's—final impenitence. Aquinas, however, sees it rather differently:

the sin against the Holy Ghost is said to be unpardonable, by reason of its nature, in so far as it removes those things which are a
means towards the pardon of sins. This does not, however, close
the way of forgiveness and healing to an all-powerful and merciful
God, Who, sometimes, by a miracle, so to speak, restores spiritual
health to such men.[4]

Aquinas denies, however, that the sin is therefore pardonable and that
man, by means of his free will can return from it to a state of grace:

In this life the free-will does indeed ever remain subject to change:
yet sometimes it rejects that whereby, so far as it is concerned, it

can be turned to good. Hence considered in itself this sin is unpardonable, although God can pardon it.[5]

Here again is the mystery of God's judgment and again, as in *Robert le Dyable*, the playwright has made the mystery disappear. Though the Virgin's reclaiming of the pact from the devil is as miraculous an incident as one could wish for, the restoration to spiritual health represented theatrically by Théophile's repentance is not shown to be the result of "a miracle, so to speak" and the audience is, therefore, free to assume that it is the result of the exercise of Théophile's will and yet the play does not violate the spirit of Saint Thomas's optimism, for both assert that God may pardon even the unpardonable sin.

Calvin's consideration of the problem of the sin against the Holy Ghost makes a good starting point for any attempt to analyze the difference between the Catholic and Reformation attitudes toward the mystery of God's judgments. What constitutes the problem for Augustine and Aquinas is clear enough. How can a sin be unpardonable if any sin is pardonable when it is repented of? For Augustine the answer is that a sin cannot be repented of once the sinner is dead. For Aquinas a sin cannot be repented of if repentance is precluded by the sin itself— but even such a sin can be pardoned and repented of if God wishes to pardon it. For Calvin, the problem is not so difficult because of his quite different view of the relationship between God and man, between God's will and man's will. He finds it easy to identify the sin against the Holy Ghost. It is apostasy—the turning away from God by men who know the truth but reject it: "they whose conscience is convinced, that it is the worde of God which they forsake and fight againste, and yet cease not to fight against it, they are said to blaspheme the holy Ghost."[6] Such sinners are guilty of "the Apostasie of the whole man," of "the universall departing whereby the reprobate doe forsake salvation." And by their action they *reveal* that they are among the reprobate, one of those sinners whom God has selected, from eternity, to serve as vessels for his wrath. We may be certain that for such unfortunates there is no forgiveness either in this world or the next.

In the late 1580s, three hundred years after Rutebeuf's *Théophile*, two hundred after *Robert le Dyable*, an English clergyman named

Nathaniel Woodes embodied Calvin's doctrine of the unforgivable sin in a morality play called *The Conflict of Conscience*.[7] The result is lamentable in every way, including, to be fair, the way in which the author intended it to be, but it is a rare and useful, if artistically unsuccessful, example of Calvinist didacticism in the theater. The story which Woodes tells is taken from a famous real-life case of conscience, the "notable and marveilous" example of Francis Spira, an Italian Protestant who, under pressure from the Inquisition, renounced his faith and fell, as a result, into an absolutely unshakable despair.[8] His story was written by, among others, one Matteo Gribaldi, published with a preface by John Calvin, translated and published in England in 1550 with a second edition about 1570.[9]

In adapting Spira's story for the stage, Woodes first allegorizes it. Italy becomes an everywhere, but one very much like what a good Protestant might fear that Elizabethan England would become if the Catholics returned to power. Spira is transformed into Philologus— though the Prologue is careful to point out that he is really Spira but that he is called Philologus in order to universalize him and make his experience relevant to each member of the audience. Satan opens the play proper by proclaiming that he must preserve his kingdom by coming to the aid of his vicar on earth, the pope ("my darlyng deare, / My eldest boy, in whom I doo delight.") Unkind men are threatening the pope's power, so the devil will help him out by sending Tyranny, Avarice and Hypocrisy to his aid.

We are next introduced to Philologus, who is having a godly conversation with his friend Mathetes. Their subject, appropriately in view of Satan's plans, is the problem of why God sends afflictions to the pious. True to his name, Philologus waxes eloquent and Mathetes is instructed. God, we learn, sends tribulations in order to preserve men from complacency, to make them abjure their sins, to prove their constancy, but also, and rather ominously, simply in order to display his power. As Tyranny, Avarice, and Hypocrisy gather and begin their work, it soon becomes clear that Philologus himself will be called on to serve as an example of God's judgments here below. Up to this point he has been much blessed with the things of this world. He is rich and has many friends and a wife and children of whom he is very fond. As a prominent Protestant he quickly finds himself turned in to the authorities by his local parson—one Caconos, who speaks with a thick northern accent and is devoted to the old popish ways.

Called before a cardinal, Philologus is questioned on his attitudes toward papal supremacy and the doctrine of the real presence. His replies are entirely unsatisfactory and the cardinal orders that Philologus's goods should be seized. For a time Philologus stands firm in the faith, but then Sensual Suggestion enters and gives a pitiful description of the sorrows of Philologus's wife. Philologus begins to weaken and when Suggestion shows him a vision of worldly joys in a mirror, he capitulates and agrees to a public recantation. But the unpardonable sin has not yet been committed. Spirit enters with a warning from God telling Philologus to stop while there is still time. He is followed by Conscience who wrestles with Philologus's evil inclinations, but in the end Sensual Suggestion is too much for him and, by tempting Philologus to presume upon God's mercy, finally brings him to forsake God completely.

The horror of the results is dramatically effective in spite of the almost total incompetence of the author. After a few brief moments in which Philologus congratulates himself on being elevated to the top of Fortune's wheel, a new character enters:

> My name is calde *Confusion* and *horror* of the mynde,
> And to correct impenitents, of God I am assignde.
> (Ll. 1968–1969)

Horror's function, which we would see as that of a diseased superego, is to replace the promptings of conscience with diabolical mental torments. Philologus has sinned against the Holy Ghost, has "extinguished, the holy Spirit of God." As a result God has forsaken him:

> He will no lenger in thy soule, and spirit make abode:
> But with the Graces, which he gave to thee, now is he gone,
> So that to Godwarde, by Christes death, rejoysing thou hast none.
> (Ll. 1979–1981)

The result of this visitation is to throw Philologus into an absolutely uncurable despair. Two godly comforters, Theologus and Eusebius, rush to assure him of God's plenteous mercy. He listens patiently and assures them that he believes that these comforts come from God. The devils in hell also believe it, but they continue to despair. Because he is one of the reprobate, Philologus too can only despair. He is quite willing to repeat the Lord's Prayer and does so. Theologus rejoices at this evidence that God has mollified Philologus's heart:

> These are not tokens unto us of your reprobation,
> You morne with teares, and sue for grace, wherefore be certified,
> That God in mercy giveth eare, unto your supplication.
>
> (Ll. 2137–2139)

But Philologus soon disabuses him. They "only heare and see the outward part." And when Eusebius again points out that God has said that he will always pardon the truly repentant, Philologus assures him that his own grasp of theology is at least as firm as Eusebius's:

> You cannot say so much to me, as herein I do knowe,
> That by the mercyes of the Lord, all sinnes are don awaye,
> And unto them that have true fayth, aboundantly it flowe,
> But whence do this true fayth proceede to us, I do you pray,
> It is the only gift of God, from him it comes alwaye.
>
> (Ll. 2160–2164)

We have arrived again at the mystery of God's judgment but here the mystery, instead of being concealed as in the medieval miracle plays, is insisted on. Man's will, in the world of the Reformation play, far from being of paramount importance, is shown to be absolutely dependent upon God's will.

In considering how he came to abjure the true faith, Philologus arrives at an interesting conclusion. The very Protestant insistence upon the necessity for faith as against works in the achievement of salvation has led Philologus, he says, to presume that since he believed in Christ he could with impunity commit the "work" of apostasy, but when he had done so he found that the grace to believe had been taken from him. This apparent denigration of the *"sola fides"* rather shocks Eusebius but Theologus assures him that Philologus only means to warn good Protestants against presumption. In any case we soon arrive at the heart of the matter. Eusebius, in a last effort to raise some hope in Philologus, cites the case of King David:

> Eus. Consider *David* which did sinne in lust, and murther too:
>   Yet was he pardoned of his sinnes, and so shalt thou also.
> Phil. King *David* alwaies, was elect, but I am reprobate,
>   And therefore I can finde small ease, by waighing his estate.
>   (Ll. 2302–2305)

Here we have come to the first cause, and it is uncompromisingly Calvinist. Against God's eternal decree there is no arguing and no appeal. Philologus's despair is clearly beyond the reach of human reason. He exits, accompanied by his sons, and Nuntius enters to pronounce the tragic conclusion:

> Oh dolefull newes, which I report, and bring into your eares,
> *Philologus* by deepe dispaire hath hanged himselfe with coard.
>   (Ll. 2411–2412)

The Conflict of Conscience is a thoroughly bad tragedy, but it is a tragedy. Its action presents us with a protagonist who makes a wrong choice and falls from felicity to total destruction. The wrong choice is not an obvious miscalculation, or an incompetent missing of the mark. From the point of view of the world and of nature Philologus's choice is intelligent. He refuses to let goods and kindred go and, at least insofar as he acts to shield his wife and children from suffering, he acts admirably. But in doing so he knowingly acts in direct opposition to divine power. His knuckling under to the papacy is a Calvinist equivalent to signing a pact with the Devil. The servants of the pope are in fact the servants of the Devil, the pope is identified as the "son" of Satan and Satan himself presides over the action. As a result Philologus commits the sin against the Holy Ghost. Like Theophilus of Adana and Doctor Faustus he consciously switches allegiance from God to Satan in exchange for worldly felicity. But the results of this choice are very unlike the results of Theophilus's. The comedy of the medieval play becomes the tragedy of the Reformation play because the similar actions unfold in very different dramatic worlds.

One basic difference is in the nature of the wills of the protagonists.

Theophilus is free to revoke his original choice and does so. Philologus cannot revoke his original choice because God, in order to punish the choice, withdraws from the sinner the grace that alone makes the choice of good possible. We have seen that doctrinally this prevenient grace was a necessity for the medieval protagonist too, but that the medieval dramatist, if he was conscious of the necessity at all, concealed it for artistic and didactic reasons. The Calvinist playwright could not but be conscious of the necessity. It was central to his theology. Once having decided to dramatize a case of conscience like Francis Spira's, he could not avoid the Protestant confrontation of the mystery of God's judgments. Nathaniel Woodes learned his Calvinism in the best of schools. He took his B.A. from Corpus Christi in Cambridge in 1571, his M.A. in 1574, and at the time Cambridge was a notorious source of pure Calvinist truth.

For early Protestants the mystery of grace and free will had been solved by Luther when he denied the freedom of the will in *De Servo Arbitrio*, a counterblast to Erasmus. In it Luther congratulated his opponent on having seen that the denial of free will was at the basis of nascent Lutheran theology:

> You have not wearied me with those extraneous issues about the Papacy, purgatory, indulgences and such like—trifles, rather than issues—in respect of which almost all to date have sought my blood (though without success); you, and you alone, have seen the hinge on which all turns, and aimed for the vital spot. For that I heartily thank you.[10]

But I have so far been discussing *The Conflict of Conscience* as if its protagonist made a wrong free choice which was then punished by the withdrawal of the power of free choice. If this were in fact the case, the play and its theology would be at no great distance from Aquinas who sees the unpardonable sin as guaranteeing its own unpardonableness by its rejection of that grace which alone can pardon it. Protestant theology goes beyond this, however, and under the guidance of Calvin goes far beyond it. Both Luther and Calvin see men not simply as losing free will, but as never possessing it, and Calvin in particular stresses that man's radical lack of freedom is the result of God's will—a will that has determined, in eternity, what the eternal fate of every man will be. We have come to the second aspect of the mystery of God's judgments: election and reprobation.

A firm belief in election characterizes both orthodox Catholicism and reformation Protestantism. As a result of God's love for certain of his creatures, they attain salvation. Election is the decree by which God intends to give to those whom he predestines to glory the grace and merit needed to attain that glory.[11] Orthodox Catholicism maintains steadfastly, against all temptations to semi-Pelagianism, that such election is the result of divine choice and is in no way merited by the creatures who benefit from it, not even by God's foreknowledge of the virtuous actions that the elect will perform. But this recognition and definition of the elect clearly leads directly to another subject. What of those who are not among the elect? Their fate is clear enough. They will go to hell. But, again according to Catholic theology, they are not predestined to go to hell. Those of us who go to heaven are predestined to do so. Those of us who are not predestined to go to heaven, go to hell, but are not predestined to do so. Again we are in the presence of the mystery. Salvation is given to those who are saved. Perdition is merited by those who perish: "Autant ces deux grandes vérités indiscutables sont fermement affirmées par le sens chretien, autant leur intime conciliation reste mystérieuse."[12] The Protestant reformers agree enthusiastically that salvation is unmerited and perdition is deserved, but just as they "solve" the mystery of grace versus free will be declaring that free will does not exist, so they solve the problem of election and reprobation by deciding that reprobation from eternity does exist. Calvin is memorably eloquent on the subject:

Againe I aske: how came it to passe, that the fall of Adam did wrap up in eternall death so many nations with their children being infants, without remedie, but because it so pleased God? Here their tongues which are otherwise so pratling, must of necessity be dumme. It is a terrible decree, I graunt: yet no man shalbe able to denie, but that God foreknewe what end man should have ere he created him, and therefore foreknewe it because he had so ordeined by his decree.[13]

31

Reprobation, the terrible decree, *decretum horribile*, is described with an even more uncompromising clarity in an undated leaflet entitled *Articles concerning Predestination:*

> Before the first man was created, God in his eternal counsel had determined what he willed to be done with the whole human race.
>
> In the hidden counsel of God it was determined that Adam should fall from the unimpaired condition of his nature, and by his defection should involve all his posterity in sentence of eternal death.
>
> Upon the same decree depends the distinction between elect and reprobate: as he adopted some for himself for salvation, he destined others for eternal ruin.
>
> While the reprobate are the vessels of the just wrath of God, and the elect vessels of his compassion, the ground of the distinction is to be sought in the pure will of God alone, which is the supreme rule of justice.[14]

There is in all this a terrible clarity and yet the mystery of God's judgments does not disappear as a result of the doctrines of the Reformation. The mystery changes its nature but in the process becomes more intensely terrifying than it was in its Catholic version, for how can we possibly call just the judgments of the God described to us by Calvin? Luther urges us to have faith:

> Keep in view three lights: the light of nature, the light of grace, and the light of glory. . . . By the light of nature, it is inexplicable that it should be just for the good to be afflicted and the bad to prosper; but the light of grace explains it. By the light of grace, it is inexplicable how God can damn him who by his own strength can do nothing but sin and become guilty. Both the light of nature and the light of grace here insist that the fault lies not in the wretchedness of man, but in the injustice of God; nor can they judge otherwise of a God who crowns the ungodly freely, without merit, and does not crown, but damns another, who is perhaps less, and certainly not more, ungodly. But the light of glory insists other-

wise, and will one day reveal God, to whom alone belongs a judgment whose justice is incomprehensible, as a God Whose justice is most righteous and evident—provided only that in the meanwhile we *believe* it.[15]

"In the meanwhile," here and now, we must perforce live by the lights of nature and grace and by those lights Luther by his own admission presents us with an unjust God—one who may have condemned us to an eternity of torment before we came into existence and against whose decree we are powerless. Fear and trembling hardly suffice to describe the emotions evoked by such a vision in those who believe in its possible truth, and even Calvin, whose grim satisfaction in the truths he is discovering is always evident, allows for the terror inherent in a God who moves men to do the evil deeds for which he will then punish them, and he justifies the vision by reference to the authority of Saint Augustine:

If any be more combered with this that we nowe saye, that there is no consent of God with man, where man by the righteous moving of God doeth that which is not lawfull, let them remember that which Augustine saith in another place: Who shall not tremble at these judgements, where God worketh even in the hearts of evil men whatsoever he will, and yet rendreth to them according to their deservings?[16]

The Reformation solutions to the mystery of God's judgments have always been inherent in orthodox Catholic theology, particularly since the definitions of grace called forth by Augustine's fight against Pelagianism. Proto-Calvinist heresies and controversies exist long before the sixteenth century. But the political success of the reformers and the availability of the printing press guarantee that their ideas will become a part of the consciousness of intelligent laymen. In the sixteenth century the Christian was presented with a choice of worlds to live in. He could believe himself to inhabit a world of free choice, in which he exercised his will in an effort to achieve his salvation. Or he could believe that he lived as the member of a race already divided into elect and reprobate and that by an examination of his conscience and consciousness he might discover (though only with doubtful certainty) the category into which he fell. Or, inevitable alternative, he might not know what to believe.

Nowhere was such uncertainty more likely than in England. The Anglican settlement did not proclaim either of these alternatives as the truth, nor did it attempt a rational reconciliation of the two. Rather it tried to permit their coexistence. For example, the tenth article of religion, "Of Free Will," does not say whether its subject exists or not, but affirms that only God's prevenient grace makes it possible for us to have a good will. Article XVII, "Of Predestination and Election," describes the nature and condition of the elect in some detail, but leaves the Anglican free to believe what he wants about the reprobate.[17] The Elizabethan Christian found the usual mystery of the nature of God and man's relationship to him compounded by the possibility of two answers.

I do not want to suggest that the average Elizabethan was a tormented creature, devoured by doubt. Sixteenth-century Englishmen were no more neurotic than human beings have ever been. But intelligent Christians were as always faced with mysteries and more than usually these mysteries were forced upon their attention during the Reformation. It was necessary to cope with them. Theologians coped by theorizing and polemicizing. Laymen coped by not thinking about it or by deciding to be as good as possible and hope for the best. Artists—literary artists—coped as artists always do, by making art. The dramatists, I shall suggest, found in the doubts and fears about God and his creatures that are aroused by the controversies of the Reformation the raw material for art. Their own doubts and fears could be given form and consequently relieved by making drama out of them, and because these particular doubts and fears were the common property of artist and audience, the writer could use them as a means to his end—the creation of drama. The fear that one may be living a life predetermined by an apparently unjust God and that that life may be succeeded by an unavoidable eternity of torment is clearly a fear that tragedy can be made out of. Belief in such a view is not necessary. If the fear of the possibility is there, in artist and in audience, it can be evoked as tragic terror and coped with through the familiar therapeutic process of tragedy.

Nathaniel Woodes was a theologian who tried very unsuccessfully to write a tragic morality play. His motives would seem to have been largely didactic. He wanted to teach men the truth about their condition and warn them of the dangers of apostasy. But frustration is an inherent condition for the Calvinist didact. Even Calvin, when he comes to justify the preaching of predestination, though he quotes copiously from Augustine, does not succeed in making a great deal of sense. It is clearly hard to find a rational explanation of why one should exhort his fellows to be something they cannot choose to be, and yet Calvinist preaching is highly effective in persuading men to behave themselves. The fact that you cannot choose to be one of the elect makes it a matter of desperate necessity to convince yourself that you are, and works are one sign that you are. They are, of course, also a sign that you aren't, and in dramatizing the story of Spira, Woodes is putting on the stage the story of a man whose acts revealed to himself that he is damned from eternity. To conceive of such a man as an intellectual possibility is disquieting, to read of his actual existence is frightening. To put him on stage is to vivify a terrible possibility and even when it is done incompetently, as it is by Woodes, the terror comes through. Terror can, of course, be read as a sign of truth: the sincerity and intensity of the fear appears to demonstrate that it must be inspired by a reality and, in fact, the learned Catholic scholars who tried to reason Spira out of his despair were themselves converted to Protestantism. But terror can also repel. The spectacle of Spira's sufferings can cause an audience to rebel against the God of the play and to refuse to grant belief to a God conceived of as having created and destroyed the protagonist of such an action.

A reaction of this kind may explain the most curious aspect of *The Conflict of Conscience:* it has two endings. It was originally issued with the unremittingly tragic conclusion I have already described. But then it was apparently reissued immediately with a new prologue and a last page which provides a quite different catastrophe:

NUNTIUS. Oh joyfull newes, which I report, and bring into your eares,
    Philologus, that would have hangde himselfe with coard,
    Is nowe converted unto God, with manie bitter teares,
    By godly councell he was woon, all prayse be to the Lorde,

His errours all, he did renounce, his blasphemies he abhorde:
And being converted, left his lyfe, exhorting foe and friend,
That do professe the fayth of Christ, to be constant to the ende.

(Ll. 2410–2417)

Blessed are the dramatists, for they shall play God. The change is ludicrous but interesting. There is no evidence whatever for why the alteration was made. It may not have been the result of the author's decision. The censor of printed books—the bishop of London—might have concluded that the play as it stood originally was so uncompromisingly Calvinist that it could lead to doctrinal contentions, or so clear in its presentation of the terrifying mysteries of predestination as to be upsetting to the unsuspecting laymen who would come into contact with it. If so, the change made would do much to solve such problems. By altering its ending, the author gives his play the form of the medieval miracle play of forgiveness, of *Théophile* and *Robert le Dyable*. God grants his grace to the sinning protagonist of both the Protestant and the Catholic plays but, of course, there is a difference. The grace received by Robert and Théophile is the result of and reward for their repentance. The grace God grants to the "comic" Philologus is prevenient grace—the grace that makes repentance possible. The "Disons: Te Deum Laudamus" of *Théophile*'s conclusion and the "all prayse be to the Lorde" of this ending are praises for rather different gifts.

The original prologue of Woodes's play describes what happens to Philologus as follows:

From state of grace wherein he stoode, he is cleane overthrowne,
So that he had no power at all, in heart firme fayth to have,
Being urgde to praye unto the Lorde, his mercyes for to crave.

(Ll. 33–35)

In the second issue, this becomes:

From state of grace wherein he stoode, was almost overthrowne:
So that he had no power at all, in heart firme fayth to have,
Tyll at the last, God chaungd his mynde his mercies for to crave.

(Ll. 33–35)

Even in his "comic" version of the action Woodes avoids the implicit semi-Pelagianism of the medieval playwright. God's will is responsible for the change in Philologus's mind. And yet the change makes possible an interpretation of the play according to Aquinas (a Protestant Aquinas of course): Philologus commits the sin against the Holy Ghost, but God forgives it, "by a miracle, so to speak." Nonetheless, a Calvinist interpretation remains simultaneously possible: Philologus's sin has been shown to be close to but not quite the "apostasy of the whole man," his loss of grace is "almost," and in the end he stands revealed as one of the elect after all. In making possible the coexistence of these two views, the play has become "Anglican"—at least by the lights of the 1580s.

This "Anglicanization" need not have been the effect of a decision imposed on the author from outside, however. It is quite possible that Woodes, having gone through the imaginative experience of creating a reprobate protagonist, was disturbed enough by what that act of creation taught him to have undergone a change of heart and mind that led to an alteration of his play's meaning.

Woodes is a theologian and a Calvinist didact whose lesson may have been rejected by authority or who may himself have learned from the attempt to teach. Shakespeare is not a theologian or a Calvinist or a didact. For him the mystery of God's judgments is not a problem to be solved or a solution to be taught. I think, however, that he is well aware of the mystery's existence and I think that he uses the mystery in the creation of some of his tragedies—uses it emotionally to create pity and terror in his spectators. But he also uses it intellectually in the creation of the artistic analogues to reality that we call the worlds of his plays. These worlds, however, do not embody even tentative or aesthetic solutions to the mystery. Rather they aim to present it, and a full intellectual and emotional experience of mystery is, I shall maintain, their final cause.

What Shakespeare is doing is clearer, I think, in Marlowe, above all in *Doctor Faustus*. This is not because Marlowe is clearer, but because he is less subtle. His means are more obvious. *Faustus* is a theological play. Its employment of the incomprehensibilities of Christian doctrine is overt. The Shakespearean tragedies I discuss, though all but *Lear* are

Christian in setting, are secular in subject and the eternal fates of their protagonists are uncertain. Theological concepts are rarely referred to. They do their work by inference. It seems to me, however, that what Marlowe and Shakespeare do and how they do it in these plays, their aims and methods, are similar, and that an examination of *Dr. Faustus* from the point of view I am adopting should be illuminating for *Richard III*, *Hamlet*, *Othello*, *Macbeth*, and *King Lear*.

CHAPTER 3

Dr. Faustus

SEMI-PELAGIANISM is the natural condition of popular theology. The ordinary Christian believes in original sin—in Adam's fall we sinned all—but he also thinks that it is up to him to be as good as possible and he feels that if he does his best, it will probably be none too good, but God will understand. The medieval miracle plays are designed so as to instruct the layman without contradicting this view of life. They emphasize the necessity for contrition as the means to grace and urge the sinner never to despair. In doing so the plays do not, on the other hand, contradict the anti-Pelagian orthodoxy that derives from Augustine—that would be heresy after all. Instead the plays simply disregard the comparatively esoteric problems raised by the concept of prevenient grace and its challenge to the freedom of the will, or by the doctrine of election and the doctrine of reprobation which it apparently implies. The result is an artistic form and an imaginative vision of life that are essentially comic, and I have maintained in another book that secularized versions of the form and vision are present in some of the comedies of Shakespeare and his contemporaries.

Disregarding the mystery of God's judgments was made more difficult for ordinary Christians by the Reformation. Luther and Calvin saw themselves as true Augustinians (whether Augustine would have agreed is another matter). They "solved" the mysteries of free will and reprobation and in proclaiming their solutions called attention both to the existence of the old mysteries and to the new ones that their solutions had brought them to. Their activities must have made the undisturbed possession of semi-Pelagian views harder for their contemporaries to retain and yet we can be sure that a great many of them managed to do so. Such unreflecting Christians would have made up a sizable portion of the fellow countrymen of Marlowe, Shakespeare, and the other Elizabethan writers of tragedy. At the opposite end of the spectrum of Elizabethan belief were the convinced and informed Calvinists. In the center came the non-Pelagian, non-Calvinist adherents to past orthodoxy whom

I shall lump together and, loosely and in quotation marks, call "Augustinians." They could be recusants or Anglicans, but if Anglicans, they would be no more nor less Anglican than the Calvinists who also subscribed to the Thirty-Nine Articles for, as I pointed out in the last chapter, those articles had been devised so carefully that both Calvinists and "Augustinians" could safely subscribe to them. According to the tenth of the Articles of Religion, then entitled "Of Free Will,"

> we have no power to do good works, pleasant and acceptable to God, without the grace of God by Christ preventing us, that we may have a good will, and working with us, when we have that good will.[1]

To this statement the reaction of both Calvinist and "Augustinian" would, I think, be, "To be sure." The Church of England deals with the problem of free will by asserting the doctrine of prevenient grace. Both Calvinism and Romanism hold such grace to be a necessity for justification, but whereas the Calvinist sees the logical corollary of that necessity to be the absence of free will, the Augustinian insists that the necessity for prevenient grace does not destroy the freedom of the human will. The Anglican article deals with the conflict by disregarding it.

The eleventh of the Thirty-Nine Articles is called "Of the Justification of Man" and is a restatement of Luther's doctrine of justification by faith alone:

> We are accounted righteous before God, only for the merit of our Lord and Saviour Jesus Christ by Faith, and not for our own works or deservings. Wherefore, that we are justified by faith only is a most wholesome doctrine, and very full of comfort.[2]

This leaves open the question raised by the preceding article of whether such justifying faith is the gift of God or the result of our own free will to believe. The article ends with the assurance that the nature of the doctrine "more largely is expressed in the Homily of Justification." When we turn to that Homily for the resolution of our doubts, we seem to discover that a man's justifying faith is attributable to God alone: "true and lively faith in the merits of Jesus Christ, which yet is not ours, but by GODS working in us." And this is reemphasized a few lines later: "a true and lively faith, which neverthelesse is the gift of GOD, and not mans onely worke, without GOD." But what is the adjective "only" intended to suggest here? That faith is partly man's work without God? This possibility seems to be reinforced by the exhortations at the beginning and end of the sermon where we are told that sinners are washed from their sins by Christ's sacrifice "when they turne againe to GOD unfaynedly" and the great and merciful benefits of God "moove us to render our selves unto GOD wholly with all our will, hearts, might and power."[3]

As for the mystery of election and reprobation the official church of England position, as stated in the seventeenth article of religion, "Of Predestination and Election," is to leave the problem as undefined as possible. The article begins with a succinct and eloquent statement of the meaning of Predestination to Salvation:

> Predestination to Life is the everlasting purpose of God, where-by (before the foundations of the world were laid) he hath constantly decreed by his counsel, secret to us, to deliver from curse and damnation those whom he hath chosen in Christ out of mankind, and to bring them by Christ to everlasting salvation, as vessels made to honour.[4]

The article goes on to expatiate on the felicity of those lucky vessels, but the fate of those less lucky, a subject that might strike even those of us who are not theologically alert as apropos at this point, is not touched upon. Instead the article concludes by pointing out that consideration of predestination is full of unspeakable comfort to godly persons, but that for the curious and carnal it can be a most dangerous downfall.

The articles of Free Will, Justification, and Predestination were annoyingly unspecific to a good Calvinist, and by the 1590s, when what was later to be called the Arminian reaction against orthodox Calvinism was beginning to pick up strength, the Calvinist party within the Church of England attempted to clarify its opponents out of existence by substituting the so-called Lambeth Articles for the deliberate vagueness of earlier statements of dogma. These articles, which were enthusiastically approved by the archbishops of Canterbury and York, are a succinct statement of the view of God and man which was held by a powerful force within the Church of England in Marlowe's and Shakespeare's time. The first four of them are worth quoting in full:

    I.   God from eternity hath predestinated some to life, some He hath reprobated to death.

    II.   The moving or efficient cause of predestination to life is not the prevision of faith, or of perseverance, or of good works, or of anything which may be in the persons predestinated, but only the will of the good pleasure of God.

    III.   Of the predestinated there is a forelimited and certain number which can neither be diminished nor increased.

    IV.   They who are not predestinated to salvation will be necessarily condemned on account of their sins.[5]

Obviously the Calvinists within the Church of England were strong enough to think, with some justification, that they could force a Genevan conformity upon their contemporaries. They were wrong. When the archbishops approved the articles, in November of 1595, and submitted them to the queen, Elizabeth was furious. Her anger does not seem to have been directed at the Calvinist content—she was at least equally annoyed with the proto-Arminian party to the quarrel—but at the threat to theological peace and quiet inevitably caused by an insistence upon absolute clarity.

    The enforced coexistence of diametrically opposed points of view within England's only church would necessarily draw the attention of the intelligent Elizabethan to the theological difficulties I am calling the mystery of God's judgments. The dramatist who was writing for a Christian audience during Shakespeare's lifetime was not, as a result, writing for an audience of singleminded true believers all of whom thought the same thing. He was writing for semi-Pelagians, "Augustinians" and Calvinists. And he was also writing for men and women who did not know quite what to think. Conflicting certainties, doubts, and uncertainties were his raw material, both within his own mind and within the minds of the audience whose responses he was playing upon. If I interpret Shakespeare's overtly Christian tragedies correctly, they were not written for or from any single point of view. Rather they use the diversity of points of view and the doubt inspired by such diversity in order to create tragedy.

Marlowe does the same—did it, indeed, before Shakespeare did. I shall try to demonstrate how *Dr. Faustus* can be made sense of by semi-Pelagian, "Augustinian" and Calvinist alike and how also each variety of believer would find terror, mystery, and perhaps even doubt inspired by the spectacle Marlowe presents him with. The necessary ingredient for this result is, I think, the Calvinist conception of God. The presence of a Calvinist possibility (not certainty) in this tragedy makes it terrifying beyond what it could otherwise be. Even (perhaps especially) to the non-Calvinist, the Calvinist God, once understood, is uniquely frightening. Lord Burghley's non-Calvinist reaction to the Calvinist possibility as expressed by the Lambeth Articles has been preserved:

> [He] seemed to dislike of the propositions concerning predestination, and did reason somewhat against Dr. Whitaker in them, drawing by a similitude a reason from an earthly prince, inferring thereby they charged God of cruelty and might cause men to be desperate in their wickedness. Master Dr. Whitaker seeing then his Lordship's weakness, did in wisdom forebear to answer my Lord.[6]

Burghley was not a theologian, but he knew all that experience has to teach about earthly princes, desperate men, and the exercise of power. He responds to the Calvinist glad tidings as a man and as a politician. An artist, we may assume, will respond to them as a man and as an artist. A playwright will tend to make plays out of them.

Marlowe was trained to be a theologian before he became the artist that he was by nature. As a playwright it was only natural that he should make a play out of the theology he had learned. In so doing he did not however become a theological playwright—he did not, that is, use the theater in order to make a theological statement. Instead he used theology in order to make a theatrical statement. So, of course, did the authors of the medieval mystery plays. But while these men are writing comedies, and using theology in order to give their audiences the sense that God is good and that all manner of things shall be well, Marlowe, in *Dr. Faustus*, is writing a tragedy. He uses theology to quite different ends, to inspire pity and terror, and, by playing upon the doubts aroused by religious controversy, he is able to leave his audience confronted with a terrible mystery at the end of a tragic experience whose intensity is increased by the fact that its creator has manufactured it out of the religious beliefs and doubts of the men and women watching it. And, of course, out of his own beliefs and doubts as well. A playwright terrifies us by sharing his terrors with us.

In order to achieve this end, Marlowe draws upon the full spectrum of Christian belief in his time. Semi-Pelagian, "Augustinian," and Calvinist could sit side-by-side at the same performance of *Dr. Faustus* and each make his separate and different theological sense of what he sees, but none of these reductions of the play to theological order would in fact equal the significance of the play—and none of them would explain away the terror it inspires, and thus no single theology will account for the tragedy of Faustus to the exclusion of all other Christian orthodoxies. Marlowe denies us both the comfort of sharing certainty with him and the corollary comfort of despising his certainty should we happen not to share it.

Marlowe begins his play with a prologue emphasizing the oddity of his protagonist—not a warrior or a lover or a courtier, but a theologian:

> So soone hee profites in Divinitie,
> The fruitfull plot of Scholerisme grac't,
> That shortly he was grac't with Doctors name.[7]
>
> (A text, ll. 16–18)

Editors of the play gloss the second of these lines "the fruitful garden of scholarship being adorned by him,"[8] but I think it rather stands in apposition to "Divinitie." Divinity, when graced, is the fruitful plot of scholarism. What we are about to see is what theology becomes when no grace accompanies it. The line is a small ironic piety, the first of many, and the first of many to be dropped from or altered in the B text of the play. But the future as well as the past of the protagonist is presented in a stock emblem for tragedy, the fall of Icarus:

Till swolne with cunning, of a selfe conceit,
His waxen wings did mount above his reach,
And melting, heavens conspir'd his over-throw.
(B text, ll. 20–22)

Faustus, according to the implications of this image, destroys himself by
aspiring to a superhuman condition which his mere humanity is unable
to attain. The forces which destroy him are laws of nature—wax has a
certain melting point; what goes up must come down. But then Marlowe contradicts this lack of intention in the forces which destroy Faustus by his choice of verb: "heavens *conspir'd* his over-throw." Did
divine power act deliberately, and with forethought, plotting the destruction of Faustus beforehand? Was grace withheld from Faustus's study
of theology, turning it sterile and destructive? Such possibilities are only
just present in the prologue, but they are there.

However, the primary concern of the prologue and the opening scenes
is the character of the play's protagonist rather than the nature of the
God of the play's world and Marlowe's achievement in creating Faustus
seems to me both brilliant and different from the achievement he is
usually credited with—so different that I should warn the reader at
once of what may be an idiosyncratic response to Marlowe's artifact. In
a word, Faustus strikes me as silly. Magnificently silly, of course—ex-
travagantly and heroically absurd, but a protagonist much more in the
half-comic, half-tragic tradition of Barrabas, Richard III, and Volpone
than in that of Hamlet, Macbeth, and Othello. I do not however use
the word with any intention to suggest a lack of human sympathy
for Marlowe's "hero." I mean it rather as Auden meant it when he used
the word of Yeats. Faustus is "silly like us." His absurdity has its source
in our common humanity and it links us to him, making his final damnation all the more intimately horrible.

When we first see him Faustus is bored. Bored with life and bored,
above all, with scholarship. All the disciplines are trivial. Philosophy is
logic-chopping. Medicine is pill-rolling. Law is pettifogging. The human condition is boring: "Yet art thou still but *Faustus*, and a man"
(A, l. 53). The dismissal of divinity when it comes, though just as
sophomoric, is of central importance for the significance of the play:

45

> when all is done, Divinitie is best.
> *Jeromes* Bible, *Faustus*, view it well.
> *Stipendium peccati mors est:* ha, *Stipendium, &c.*
> The reward of sinne is death: thats hard.
> *Si peccasse negamus, fallimur, & nulla est in nobis veritas.*
> If we say that we have no sinne,
> We deceive our selves, and theres no truth in us.
> Why then belike we must sinne,
> And so consequently die.
> I, we must die an everlasting death:
> What doctrine call you this, *Che sera, sera,*
> What wil be, shall be? Divinitie, adieu.
>
> (A, i. 67–78)

What is the meaning of this ridiculous performance? Faustus opens the Vulgate to Romans 6 : 23 and reads the first half of the verse. Then he flips to 1 John 1 : 8 and reads all of it. The sentence from Saint Paul is completed by the clause "but the gifte of God is eternal life through Jesus Christ our Lord." The latter half of 1 John 1 : 7 reads "the blood of Jesus Christ his Sonne clenseth us from all sinne."[9] What has slipped the absentminded professor's towering Renaissance intellect at this point is the central doctrine of Christianity. If we wish to interpret the incident as a moment of psychological realism we can only assume what is in fact true—that Faustus is literally hell-bent to destroy himself. The psychopathology of his everyday life is psychopathic to the point where he effectively represses the sight of words that are before his very eyes. But it is more rewarding to ask what Marlowe, as opposed to his protagonist, is up to here. For one thing, he is making it clear what Faustus is up to. Even the dullest catechumen will suspect that Faustus is leaving something out of his syllogism and most Christians will realize that the missing ingredient is Christ's atonement for the sins of humanity. But Marlowe is writing for Cambridge graduates (himself included) as well as duller catechumens and Faustus's odd lapse of memory is designed, I suspect, to raise a basic theological question—a question that can be formulated quite simply as, "Who are 'we'?" Who, that is, are the "we" referred to in the passages which Faustus cites—and fails to cite?

The "we" in the words Faustus actually quotes are all mankind. We are all sinners and we have all earned the wages of sin. But does this hold for the portions of the passages he does not quote? Are we all cleansed from sin by the blood of Christ? Is the gift of God—his grace —given to all men? This is a question that seems to be answered unequivocally in 1 Timothy 2 : 4, where Saint Paul tells us that God "will that all men shalbe saved, and come unto the knowledge of the trueth," but Augustine for one denies that *all* is meant by "all" here: " 'God wills all men to be saved,' may be understood of all the predestined, because every type of man is among them."[10] And Calvin, with a slight change of emphasis, agrees, "Whereby verily hee signifieth nothing else but that he hath stopped up the way unto salvation to no degree of men."[11] In other words "all" means "some of each kind," or, as the shoulder note to the Geneva Bible's version of the text puts it "Jewe & Gentile, poore and riche."

William Perkins, the great Puritan polemicist, who was at Cambridge throughout the six-and-a-half years of Marlowe's residence there, presents the Calvinist position with admirable clarity:

> it is untrue, that God would have al men saved in Christ. For no man can be saide to be elected, if God will that all men should be elected in Christ. For election is a singling out of some from others. . . . If any man reason out of I Tim. 2.4. *That God would that all men should be saved.* He must know, that this sentence is not generallye ment of all men, but indefinitely of some. . . . it is not true, that all men are called to salvation: and that therefore that grace which is in Christ, is offred to all.[12]

According to Calvinism, then, the gift of God *to the elect* is eternal life through Jesus Christ and the blood of Jesus Christ cleanses *the elect* from all sin. The syllogism Faustus makes from his texts is not quite so absurd from this point of view. His eye has lit upon the texts which refer to him along with all other men, but he has failed to see those doctrinal comforts which apply, according to Calvinism, to the elect alone. If the "we" of Faustus's unquoted texts means the elect, then the "we" of Faustus's syllogism can mean the reprobate. The elect and the reprobate must sin and both will die, but only the reprobate will die an everlasting death.

Marlowe has so presented the moment of Faustus's renunciation of theology that it can have varying significances for the various kinds of Christian in his audience. The unreflecting semi-Pelagian will suspect that Faustus ought to search the Scriptures a little more thoroughly before jumping to conclusions about the inevitability of the damnation of all sinners. The Catholic or non-Calvinist Anglican, the "Augustinian" Roman or Arminian, will see in Faustus's forgetfulness the corrupt will and perverse reason of a sinner in danger of failing to respond to God's proffered grace. Corruption and perversity will be apparent to the Calvinist, too, but he will see in them signs of a reprobate nature and in the syllogism Faustus forms out of the half-truths of half-texts a terrifyingly ironic possibility: perhaps Faustus must die an everlasting death. Perhaps he is one of those whom "God from eternity . . . hath reprobated to death." *Che sera, sera.*

This playing upon the entire range of response within his Christian audience and within some single members of that audience is typical of Marlowe's method in *Dr. Faustus*—though the employment of it was probably not so fully conscious as a critical analysis of it must necessarily suggest. The result is a play—and a climactic scene, above all— of extraordinary power. The tragedy is, so to speak, chivying us toward a moment in which we will be forced to confront intensely terrifying possibilities in the brilliantly imagined and executed destruction of a fellow human being by a frighteningly mysterious omnipotent force. That a good deal too much of the drama that fills the space between beginning and end is a failure even by the lowest standards does not finally nullify what the play manages to achieve.

Faustus's psychomachy is sometimes fascinating and usually suspenseful, though again the precise nature of what one is feeling suspense about will vary from believer to believer. The semi-Pelagian will wonder if Faustus is going to find within himself the strength to turn to God. The "Augustinian" will ask himself if Faustus will be given the grace to accept grace. The Calvinist will find his original suspicions of Faustus's reprobation continually strengthened. But by contrast with the other two views, the Calvinist perception of the nature of human action, whether accepted as a truth or a possibility, changes fundamentally a spectator's sense of what he sees on stage in a play like *Dr. Faustus*. If you believe that all men, good as well as evil, have been or may have been predestined to their individual fates from eternity, if you think that the outcome of the mental battle was decided before the existence of the battlefield, then the struggle alters its nature. Psychomachy becomes sciamachy—a battle of shadows—and the familiar "all the world's a stage" metaphor for human life takes on its profoundest meaning. We all know that when we act, we often "act"—that is we knowingly pretend to emotions and motives we do not possess. But the sciamachic view of life asserts that when we act in what we think is the profoundest sincerity, we also "act"—we repeat a script which we do not remember having learned. This view or fear of what life may be is hardly the exclusive possession of the Calvinist, but Calvinism is one way of arriving at it. A contemplation of the mystery of God's judgments leads to the possibility that the world is a theater of God's judgments in a fully literal sense. All the men and women are merely players—who will be awarded eternal bliss or eternal torment for having done what they have had to do in the course of playing the roles they have been assigned. A potential intensification of this ironic sense of what we are—or what we may be—is always possible in the theater and in Elizabethan tragedy the possibility is sometimes realized, as it is in *Dr. Faustus*.

If the will of God is the only reality, then Faustus, in rejecting "divinity" is rejecting the only reality and the only means of arriving at an understanding of reality. Marlowe could not make it clearer that magic in this play is a ridiculous illusion, which only a man who has lost his sense of the true nature of the first cause could believe in. As a result of believing in it, Faustus begins to live in a world of shadows, failing to see what is before his eyes, failing to hear what he is plainly told and believing in the reality of what is shown to be unreal—magic. Faustus goes through his mumbo-jumbo and, to be sure, Mephostophilis makes his predicted appearance—an appearance as a devil, the sign of a reality that Faustus significantly refuses to accept, demanding and getting an old Franciscan friar instead. But the illusory form speaks the truth.

Mephostophilis will do what Faustus wants, not because the magician wants him to, but because Lucifer wants him to. As for the power of magic to "raise" him:

> That was the cause, but yet per accident,
> For when we heare one racke the name of God,
> Abjure the scriptures, and his Saviour Christ,
> Wee flye, in hope to get his glorious soule,
> Nor will we come, unlesse he use such meanes
> Whereby he is in danger to be damnd:
> Therefore the shortest cut for conjuring
> Is stoutly to abjure the Trinitie,
> And pray devoutly to the prince of hell.
>
> (A, ll. 291–299)

This could hardly be clearer. If you want superhuman powers, you can get them only by committing something like the sin against the Holy Ghost, by damning yourself through "the Apostasie of the whole man." Faustus counters this revelation of the real nature of the power of magic by espousing a particularly fatuous new illusion:

> This word Damnation, terrifies not me,
> For I confound hell in *Elizium:*
> My Ghost be with the old Phylosophers.
>
> (B, ll. 284–286)

But Mephostophilis embodies the damnation that Faustus wants to deny and after hearing a speech of extraordinary power on the nature of it ("Why this is hell: nor am I out of it") Faustus again shifts his ground—back perhaps to his starting point:

> Go beare these tydings to great Lucifer,
> Seeing *Faustus* hath incur'd eternall death,
> By desperate thoughts against *Joves* Deity:
> Say he surrenders up to him his soule,
> So he will spare him foure and twenty yeares,
> Letting him live in all voluptuousnesse.
>
> (B, ll. 312–317)

Faustus now claims to believe that, in effect, the pact has already been signed, the sin against the Holy Ghost committed. *Che sera, sera*. This is a return to the dismissal of theology, with the difference that Faustus now believes himself to have committed specific sins which will insure his "everlasting death." As with the original perverse syllogism, Faustus's pessimism is open to more than one possible interpretation. If Augustine is right and only final impenitence is beyond forgiveness, then Faustus is wrong. He has not incurr'd eternal death. If Aquinas is right and if Faustus is right in equating his desperate thoughts with the unpardonable sin against the Holy Ghost, Faustus is still wrong because God can still pardon him, as he pardoned Theophilus or the "comic" version of Philologus in *The Conflict of Conscience*. But if Calvin is right and if Faustus is right in assuming his "thoughts against Joves Deity" to be the unpardonable sin, then Faustus is right in deeming himself already damned. His very thinking so suggests that he has already been numbered among the reprobate and the pact he signs will only ratify a divine decision taken in eternity.

After some high jinks from the clowns, Faustus reenters for the first of his three attempts to repent his rejection of God and for the last of his mental battles before the signing away of his soul:

> Now Faustus must thou needes be damnd,
> And canst thou not be saved?
> what bootes it then to thinke of God or heaven?
> Away with such vaine fancies and despaire,
> Despaire in God, and trust in Belsabub:
> Now go not backeward: no Faustus, be resolute,
> why waverest thou? O something soundeth in mine eares:
> Abjure this Magicke, turne to God againe,
> I and Faustus wil turne to God againe.
> To God? he loves thee not,
> The god thou servest is thine owne appetite.

(A, ll. 438–448)

Whether psychomachy or sciamachy, the attempt to turn to God fails. And yet it occurs. Faustus wills it, but cannot accomplish it. Why not? For the semi-Pelagian the answer will have to do with the quality of

Faustus's reason and will. The corrupt reason of a fallen man has led him to believe that he is beyond the mercy of God—has indeed led him to want to believe so, since Marlowe makes it clear that Faustus is trying to despair in order to justify to himself the signing of the pact. But his conscience, the voice of God within him, is still able to contradict his mistaken reason. Unfortunately, however, his free will does not have the power to respond strongly enough to the impulse toward contrition. Faustus's irrationality and weakness are responsible for his failure. For the "Augustinian," Faustus's responsibility is no doubt clear, but his failure to achieve grace raises another problem. Was the grace there for him to achieve? Is prevenient grace at work in Faustus's mind and soul at this moment? Presumably it is not, or Faustus's attempt would have succeeded. The Augustinian has arrived at the mystery of God's judgments. Faustus's will is free, but its ability to will the good is dependent upon grace. In watching Faustus try and fail to achieve contrition the "Augustinian" watches a terrifying and mysterious event. Whoever prepared the manuscript for the B text of the play was aware of that mystery and terror and did his best to soften it by striking out the essential line: "I and Faustus wil turne to God againe," thus changing Faustus's failure into a willful refusal to listen to the voice of God within him. For the Calvinist, the terror is there but the mystery has been largely eliminated. Once again he finds his suspicions of Faustus's reprobation confirmed. There is no mystery in that terrible decree, but there is surely terror in the sight of a human being trying to extricate himself from the most horrible of all imaginable situations and being without any hope of doing so.

Marlowe presents on his stage an imitation of the world stage—the theater of God's judgments. The emotional experience of that imitation, the response to the artifact, will not vary substantially from one member of the audience to the next except at those points where each member attempts to define the meaning of what he experiences or, when the play is over, of what he has experienced. At these moments of reflection, responses will tend to diverge in accordance with what the viewer believes to be the significance of the object being imitated. One of the options of the literary artist lies in his deciding where he will relinquish his control of the work. The didactic writer—Shaw, Bunyan—will insist on full control, and quite rightly so, since precise significance, the imaginative statement of an abstract truth, is the aim of his art. Other artists, notably Shakespeare, have as their aim the construction of "percepts," of objects for contemplation whose meanings are multiple and change with the beholder. About such works it is incorrect to say that they can only mean thus and so. We must attempt to discover all that they can and cannot mean and we must accept as integral to their meaning the doubts they inspire.

Dr. Faustus, by being able simultaneously to mean contradictory things, can inspire a stronger certainty in the mind of the true believer who opts for his previous conviction and strengthens it by rejecting other possibilities. It can also inspire a potentially terrifying doubt in the mind of a believer whose convictions are open to challenge. Such believers are most likely to exist in the middle of our spectrum, are likely to be Romanist/Arminian/Anglican nonfanatics who wish to avoid what are to them the apparent errors of Pelagianism on the one hand and of radical Protestantism on the other. Pascal advances their creed at the end of his *Écrits sur la Grâce:*

> Apprenons . . . à défendre tout ensemble la puissance de la nature contre les Luthériens, et l'impuissance de la nature contre les Pélagiens; la force de la grâce contre les Luthériens, et la nécessité de la grâce contre les Pélagiens, sans ruiner le libre arbitre par la grâce, comme les Luthériens, et sans ruiner la grâce par le libre arbitre, comme les Pélagiens.
>
> Et ne pensons pas qu'il suffise de fuir une de ces erreurs pour être dans la vérité.[13]

An important part of the power of a work like *Faustus* lies in its ability to inspire in a rational and unfanatical Christian the desire to run in opposite directions simultaneously. (And I would add parenthetically that the peculiar power of *King Lear* arises from the desire it inspires to run in all directions simultaneously.) The semi-Pelagian view of Faustus impels us to recognize that human nature is primarily characterized by self-destructive fatuity, while this depressing insight is more than matched by the monstrousness of the God who results from a Calvinist interpretation of the play. But the Christian who takes Pascal's advice and flies from both "errors" can do so honestly only if he confronts the enigma of grace versus free will.

Shortly after signing his pact with Lucifer, Faustus returns from Olympus where he has gone with Mephostophilis on an expedition to "prove Cosmography." The sight of the heavens has caused him to regret his rejection of their creator and the mental struggle which results from the impulse to return to God is immediately allegorized by the appearance'of the two angels.

> FAUST. If Heaven was made for man, 'twas made for me:
> I will renounce this Magicke and repent.

> *Enter the two Angels.*

> GOOD A. *Faustus* repent, yet God will pitty thee.
> BAD A. Thou art a spirit, God cannot pity thee.
> FAUST. Who buzzeth in mine eares I am a spirit?
> Be I a devill yet God may pitty me,
> Yea, God will pitty me if I repent.
> EVILL AN. I, but *Faustus* never shall repent.   *Exit Angels.*
> FAUST. My heart is hardned, I cannot repent:
> (B, ll. 579–589)

Psychomachy or sciamachy? The angels are forces within Faustus's mind and yet not of it. They contend for possession of his consciousness and with his consciousness, presumably, his soul. Here the evil angel wins the field, and Faustus is left convinced for the moment that he will not and cannot repent. His heart is hardened. But who has hardened it? For the Pelagian the answer must be Faustus himself. Aquinas would hold that the hardening is the inevitable result of Faustus's stout abjuring of the Trinity. God permits it but does not will it and God can will its softening again. For Calvin, God wills it as he wills all things, as he wills the hardening of Pharaoh's heart in Exodus 14. If Calvin is right, the contention of Good and Evil Angels within the mind of Faustus is sciamachy, a shadowing forth of the only true reality, which is the will of God. As a result of that will or (to make room for the Catholic view) that permission, the forces of Evil possess the mind of the reprobate almost to the exclusion of all hope or comfort:

54

Scarce can I name salvation, faith, or heaven,
But feareful ecchoes thunders in mine eares,
Faustus, thou art damn'd, then swordes and knives,
Poyson, gunnes, halters, and invenomd steele
Are layde before me to dispatch my selfe.

(A, ll. 648–652)

And yet the diabolical powers who further this despair also provide
antidotes in pleasure, and Faustus now decides to anesthetize the thought
that he is incapable of repentance by discussing astronomy with Mephostophilis. The result is a domestic spat that begins with Faustus deliberately raising a question that he knows will anger his partner ("tell
me who made the world? . . . Sweete Mephastophilus tell me") and
ends with mutual recriminations and Mephostophilis storming back to
Lucifer:

FAUST. I, go accursed spirit to ugly hell:
　　　'Tis thou hast damn'd distressed Faustus soule.
　　　　　　　Ist not too late?

Enter the two Angels.

BAD. Too late.
GOOD. Never too late, if *Faustus* will repent.
BAD. If thou repent, devils will teare thee in peeces.
　　GOOD. Repent and they shall never raise thy skin.　　　*Ex. A.*
FAUST. O Christ my Saviour, my Saviour,
　　　Helpe to save distressed *Faustus* soule.

(B, ll. 645–653)

This time the Good Angel has the last word. The result is the play's
peripeteia, the structural equivalent of Robert le Dyable's contrition or
of Théophile's prayer to the Virgin. In terms of an audience's generic
expectation, the result of this moment will instruct us whether we are
present at a comedy of forgiveness or a tragedy of God's judgment.
Marlowe chooses to answer the question with consummate theatricality.
We may visualize Faustus on his knees, well downstage facing outward.
Then comes one of the theater's most melodramatic moments in the
"look out behind you" tradition:

Enter Lucifer, Belzebub, and Mephostophilis.

LUCIF. Christ cannot save thy soule, for he is just,
There's none but I have interest in the same.

(B, ll. 654–656)

The Bad Angel was right, it would seem. It is too late. And yet the Good Angel should be right too. It is never too late "if Faustus will repent." If the Good Angel is right, Faustus does not repent, and yet how can that appeal to "my Saviour, my Saviour" possibly be taken as insincere? But to the non-Calvinist Christian, it must fall short of true contrition. If Faustus were truly contrite, this pathetic appeal for grace would be answered by grace and not by the appearance of the forces of evil. Christ *would* help to save distressed Faustus's soul. For the Calvinist, circular reasoning is not required. Christ does not help to save Faustus's soul because God has willed that Faustus's soul should not be saved. Faustus is one of the reprobate, but this does not prevent him from feeling and expressing what appears to be true contrition. Indeed, according to Calvinism, the reprobate are capable of rather considerably more in the way of penance than Marlowe allows Faustus. Perkins describes for us

a certaine penitencie, whereby the reprobate I. Doth know his sin. II. Is pricked with the feeling of Gods wrath, for sin. III. Is greeved for the punishment of sin. IIII. Doth confesse his sin. V. Acknowledgeth God to be just in punishing sin. VI. Desireth to be saved. VII. Promiseth repentance in his miserie or affliction, in these words. *I will sin no more.*[14]

This *coup de théâtre* is the tragedy's most Calvinist moment, and in the A version of the text, the Genevan flavor is, as usual, even stronger. There the Good Angel assures Faustus that it is never too late, "if Faustus *can* repent" (A, l. 708, my italics), suggesting the possibility that he cannot. There Faustus implores Christ not to "helpe" but to "*seeke* to save distressed Faustus soule" (A, l. 712), thus eliminating the implication of the B version that salvation is the result of the co-operation of man's will with divine grace.

For the Christian who attempts to take Pascal's advice and who rejects both Pelagianism and Calvinism, the diabolical answer to Faustus's *cri de coeur* must be a painful challenge to faith. He can, of course, cope with the challenge by rejecting the art, by breaking off his involvement with the play, denying its validity as a version of the way things are. And yet, paradoxically, fear is a particularly compelling emotion in the theater, much more difficult to withdraw from, I think, than pity. Marlowe, of course, does not want withdrawal or denial and he soon gives his audience a way out of their perplexity by making it possible to see in the Faustus who grovels before Lucifer a figure who deserves the withholding of God's grace:

> pardon me in this,
> And Faustus vowes never to looke to heaven,
> Never to name God, or to pray to him,
> To burne his Scriptures, slay his Ministers,
> And make my spirites pull his churches downe.
>
> (A, ll. 724–728)

Nevertheless, that perplexing turning point has occurred and Marlowe has very deliberately devised it and included it in his play. The effect on Faustus of the quarrel with Mephostophilis is quite different in the play's source in the *Faust Book*. There when Mephostophilis leaves in a huff:

> *Faustus*, al sorrowful for that he had put forth such a question, fel to weeping and to howling bitterly, not for his sinnes towards God, but for that the Divel was departed from him so sodainely, and in such a rage.[15]

In fact, the *Faust Book* is as careful to repress perplexity as the play is to arouse it. Its Faustus cries out, "ah, woe is mee, that ever I was borne," but he is reassuringly described as

> having quite forgot his faith in Christ, never falling to repentance truly, thereby to attaine the grace *and* holy Spirit of God againe, the which would have been able to have resisted the strong assaults of Sathan.[16]

This sort of invitation to complacency is missing from Marlowe's tragedy. The strategy of the play is to terrify its audience, not to comfort it.

Uninterrupted terror would tend to work against itself however and what the play turns to, after its turning point, is buffoonery. The center of Marlowe's play gives us an equivalent to the corresponding section of *Robert le Dyable*, but whereas Robert the Devil's merry pranks were amusing or were at least not inferior in quality to the rest of the play, Dr. Faustus's merry pranks are hopelessly bad. Buffoonery is precisely what is needed at this point in the play, both as an emotional preparation for the tragedy's climactic terror and as a dramatic statement of one of the play's meanings. When he contemplates the glories of necromancy, Faustus tells us: "his dominion that exceedes in this, / Stretcheth as farre as doth the minde of man" (A, ll. 90–91). The middle section of the play shows us ironically just how far the mind of man stretches— to practical jokes and illusory fornications. This is precisely what we need to be shown, but the low quality of the showing nullifies the effect it should have on us. Something went wrong with the execution of Marlowe's intentions at this point. Perhaps they were entrusted to an incompetent collaborator or perhaps they proved to be beyond Marlowe's own powers (though the merry pranks of Barrabas, the Jew of Malta, are evidence against this). It is possible that Marlowe was murdered before he could complete this section of the play. It is possible that Marlovian scenes were rejected by the censor. In any case, I find it necessary to speculate, quite illegitimately no doubt, as to what the present middle section of the play should have been.

Faustus's terror at the appearance of Lucifer and his cohorts is calmed and compensated for by an allegorical presentation of the Seven Deadly Sins. This opens with a male embodiment of Pride and ends with a female embodiment of Lust. The central section of the play opens with a (verbally slightly inferior) Marlovian scene in Rome which includes the sight of the pope of Rome ascending to his throne by stepping on the back of Saxon Bruno, his rival of Avignon. This, I suggest, is a brilliantly Marlovian emblem for Pride. The middle section ends with the Helen of Troy episode—one of the greatest Marlowe ever wrote and a gorgeously ironic emblem for the destructive glories of Lust. It seems to me likely that the rest of the middle section of the play was intended to complete this "perceptual" reprise of the conceptual allegory of the Seven Deadly Sins. Its loss or failure to materialize weakens the play almost—though not quite—to the point of destroying its effectiveness.

Nothing could destroy the effectiveness of the scene of Faustus's damnation. The psychomachy which immediately precedes it epitomizes the inner struggle of Marlowe's protagonist throughout the play. The Old Man's exhortations lead Faustus once more to "a certain penitencie" though this is significantly weaker than formerly:

> FAU. Accursed Faustus, where is mercie now?
> I do repent, and yet I do dispaire.
>
> (A, ll. 1329–1330)

This is an intense and compact summation of the spiritual condition of a sinner who cannot find grace, and as such it is a strong challenge to semi-Pelagian complacency—a challenge that is typically softened by the B text, which changes Faustus's question to "wretch what hast thou done?" The earlier seemingly unalloyed contrition of "O Christ my Saviour, my Saviour" is not repeated and the threat of pain from Mephostophilis brings Faustus quickly back into line. The juxtaposition of Faustus and the Old Man, the reprobate and the elect, emphasizes the mysteriousness of grace. "His faith is great, I cannot touch his soule," (B, l. 1860) Mephostophilis says of the Old Man, leaving us to wonder about the source and the absence of such faith. But Faustus has his reward in the Seventh Deadly Sin, in the arms of Helen of Troy. He also has a moment of something like heroic stature in his prose scene of farewell to his fellow scholars, a moment that gives him a humanity and dignity that are necessary for our full participation in the terrors that lie ahead of him. This is followed by two incidents which are present only in the B text and which W. W. Greg maintains are not by Marlowe. In the first of these Mephostophilis triumphs over the man he has served:

> FAUST. Oh thou bewitching fiend, 'twas thy temptation,
> Hath rob'd me of eternall happinesse.
> MEPH. I doe confesse it *Faustus*, and rejoyce;
> 'Twas I, that when thou wer't i' the way to heaven,

Damb'd up thy passage, when thou took'st the booke,
To view the Scriptures, then I turn'd the leaves
And led thine eye.
What weep'st thou? 'tis too late, despaire, farewell,
Fooles that will laugh on earth, most weepe in hell.   *Exit*

(B, ll. 1986–1994)

This is highly unlike the usual Mephostophilean tone, but then the moment is an unusual one in his career. But what of the boast that before the pact had been conceived, the powers of evil were so strongly in control of Faustus's mind that they could prevent him from seeing the saving truths that were in front of him? If the passage belongs in the play, what is it doing there? To the non-Calvinist it strongly dramatizes the terrifying power of Satan, who cannot only inspire evil thoughts, but can, it would seem, prevent good ones. It may be that the lines were intended somehow to absolve God of any responsibility for the failure of Faustus's reason at the moment of his rejection of divinity. The fault, it would seem, is Satan's. This is not, however, the effect the lines would have upon a well-informed and true-believing Calvinist. If Mephostophilis is telling the truth, then he is really boasting, though he may not know it, of serving the will of God: "I grant that God doth often times worke in the reprobate by Satans service as a meane, but yet so that Satan doeth his office by Gods moving, and proceedeth so farre as is given him."[17] By this interpretation, Mephostophilis is here revealing a divinely inspired diabolical control over the mind of the reprobate.

The validity of so fatalistic an explanation is immediately challenged by the second possibly interpolated incident. In the most piously Pelagian moment in the tragedy, the Good and Evil Angels enter to indulge in atypically lengthy moralizations which place the blame for his plight entirely on Faustus:

GOOD. Oh *Faustus*, if thou hadst given eare to me,
Innumerable joyes had followed thee.
But thou didst love the world.
BAD. Gave eare to me,
And now must taste hels paines perpetually.

(B, ll. 1997–2001)

This comfort to the believers in man's free will would not, of course, trouble the true Calvinist. That God has reprobated Faustus to eternal death before creating him does not, according to Calvinist thinking on the matter, make Faustus less to blame for the sins he commits. That he commits them, even without free will, is what makes his eternal damnation just.

But theological controversies and comforts tend to dissolve in the terror of what follows. The impassioned but essentially intellectual theorizing of generations of Christian theologians, from Augustine to Calvin, is here embodied by the imagination of a poet of genius. The reprobate whose fate the theologians have so often and often so airily proclaimed and justified, is here given the form of a vain, silly man whose "evil," with regard to his fellows, has never gone beyond spitefulness, but who has deliberately offended his omnipotent creator, though whether the deliberation involved is the result of the exercise of Faustus's free will or of the offended God's eternal, terrible decree is a matter on which the play is careful not to pronounce. At any rate a doomed human being is presented to us: "The divel wil come, and Faustus must be damnd" (A, l. 1461).

Faced with the horror of eternal damnation, Faustus makes his third and last futile attempt at repentance:

> O Ile leape up to my God: who pulles me downe?
> See see where Christs blood streames in the firmament,
> One drop would save my soule, halfe a drop, ah my Christ,
> Ah rend not my heart for naming of my Christ,
> Yet wil I call on him, oh spare me *Lucifer*!
> Where is it now? tis gone:
> And see where God stretcheth out his arme,
> And bends his irefull browes.
>
> (A, ll. 1462–1469)

Nothing makes clearer what these lines are doing and how they are doing it than the juxtaposition of them against their emasculated equivalents in the B text of the play:

> O I'le leape up to heaven: who puls me downe?
> One drop of bloud will save me; oh my Christ,

> Rend not my heart, for naming of my Christ.
> Yet will I call on him: O spare me *Lucifer*.
> Where is it now? 'tis gone.
> And see a threatning Arme, an angry Brow.
>
> (B, ll. 2048–2053)

Marlowe is returning God to the scene in the A version of this play. At the moment of judgment God enters the theater of God's judgments. He is visible only to the damned protagonist, but the vision is communicated to us. The two visions, in fact. First Faustus sees God's grace, his mercy in the form of Christ's blood. This vision disappears completely from the B version of the play. It also disappears from Faustus's sight in the A version and is replaced by the terrible vision of God's other nature—the just and vengeful God. Again this terror is mitigated in the B version, its vividness generalized out of existence. What Marlowe is doing in the A version is characterizing the God who sends his creatures to hell and this the B version will not allow.

The God of grace is replaced by the God of wrath. Why? Because Faustus attempts to unite himself with the benevolent image of his creator and saviour. But God does not reject men merely because they wish to come to him. Quite the contrary. Why, then, does he reject Faustus? Here again we get the divergence of explanation that we have seen operating throughout the play. To begin with, a third force is present at this damnation. The devils have long before entered to watch Faustus's performance—"To marke him how he doth demeane himselfe" (B, l. 1905, there is no equivalent stage direction in A). When Faustus calls upon Christ for mercy, the forces of evil intervene and exercise their dominion over man by rending Faustus's heart. This is precisely what they have done previously to the Old Man:

> Sathan begins to sift me with his pride,
> As in this furnace God shal try my faith,
> My faith, vile hel, shal triumph over thee,
> Ambitious fiends, see how the heavens smiles
> At your repulse, and laughs your state to scorne,
> Hence hel, for hence I flie unto my God.
>
> (A, l. 1381–1386)

Faustus, by contrast, gives up the fight. He calls upon Christ once more and then his stock of perseverance is exhausted and he appeals to Lucifer. The effect is immediate. The God of grace becomes the God of wrath. The Pelagian knows why. Faustus is a weak and wicked man. Rend his heart a few times and he turns from God. The non-Pelagian is far less sure because he is, like Saint Augustine, far more conscious of his own weakness. He believes that without God's grace no man can stand up against the powers of evil and he must suspect that he has just seen a fellow creature begging for grace—for half a drop of Christ's blood—and being refused. When he asks why, if he is not a Calvinist, he must confront the mystery of God's judgments though he may sometimes delay that confrontation by appealing to the mystery of God's omniscience, by pointing out that God from eternity foresaw the wickedness of Faustus, including his appeal to Lucifer, and withholds his grace because of what he has foreseen. But, of course, God's foreseeing cannot make that wickedness a necessity if free will is to survive and so the mystery remains.

The Calvinist, more obsessed with the omnipotence of God's will and the total depravity of all mankind, will "solve" the mystery by jettisoning free will and invoking the concept of reprobation. The spectacle of God granting grace to the Old Man and withholding it from Faustus will become for him a striking example of the *decretrum horribile* in action. God has willed the election of one and the reprobation of the other. No more need be said. Except as to the justice of what Marlowe is here so vividly dramatizing. Of course, the Calvinist has an answer:

> Neither must any thinke it to be crueltie in God to forsake his creature which hee hath made: for he is soveraigne Lord over all his workes: and for that cause he is not bound to any; and he may doe with his owne whatsoever he will. And this his will is not to be blamed: for men are not to imagine, that a thing must first bee just and then afterward that God doth will it: but contrariwise, first God wils a thing, and thereupon it becomes just.[18]

In the study or even from the pulpit it may be possible to proclaim such a God as worthy of worship, but in the theater he is, at best, what Burghley suggested he was, a tyrant. Faustus's impulse, faced with this

"Justice" is, not surprisingly, to "run into the earth" but his sense of time's passage makes him turn to God again in one last appeal:

> Oh God, if thou wilt not have mercy on my soule,
> Yet for Christs sake, whose bloud hath ransomd me,
> Impose some end to my incessant paine.
>
> (A, ll. 1483–1485)

But God does not have mercy and the ransom paid in Christ's blood appears not to have been paid for Faustus, just as one might have suspected from the syllogism which Faustus constructed out of his biblical half-texts at the play's beginning. One would suppose that a God who damns eternally the speaker of these lines is too horrible a concept to bear thinking about by a believing Christian. Surely the hardiest Calvinist must want to retreat before this vision and whoever was responsible for the alterations in the B text—and it may have been Marlowe himself, after all—simply eliminated this God from the play. These lines are changed to read: "O, if my soule must suffer for my sinne, / Impose some end to my incessant paine" (B, ll. 2067–2068). The responsibility becomes unequivocally Faustus's. His suffering is seen as the necessary punishment for his sin. The memory of Christ's sacrifice is suppressed as efficiently as it was in Faustus's original foolish syllogism.

But the God of the A text is, I suspect, the true and original God of this tragedy. To remove him, as the B text does, is to give comfort to the Pelagian without offending the Calvinist. There is no comfort for anyone in the A text lines. Without the aid of grace, no attempt at contrition, no attempt at faith can save a man from the heavy wrath of God. And this of course is precisely what all non-Pelagian Christian theology in Marlowe's time maintained, whether Calvinist, Romanist, or Anglican. What the play is doing here is to force the believing Christians of the Elizabethan era to face the full reality—emotional as well as intellectual—of their beliefs. It is generally assumed that this tragedy's didactic purpose was to terrify its audience into faith and godliness. I am not convinced that the play has a didactic purpose, but I think that one of its possible didactic effects would be precisely to terrify the more intelligent and informed of its beholders out of their beliefs or at least into a serious examination of them. Such an examination was going on, of course, with or without the help of *Dr. Faustus*. The most profoundly imaginative Christians among Marlowe's Anglican contemporaries— men like Andrewes, Hooker, and, later, Donne—were attempting to conceive a less monstrous God than the one who rules the world of *Dr. Faustus*.

Faustus, however, is not given the privilege of constructing a different world from the one Marlowe has devised for him out of theological concepts. *"Pythagoras Metemsycosis"* is not true, and Faustus is dragged off to hell. But of course, the play is not over. The chorus must pronounce some sort of moral, and at first hearing this concluding didacticism sounds peculiarly unsatisfactory:

> *Faustus* is gone, regard his hellish fall,
> Whose fiendfull fortune may exhort the wise
> Onely to wonder at unlawfull things:
> Whose deepnesse doth intice such forward wits,
> To practise more then heavenly power permits.
> (B, ll. 2117–2121)

In other words, "Behave yourselves." But surely one of the major points of the play is that we cannot behave ourselves. We must sin. "Si peccasse negamus, fallimur." Try as we may not to, we will always practice more than heavenly power permits. And so the play leaves us back where we started, though with a frightening knowledge gained from imaginative experience of just what the human inability to obey divine commands may mean. There is however another sense in which the chorus's words can be taken. Faustus's tragedy exhorts the wise only to wonder at unlawful things. The obvious reference is to magic, to the attempt to exercise supernatural power. But a second reference is possible, I think. The tragedy of Faustus causes us to do what, in the course of this essay, I have been assuming that Elizabethans did—to wonder what Faustus's tragedy reveals about the nature of the God who, according to Christianity, has created and will judge us. Too much wondering about that subject is an unlawful thing. On this all theologies agree, even Calvin's:

Wherefore let us rather beholde an evident cause of damnation in the corrupted nature of mankind, which is neerer to us, than search for a hidden and utterly incomprehensible cause therof in the pre-destination of GOD. Neither let it grieve us so farre to submitt our wit to the unmeasurable wisedom of God, that it may yeelde in many secretes of his. For, of those thinges which it is neither graunted nor lawfull to knowe, the ignorance is well learned: the coveting of knowledge, is a kinde of madnesse.[19]

It is quite like Marlowe to devise his tragedy out of the terrors inspired by the controversial certainties and final mysteries of Christian theology and then to turn around and exhort his audience not to think about what he has forced them to think about. He has forced upon us "the coveting of knowledge"—which is precisely Faustus's kind of madness. As a result he forces his Christian audience to examine imaginatively what it is they believe and to discover, if they can stand the knowledge, that what they believe is a mystery both terrifying and incomprehensible.

CHAPTER 4
Richard III

WE REGARD the hellish fall of Dr. Faustus and wonder at the forces that explain it, particularly at the mysteries of grace and free will, of election and reprobation. The hellish fall of Richard the Third directs our minds toward the same unlawful things, but Shakespeare's first great tragic protagonist is the protagonist of something more (or other) than tragedy. The Richard III plays (I shall be considering *Henry VI, Part Three* as well as *Richard III*) are doubly generic—tragic history within comic history—and the tragic destruction of Richard is simultaneously the comedy of England's salvation. Evil is done but good comes of it. Divine providence is necessarily among Shakespeare's subjects. The mysteries of grace and free will, of election and reprobation are contained within the mysteries of providence and predestination. The result is a work of art more complex than Marlowe's.

Not that the explanation for the increase in complexity is to be found wholly or even largely in the theological concepts evoked. Shakespeare is making art out of history and Northrop Frye is right when he maintains that "the poet . . . can deal with history only to the extent that history supplies him with, or affords a pretext for, the comic, tragic, romantic or ironic myths that he actually uses."[1] Nonetheless, once the artist declares himself a writer of history he can achieve "the integrity or consistency of his verbal structure" only by accommodating his mythic urges to those facts which are too well known to be altered and by producing characters who are moved by impulses human enough to be reconcilable with the historical nature of the events which form the mythic pattern. Thus in the Henry IV plays Shakespeare must reconcile his mythic Hal—the legendary prodigal prince—with the Machiavellian power struggle which makes up the history he is dramatizing. The result of the effort is a Machiavellian prodigal, a character more complex and significant than the Henry of Monmouth produced by either popular legend or official history, and to create this figure Shakespeare invents one of his greatest mythic actions—the story of Falstaff and Prince Hal.

The accommodation of the legendary Richard III, the murderous Machiavel, to the facts of history had largely been done before Shakespeare took on the job. Indeed the legendary figure had been to some degree created by the historians and declared a fact by royal authority in order to validate what has since been called the Tudor myth. That pious version of the past held that the coronation of Henry VII (i.e., the arrival of the Tudor dynasty out of genealogical left field) was the happy ending of God's providential plan for sinful, suffering England, a plan that necessarily included the agonies inflicted upon the English by the villainy of the supplanted king. I do not believe that the propagation of this quaint notion was Shakespeare's overriding purpose in the Histories. The providential view is, however, among the materials Shakespeare had to deal with in making these plays and he did not choose to deal with it by eliminating it. On the contrary he used it as an essential ingredient for transforming what the historians presented him with—a melodrama about a melodramatic villain—into a tragedy with a tragic protagonist.

Authorized historical legend presented Shakespeare with a villainous instrument of God's beneficent providence. Shakespeare proceeded to discover the tragic meaning of such a figure by creating him through action. But in order to do so, it was necessary for Shakespeare to create a complicated work of art—complicated primarily in its sense of cause. The actions of the play must take place within a dramatic version of what we may call the world of second causes. What happens in that imagined world must be clearly the result of acceptable artistic imitations of those emotional and political forces with which, as creatures who inhabit the real world of second causes, we are altogether too familiar. But because the world in which the action of the play unfolds is proclaimed to be providentially ordered, the play must also make us aware that those very psychological and political forces are themselves caused and that their first cause is the nature and will of the God who has created and now governs that world—or Shakespeare's imitation of it. And what is true of action must be true of character also. Richard III is a vividly imagined expressionistic imitation of a man. Shakespeare has selected, emphasized, and repressed the various elements of human nature to create a brilliant artifact. But he has also imagined for this creation a creator other than the playwright himself. Richard the Third is presented as a manifestation of the first cause of the world he inhabits. Both action and character in the earlier histories are evidence of the nature of the God who governs the world of these plays, and the nature of the God they bear witness to is an important source of tragic terror for the audience at Richard's tragedy. By looking first at some aspects of the action of the plays and then at the character of the protagonist, I would like to try to discover what these tragical histories suggest about the nature of the God who creates and destroys Richard.

Not that divine nature is constantly being forced upon our attention in the Histories. God's existence is easy to forget, so completely does the action of these plays appear at times to be entirely the outcome of the characters' lust for power. Before the emergence of Richard, Warwick the King-maker is the most important human determiner of the design of these plays, the human God of the political world of *Henry VI, Part III*. Indeed, he is described more than once in terms that make him appear to be a human embodiment of Fortune, a man who, like Marlowe's Mortimer, "makes Fortune's wheel turn as he please," or seems to. Queen Margaret calls him the "Proud setter up, and puller downe of Kings" (*3H6*.3.3.157), and on the occasion of his final fall Warwick finds it necessary to remind Edward IV that he owes his royalty to the talents of the King-maker: "Confesse who set thee up, and pluckt thee downe" (*3H6*.5.1.26).

With these images of royal rise and fall, Warwick is being associated with the goddess Fortuna, and by the association Shakespeare is saying something about the nature of Fortune as well as of Warwick. From one point of view, the force which moves these characters to catastrophe and success is blind chance, an unseeing goddess mindlessly turning a meaningless wheel. Looked at from another perspective, however, Fortune appears to own the features of Warwick, and the motivating force of these plays is the human drive for power. The tragic rises and falls result from the Machiavellian skills which the various characters bring to the political struggle the plays dramatize. This way of seeing explains the action by presenting it as a series of cause and effect relationships and thus satisfies our need to find a structure in the chaos of our lives. It does not, however, quite satisfy our need to find a meaning. The political perspective tells us that event is consequence, but we know that the coinciding of consequence and justice is rare and usually accidental. We want what happens in drama to be what, morally and ethically, should happen and Shakespeare presumably shares this desire. At any rate, he certainly plays with it, using it for the purposes of creating his tragic effect. He allows us to perceive that a design formed by the assertion of human will coexists in tragedy with the mindless revolutions of Fortune's wheel. But coexisting with both these patterns and transcending them both is a pattern determined by the exercise of the omniscient and omnipotent will of God. The plays suggest that chance and consequence have first and final causes and that they are appearances which conceal the reality of divine providential justice. The dramatic action is thus made meaningful and we are made happy, our need for meaning satisfied. But Shakespeare's tragedies are never content simply to achieve our happiness. The art then goes on to show us that the meaning which has pleased us is, in fact, incomprehensible and terrifying. If we choose to contemplate the vision of divine providence that these early histories present us with, we find that there is little in it for our comfort. What we confront is a mystery and when we attempt to solve that mystery by embodying in a god the logical conclusions toward which the clues in the art direct us, we find our reason bringing forth monsters. Thus we can discover if we wish to that our need for meaning leads us to terror and a knowledge of our ignorance. We learn from tragedy what we have been told by theology: the coveting of knowledge is a kind of madness.

We are mightily assisted in our first attempts at understanding by the fact that the men and women around Richard are also trying to discover a transcendent meaning for their more or less horrible lives. As a result, the various characters present us with a series of versions of God and of a divine providence whose existence will explain away the meaningless injustice that is inherent in accident or mere consequence. This is true even of Warwick. As a preeminently political man, he is usually content with political meaning, but he is also conscious of divine power—though far more conscious of his own—and can appeal to it in moments of unusual stress:

Why stand we like soft-hearted women heere,
Wayling our losses, whiles the Foe doth Rage,
And looke upon, as if the Tragedie
Were plaid in jest, by counterfetting Actors.
Heere on my knee, I vow to God above,
Ile never pawse againe, never stand still,
Till either death hath clos'd these eyes of mine,
Or Fortune given me measure of Revenge.
(*3H6*.2.3.25–32)

The effect of this bombast is more than ordinarily complex for a play so early in the canon. Warwick's theatrical metaphor reminds us that he is wrong—the tragedy *is* played in jest by counterfeiting actors. But the action and speech that follow the metaphor remind us that he is doubly wrong. Prayers in the theater are usually addressed to the second balcony. By falling to his knees and calling God to witness, Warwick suggests that there is a divine spectator within the play's world for whom the imitated reality takes place in the theater of God's judgments. For the God of the play the action may be as much as drama as it is for us, the "children of paradise," the human audience in the theater. Edward extends that sense by joining Warwick and further defining the power to which both appeal:

Oh Warwicke, I do bend my knee with thine,
And in this vow do chaine my soule to thine:
And ere my knee rise from the Earths cold face,
I throw my hands, mine eyes, my heart to thee,
Thou setter up, and plucker downe of Kings:
Beseeching thee (if with thy will it stands)
That to my Foes this body must be prey,
Yet that thy brazen gates of heaven may ope,
And give sweet passage to my sinfull soule.
(*3H6*.2.3.33–41)

Warwick vows; Edward also prays, and that characterizes both men. But in praying Edward modifies Warwick's vow. For Warwick, God is

71

a spectator at the theater of His judgments; for Edward, He is the all-powerful actor in it. Warwick looks to Fortune for revenge. Edward looks beyond, defining Fortune's true nature. As we have seen, the phrase "Thou setter up, and plucker downe of Kings" could serve nicely to describe Fortuna and her wheel. It does serve to describe Warwick the King-maker, but in using it Edward is talking about neither Fortune nor Warwick. He is describing divine will, the ultimate reality which contains the meaning both of blind chance and of human will.

The pattern of royal rise and fall, which can be ascribed to the random working of blind Fortune, can also be seen as the result of such human power drives and political skills as are embodied in Warwick. But just as the appearance of Fortune is rejected by the more pious for the reality of divine will, so is the appearance of human freedom and control, and appropriately enough it is the pious Henry who defines the true relationship with precision:

> But *Warwicke*, after God, thou set'st me free
> And chiefely therefore, I thanke God, and thee,
> He was the Author, thou the Instrument.
> (*3H6*.4.6.16–18)

To be sure, the clarity of Henry's sense of the true nature of causes does not prevent him from immediately going on with an apostrophe to Fortune and an announcement of his political intentions. For the actors in the theater of God's judgments, chance and will are realities, and though they may not be the ultimate reality, the patterns they form have a perceptible existence and coexist with the overriding design of divine providence. *One way* of looking at the drama in which Shakespeare involves us is to see it as taking place in the theater of God's judgments and Henry is here defining God's true relationship to that theater. God is more than a spectator and participant. He is the author and the characters are his characters—his instruments. His providential plot will conclude with apocalypse—joy for some, horror for others. Along the way, providential comedies and providential tragedies occur. As a human imitator of divine creation Shakespeare devises imitations of both kinds of action in the course of his career. The late Romances are supreme examples of providential comedy but *Richard III* is a providential tragedy—

that is, a tragic action set within a providential frame, and the apparent contradiction between the agony and villainy of the protagonist and the proclaimed beneficence of the whole action inevitably raises within a Christian audience questions, doubts, and fears which Shakespeare is less interested in answering or allaying than in turning to artistic account.

Such questions arise necessarily from the material which Shakespeare has chosen to dramatize in *Henry the Sixth, Part Three* and *Richard the Third*. The Tudor myth requires that Richard be the villain protagonist of a providential action. Shakespeare accepts the myth as a "given" and pays lip service to it, but the only important enthusiast for the myth in the plays is Richmond himself—and Shakespeare has made the first of the Tudors a dramatic nonentity, a vacuum in shining armor. Richmond's repeated pieties (I count eight variations of "God and our good cause fight upon our side" in the last one hundred and sixty lines of *Richard III*) give an intellectual existence to the purely beneficent Tudor myth version of providence and create for us a God in whom it would be pleasant to believe. Like Edward's, Richmond's God is a participant in the action of the play, but far more than Edward's, he is a benevolent participant. He is ultimately responsible for the good that happens and that includes, of course, the deserved punishment of the wicked, especially of Richard himself. Richmond's God, the author of good and the enemy of evil, is the last version of divine nature we meet with in the first tetralogy of history plays and it is possible, if one has a talent for optimism, to leave the theater in undisturbed possession of something rather like the semi-Pelagianism which the medieval miracle plays promote, and which *Dr. Faustus* also permits the unreflecting Christians in its audience to retain. But like Marlowe, Shakespeare creates other possible Gods for his tragedy. Two such divinities are imag· ined by characters within the plays as possible first causes for the tragic action. Because the God-devising (or perceiving) characters in question —Queen Elizabeth and Queen Margaret—are far more vivid than Richmond and because the events that inspire their speeches are tragic rather than triumphant, their visions have an intensity and a conceptual valid· ity for the plays that Richmond's lacks.

The theological question that Elizabeth and Margaret are forced by the horror of their lives to confront is basic: is God responsible for the

73

evil which results in human suffering? For Elizabeth the answer is, "Yes, in a sense." For Margaret, "Yes, hallelujah!" The event which prompts their varying responses is Richard's murder of Elizabeth's sons, the two princes, in the Tower. The scene which explores the significance of this horror has a choral quality which is, appropriately, as much ecclesiastical as dramatic, turning it into a kind of mass for the dead with the *Kyrie eleison* of Elizabeth set against Margaret's *Dies irae*. The litany gets to its point when Elizabeth questions God's concern for the innocent:

> Qu. Wilt thou, O God, flye from such gentle Lambs,
> And throw them in the intrailes of the Wolfe?
> When didst thou sleepe, when such a deed was done?
> (*RIII*.4.4.22–24)

For the benevolent good shepherd of Richmond's version of divine power, Elizabeth is tempted to substitute a bad shepherd who abandons his flock when it is in danger. She begins, indeed, to go further and to see him throwing the innocent to the wolf. But then she turns back and modifies her accusation to one of ignorant uncaring, of sleep. The God she imagines is one who is responsible for evil only in the sense that he permits its existence and fails to prevent its effect. This, with the accusation of indifference removed, is close to the God of the theologians, like Hooker, who hold that God must permit evil in order to preserve human freedom : "all men of knowledge grant, that God is himself no author of sin. . . . And yet we must of necessity grant that there could be no evil committed, if his will did appoint or determine that none should be."[2] In terms of his control over the theater of his judgments, this God is more than Warwick's spectator, more than Richmond's benevolent participant, but less than Henry's "author." He is rather like, to punish the metaphor, a *commedia dell'arte* scenarist who leaves his characters free to improvise dialogue and invent business (especially wicked business) but who has determined both the outline of the plot and its conclusion.

Elizabeth's God is not Margaret's. Henry the Sixth's queen has done and suffered evil for so long that her sense of it is bound to make Elizabeth's appear naive by contrast. Elizabeth asks when God has slept

through a deed as evil as the murder of her children. Margaret tells us:
"When holy *Harry* dyed, and my sweet Sonne" (*RIII*.4.4.25). In Margaret's world, the slaughter of inncents is banal, and her incantations prove it:

> I had an *Edward*, till a *Richard* kill'd him:
> I had a Husband, till a *Richard* kill'd him:
> Thou had'st an *Edward*, till a *Richard* kill'd him:
> Thou had'st a *Richard*, till a *Richard* kill'd him.
> (*RIII*.4.4.39–42)

The duchess of York is also on stage and her memory is as long and her experience as rich as Margaret's. She reminds the queen and us that Margaret's role in the horrors has been far from passive:

> I had a *Richard* too, and thou did'st kill him;
> I had a *Rutland* too, thou help'st[3] to kill him.
> (*RIII*.4.4.43–44)

With the mention of Rutland, that pattern of the murder of innocent children in the two plays has been completely recalled. The Lancastrian Clifford's murder of young Rutland, the stabbing of Edward, prince of Wales, at Tewkesbury, and the murder of the little princes in the Tower form a series of events presented as doubly caused. The design results immediately from the repetitious barbarity of human impulses, but it also expresses the nature of Margaret's God, whose justice is served by such impulses even in their most barbarous forms.

Young Clifford, Margaret's chief general, is the most barbaric servant of such impulses in *Henry VI, Part III*. He comes into full dramatic being in *Henry VI, Part II* at the Battle of Saint Albans, entering immediately after the duke of York's murder of Old Clifford. Before he sees his father's body Clifford apostrophizes war:

> O Warre, thou sonne of hell,
> Whom angry heavens do make their minister,
> Throw in the frozen bosomes of our part,
> Hot Coales of Vengeance. (*2H6*.5.2.33–36)

War and the heavens answer his invitation by presenting him with the sight of Old Clifford's corpse and he replies with a demand for nothing less than apocalypse itself.

> O let the vile world end,
> And the premised Flames of the Last day,
> Knit earth and heaven together.
>
> (*2H6*.5.2.40–42)

This early but very Shakespearean invitation to chaos to come again is a sign that the heavens have chosen Clifford as a minister of their wrath against humanity. As a servant of the drive toward chaos, he will not spare the innocent:

> Henceforth, I will not have to do with pitty.
> Meet I an infant of the house of Yorke,
> Into as many gobbits will I cut it
> As wilde *Medea* yong *Absirtis* did.
>
> (*2H6*.5.2.56–59)

In *Henry VI, Part Three* he keeps his promise. He captures the twelve-year-old earl of Rutland, York's youngest son, and proceeds to slaughter him despite his pleas:

> RUTLAND. I never did thee harme: why wilt thou slay me?
> CLIFFORD. Thy Father hath.
> RUTLAND. But 'twas ere I was borne.
>   Thou hast one Sonne, for his sake pitty me,
>   Lest in revenge thereof, sith God is just,
>   He be as miserably slaine as I.
>   Ah, let me live in Prison all my dayes,
>   And when I give occasion of offence,
>   Then let me dye, for now thou hast no cause.
> CLIFFORD. No cause? thy Father slew my Father: therefore dye.
>
> (*3H6*.1.3.40–48)

When Rutland realizes that the moral argument of his own innocence will not move Clifford, he tries to influence his murderer by suggesting that vengeance breeds vengeance. Blood will have blood and the same impulses move Yorkists and Lancastrians, Shepherdsons and Grangerfords, Hatfields and McCoys. But Rutland is not arguing simply from the brutality of men. Clifford should fear for the life of his innocent son "sith God is just." By killing the innocent, men serve divine justice. But although Clifford suffers deserved death within the play, the sin of Rutlands' murderer is not visited on his posterity. Instead Queen Margaret appropriates the punishment to her own child by the enthusiasm with which she uses the death of Rutland to torment her enemy, York, before she helps Clifford to kill him:

> . . . where is your Darling, *Rutland?*
> Looke *Yorke*, I stayn'd this Napkin with the blood
> That valiant *Clifford*, with his Rapiers point,
> Made issue from the Bosome of the Boy:
> And if thine eyes can water for his death,
> I give thee this to drie thy Cheekes withall.
> (*3H6*.1.4.78–83)

The extravagance of this guarantees our memory of it, which must last on into *Richard III* if that play is to make the sense it should. It certainly lasts until the murder of Edward, prince of Wales, by York's remaining sons in act 5, scene 5 of *3 Henry VI*, where it creates a context for Margaret's agonizing that gives a grim absurdity to such assertions as "Men, ne're spend their fury on a Childe" (*3H6*.5.5.56). But it also keeps us conscious of an emerging pattern when she turns upon the murderers:

> You have no children (Butchers) if you had,
> The thought of them would have stirr'd up remorse,
> But if you ever chance to have a Childe,
> Looke in his youth to have him so cut off.
> As deathsmen you have rid this sweet yong Prince.
> (*3H6*.5.5.62–66)

Her own example (and Clifford's) invalidate the first of these sentiments. Neither maternity nor paternity is a guarantee of decent human impulses. But the death she is suffering for is clear evidence that she is right in expecting the sins of parents to be visited upon their children. Hers were visited upon her child.

Margaret is here beginning to justify her epithet: "well skilled in curses." But her virtuoso performances in the genre come only in *Richard III*. Her skill is double. She is both eloquent and accurate. Her eloquence is in part native, in part, as she explains to Elizabeth at act 4, scene 4, lines 116 and following, the result of wits sharpened by hatred. Her accuracy also has two sources: first, her ability to sense the consequences of the destructive nature of the human beings, particularly Richard, whom she hates, and second, a growing ability to perceive the pattern of divine vengeance, which becomes steadily clearer as the plays unfold. The first such moment of perception in *Richard III* comes in act 1, scene 3, when Margaret, having spied long enough on the band of wrangling pirates that the house of York has become, is amused to notice that her appearance and the memory of her evil—the death of Rutland in particular—serve to reunite the Yorkists temporarily:

> What? were you snarling all before I came,
> Ready to catch each other by the throat,
> And turne you all your hatred now on me?
> (*RIII*.1.3.188–190)

This is an important moment of analogous action. What Margaret does for the house of York, Richard will do for all England. The process of strife which originates and continues in human hatred can only be ended by human hatred. By being absolutely horrible Richard forces his society to unite in hatred against him. But this is not Margaret's perception of the future—it can only be ours, and only by hindsight. Margaret's vision is triggered by a pair of pieties from Richard and Queen Elizabeth, who see Margaret's suffering as the result of divine justice for Rutland's murder:

> RICH. . . . . God, not we, hath plagu'd thy bloody deed.
> QU. So just is God, to right the innocent.
> (*RIII*.1.3.181–182)

Now Margaret knows that her sufferings, her plagues as well as her curses, have taken the form of the suffering of the innocent—she has been punished with the murder of her innocent son and husband—and she perceives that God can be expected also to visit the sins of the house of York upon guilty and innocent alike:

> Did *Yorkes* dread Curse prevaile so much with Heaven,
> That *Henries* death, my lovely *Edwards* death,
> Their Kingdomes losse, my wofull Banishment,
> Should all but answer for that peevish Brat?
> Can Curses pierce the Clouds, and enter Heaven?
> Why then give way dull Clouds to my quick Curses.
>
> . . . .
>
> *Edward* thy Sonne, that now is Prince of Wales,
> For *Edward* our Sonne, that was Prince of Wales,
> Dye in his youth, by like untimely violence.
>
> (*RIII*.1.3.191–201)

Margaret has conceived her God, has found out the providential pattern, the design worked out by the dynamics of divine justice in this Shakespearean example of the theater of God's judgments. The principle which emerges is that of punishing the infliction of suffering upon the innocent by inflicting suffering upon the innocent. In cursing an innocent child Margaret is asking that the will of her God be done on earth.

Margaret's God is a concept shockingly foreign to the liberal humanitarianism that has characterized middle-class Christianity for at least a century. It is distinctly less foreign to Shakespeare's play and Shakespeare's time. When the innocent Rutland warns his murderer that more innocents may suffer for the crime, he does so on the grounds that God is just. And every twelve-year-old Elizabethan bright enough to memorize his catechism knew how God characterizes himself in the second commandment: "I the Lorde thy God am a jealous God, and visit the sins of the fathers upon the children, unto the thirde and fourth generation of them that hate me."[4] Such a visitation of iniquities is being presented in *3 Henry VI* and *Richard III*.

Margaret's second and final appearance in *Richard III* returns us to our starting point—the fulfillment of her curse, the murder of the princes in the Tower. It is here that her perception of the two forces—

human and divine—that shape the design of the play's horror comes into focus and presents her with a vision of Richard as the human agent of divinely willed suffering. Richard is God's enemy, "hell's black intelligencer," the "foul defacer of God's handiwork," but God is to be thanked for his existence:

> O upright, just, and true-disposing God,
> How do I thanke thee, that this carnall Curre
> Prayes on the issue of his Mothers body.
>
> (*RIII*.4.4.55–57)

It will not do to dismiss Margaret's vision of the God of her play as the ravings of a wicked woman. Her God is the inevitable corollary of Richmond's God. If the Tudor myth is to claim for Richmond the role of God's providential instrument, then it must confront the complementary possibility that Richard has previously served the same function. Before the Battle of Bosworth, Richmond prays, "Make us thy ministers of Chasticement." An instrument for chastisement is a scourge, but for the Elizabethans the term "scourge of God" connoted human guilt.[5] Richmond's innocence is a necessity for the completion of the providential pattern and so he is a minister. Richard is not innocent, but he is nonetheless an instrument of God. By slaughtering the innocent he has served the mysterious purposes of Margaret's "upright, just and true-disposing God."

That the "justice" entailed is beyond the comprehension of human reason goes without saying. And yet a belief in providence demands of the honest mind a recognition that undeserved human suffering is as much an expression of divine will as the misery of the wicked or the happiness of the good. But what is mysterious by the light of nature, as Luther puts it,[6] is comprehensible by the light of grace—that is, the innocent human suffering exemplified in the murder of Rutland and the little princes can be understood as necessary for the achievement of the benevolent purposes of providence—though in my opinion the play gives only minimal encouragement to this sort of piety. Beyond that, divine justice may be conceived of as insuring eternal compensation for temporal sufferings, but again, though so thumping a commonplace would hardly need emphasizing, this comfort is not strongly put forward by the play.

If we think of the God of *Richard III* as the first cause of the play's action, he is a terrifying figure, but one who becomes less frightening when he is viewed by the light of grace. It is when we view him as the first cause of Richard's nature that the terror is raised to tragic intensity. The pathos of innocent suffering is not finally so mysterious nor so frightening as the creation and destruction of God's evil instrument for inflicting that suffering. It is here that the light of grace fails even for the believing Christian to illuminate the mystery and leaves the spectator at the theater of God's judgments with the frightening sense that, as Luther put it, "the fault lies not in the wretchedness of man, but in the injustice of God."[7]

It is also here, I think, that the imagination of Shakespeare is most fully engaged by the material he is dramatizing. The theological problem is central: is human evil of the sort embodied in Richard the result of God's permission or God's will? Augustine insists on the former, Calvin on the latter. But the question is also psychologically central. Whether phrased theologically or not, the question of the degree to which our wills are the creatures of forces other than our own is patently at the heart of our view of ourselves and the meaning of our minds' processes. Shakespeare's fascination with creating the illusion of minds in operation made the problem central artistically as well.

The artistic problem is complex. Just as the design of the plays must be the product simultaneously of the interaction of human wills and the expression of an omnipotent divine will, so the character of the protagonist must entail an acceptable imitation of the human psyche while remaining a fated instrument for the working out of the providential design. Shakespeare solves the problem primarily through the language of Richard's soliloquies. These convince us that they are the self-presentations of a human mind while at the same time they reveal the nature of the speaker in aspects of which the speaker could not be consciously aware. The psychomachies expressed by Richard's soliloquies are sciamachies as well. They betray the presence of causes other than those which the speaker tells us about. As moderns we define these causes as unconscious motivations and we marvel, rather naively, at Shakespeare's "instinctive grasp" of psychology. If we stay within the context which I am attempting to develop for these tragedies (and I do not insist that we must or should) then we can see these "other causes" as evidence of the first cause, the nature and will of God. But however we define or account for the character who emerges from the soliloquies Shakespeare has written for Richard, we are attempting to describe Shakespeare's first brilliant work of art. Richard III and a Shakespeare who invites bardolatry come into being at the same moment.

That moment arrives in *Henry VI, Part Three*, act 3, scene 2, line 124. Richard's first soliloquy dramatizes the creation of a self. The character who emerges from the speech at the end of it is Shakespeare's first great role for Burbage—and for all the Burbages who have inhabited the theater since. Richard III, the murderous Machiavel, the reverend vice Iniquity, the player king, who can smile and murder while he smiles, exists by the time the speech is over. That Shakespeare can call so brilliant a theatrical artifact into existence demonstrates that he is as great a playwright as Marlowe, who had shown his contemporary the way by calling into existence Barrabas, the Jew of Malta. But Shakespeare does more. He not only creates Richard, he has him created and doubly created. Richard is brought into existence by himself. The Richard who speaks the opening lines is a sardonic, ambitious, destructive, hate-filled, and desperate man. His desperation has its origin in a half-conscious perception that his destructive ambition is finally self-destructive and he creates a new self as an alternative to self-destruction. This Richard is a brilliant comment on the psychic forces that move us to will ourselves into existence. But again, Shakespeare does more, for the Richard here created has a divine, a superhuman cause as well. In creating himself, Richard unwittingly creates an instrument designed to serve the will of God.

The soliloquy opens with a declaration of hate—for Edward ("Would he were wasted, Marrow, Bones and all") and for all the Plantagenets whose claims upon the throne are better than Richard's: Clarence, Henry, Edward, and the Prince of Wales "and all the unlooked-for Issue of their Bodies." Richard's enemy is human fertility—or at least Plantagenet fertility—which produces the living barriers that stand between him and the only pleasure of which he is capable, the exercise of absolute power. The frustration which has procreation for its source is bound to be intense and the brilliance of this soliloquy is founded on two similes for Richard's frustration: the images first of a man on a promontory and then of a man in a thorny wood. The first of these comes immediately after Richard's consideration of the human barriers that stand between him and the crown:

> Why then I doe but dream on Soveraigntie,
> Like one that stands upon a Promontorie,
> And spyes a farre-off shore, where hee would tread,
> Wishing his foot were equall with his eye,
> And chides the Sea, that sunders him from thence,
> Saying hee'le lade it dry, to have his way:
> So doe I wish the Crowne, being so farre off,
> And so I chide the meanes that keepes me from it,
> And so (I say) Ile cut the Causes off,
> Flattering me with impossibilities.
>
> (3H6.3.2.134–143)

Here is an early Shakespearean tragic height, an early version of the cliffs of Dover in *King Lear* or of "the cliffe, / That beetles o're his base into the sea" of *Hamlet*. The two later "heights" are associated with the self-destructive impulse and the landscape of all three is like that of Brueghel's *Fall of Icarus*.[8] The Icarus emblem, also symbolic of tragedy as self-destructive aspiration is, I think, just below the surface in Richard's case. Later, he makes it explicit, in act 5, scene 6 of *Henry VI, Part Three*, where he applies it to Prince Edward:

> Why what a peevish Foole was that of Creet,
> That taught his Sonne the office of a Fowle,
> And yet for all his wings, the Foole was drown'd.
>
> (3H6.5.6.18–20)

Henry accepts the emblem and applies it:

> I *Dedalus*, my poore Boy *Icarus*,
> Thy Father *Minos*, that deni'de our course,

83

The Sunne that sear'd the wings of my sweet Boy,
Thy Brother *Edward*, and thy Selfe, the Sea
Whose envious Gulfe did swallow up his life.
(*3H6*.5.6.21–25)

For Richard in his first soliloquy the sea is the barrier of other human lives standing between him and the crown. I would propose, however, that Henry's equation of Richard with the destroying sea indicates, in retrospect, the full meaning of the first metaphor. Richard is destroyed by other men but he is also self-destroyed by the psychic forces which impel him to step toward his "far off shore." The "envious Gulfe" into which he finally falls is as much Richard as Richmond and the event is predicted here. The image of a man on the edge of a cliff longing to take one step is an image of suicide. The total image is an emblem for, as well as from, the mind that has produced it. Richard is cliff and sea as well as man. Like Donne, he is his own precipice.

In the soliloquy Richard draws back from the suicidal vision and turns his mind to the possibilities of compensation:

Well, say there is no Kingdome then for *Richard:*
What other Pleasure can the World affoord?
Ile make my Heaven in a Ladies Lappe,
And decke my Body in gay Ornaments,
And 'witch sweet Ladies with my Words and Lookes.
Oh miserable Thought! and more unlikely,
Then to accomplish twentie Golden Crownes.
(*3H6*.3.2.146–152)

This is unduly pessimistic, as Richard's later spectacular success at "witching" the Lady Anne will prove. What Richard's self-mockery reveals is not so much the impossibility of making his way to a lady's lap as the unlikeliness of his finding heaven there. Straightforward sexual pleasure is no compensation for the frustration of a power drive as strong as Richard's and the absorption of that psychic energy in love is not a possible solution for Richard, who is capable neither of feeling nor inspiring it:

84

Why Love forswore me in my Mothers Wombe:
And for I should not deale in her soft Lawes,
Shee did corrupt frayle Nature with some Bribe,
To shrinke mine Arme up like a wither'd Shrub,
To make an envious Mountaine on my Back,
Where sits Deformitie to mocke my Body;
To shape my Legges of an unequall size,
To dis-proportion me in every part:
Like to a Chaos, or an un-lick'd Beare-whelpe,
That carryes no impression like the Damme.
And am I then a man to be belov'd?
O monstrous fault, to harbour such a thought.

(3H6.3.2.153–164)

The declaration of hate has become a declaration of self-hate. Love, we can see, in forswearing Richard, has forsworn him entirely, so that he is incapable of inspiring love for himself in himself, and his deformity, the sign of love's desertion, repels him more than it does any other character in the play. But love being absent, pity is absent too. The lines contain no element of pathetic self-display. Richard is not asking for our alms. He covers his self-hatred with sardonic self-mockery and covers it so effectively that, I believe, he conceals it from himself. Richard nowhere expresses a consciousness of the self-hatred which he here betrays —not, at least, until the very end of his life—and he does not express it because he does not know of its existence. And yet self-hatred informs his being and his actions. His deeds and desires are responses to it and this Shakespeare makes clear in the lines that follow:

Then since this Earth affoords no Joy to me,
But to command, to check, to o're-beare such,
As are of better Person then my selfe:
Ile make my Heaven to dreame upon the Crowne,
And whiles I live, t'account this World but Hell,
Untill my mis-shap'd Trunke, that beares this Head
Be round impaled with a glorious Crowne.

And yet I know not how to get the Crowne,
For many Lives stand betweene me and home.
(*3H6*.3.2.165–173)

The hatred which fills Richard can be safely diverted and even transformed to pleasure, to "joy," by directing it outward. The exercise of
power over others is the only release possible for Richard, but the frustration of his power drives forces him to fantasies of absolute power.
Yet these unrealizable fantasies, like the sexual fantasies of a prisoner,
torment their creator. Richard's self-hatred, prevented from dissipating itself in the "overbearing" of others, transforms itself into fantasy and returns to torment the self which originally inspired it. Richard is trapped
and expresses his sense of being so in a second and tremendously powerful image of frustration:

> And I, like one lost in a Thornie Wood,
> That rents the Thornes, and is rent with the Thornes,
> Seeking a way, and straying from the way,
> Not knowing how to finde the open Ayre,
> But toyling desperately to finde it out,
> Torment my selfe, to catch the English Crowne:
> And from that torment I will free my selfe,
> Or hew my way out with a bloody Axe.
> (*3H6*.3.2.174–181)

The simile gains in claustrophobic effectiveness from being the visual
and tactile opposite of the openness of the promontory image. Like the
sea, the wood is for Richard the barrier of other men, the many lives
that stand between him and home. Shakespeare uses the thorny wood
again in the play, and, as he did with the Icarus image, applies it to the
Lancastrians, Prince Edward prominently among them. Edward of York
makes the application:

> Brave followers, yonder stands the thornie Wood,
> Which by the Heavens assistance, and your strength,
> Must by the Roots be hew'ne up yet ere Night.
> (*3H6*.5.4.67–69)

For Richard's brother, the wood really is what Richard claims it is for him—an obstacle that stands between him and the throne. Edward will remove it, will hew it up. Richard is trapped inside and must hew his way out. In part this is because for Edward the thorny wood is the declared enemy—the house of Lancaster—and thus something totally other than himself. Richard's thorny wood is the house of York as well as that of Lancaster and he is trapped within the family loyalties he must destroy. There is more to the difference than that, however, and Richard comes near to discovering what it is. Richard is tormenting himself. He is using his ambition as a flagellant uses his scourge. The thorns which rend him are his own neurotic ambition, his masochism, his "self." To free yourself from self-torment, you must free yourself from yourself, and using a bloody ax to hew yourself out of yourself entails destroying yourself.

Richard does not destroy himself—at least not at this moment. What he does instead is to create a new self. It has been pointed out that the thorny wood simile is a symbolic description of birth[9] and as such it is in keeping with the birth imagery that precedes it. But Richard *is* giving birth here—to himself. As an alternative to self-destruction Richard assumes a new self, one capable of satisfying ambition by acquiring power. Shakespeare, in other words, is here creating the Richard who will serve as the villain protagonist of the tragedy to come. But the making of this magnificent bogeyman is not a creation *ex nihilo*. Shakespeare fashions the apparently inhuman Richard out of such recognizably human elements as the ambition which has hatred, and self-hatred, for its source. Thus the finished creation contains, temporarily controlled and directed outward, the self-destructive qualities that have gone into the creature's making. The process of self-creation and the nature of the self created, are hardly realistic in any documentary sense. But they are brilliantly expressionistic versions or imitations of psychic realities.

The "murtherous Machevill" who emerges from the soliloquy is a formidable instrument of destruction. Before *Henry VI, Part Three* is over he has killed two of the four men he has named as standing between him and "home." After the murder of the second, King Henry, Richard delivers a second soliloquy which is primarily a descriptive analysis of the self which we saw come into being during the first, a self which Richard characterizes as "I that have neyther pitty, love, nor feare," and, a few lines later:

> I have no Brother, I am like no Brother:
> And this word (Love) which Gray-beards call Divine,
> Be resident in men like one another,
> And not in me: I am my selfe alone.
>
> (*3H6*.5.6.80–83)

Because Richard is incapable of compassion he can be literally ruthless and this is the source of his success in gaining power. It is also the primary explanation for his almost immediate loss of it.

In order to gain the crown, Richard must perforce destroy his natural power base—the house of York. He has no compunction about this and is careful to replace the power he derived from family loyalties with the support of self-interested politicians and magnates—primarily the duke of Buckingham, and Hastings, the Lord Chamberlain. Act 1, scene 3 of *Richard III* is largely devoted to an exposition of the brilliance with which Richard works upon the rivalries, petty hatreds, and snobbism of such men in order to alienate them from Queen Elizabeth's party. Such successes require no understanding of love or pity and Richard achieves with great efficiency the destruction of the threat to his own power that is posed by the claims of young King Edward V's uncle and half-brothers to have some say in the governing of the kingdom. Thus Richard achieves unchallenged control of the kingdom as Lord Protector, but, of course, he is not satisfied with it. For him the symbolic glorious crown is even more important than the reality of power—or the reality is not complete without the symbol of it. But he discovers that in order to achieve coronation he must not only obliterate the rest of the house of York, he must also destroy his new power base as well. Lord Hastings, incomprehensibly to Richard, loved his master, Edward IV, and has transferred that love to his master's sons:

> that Ile give my voice on *Richards* side,
> To barre my Masters Heires in true Descent,
> God knowes I will not doe it, to the death.
>
> (*RIII*.3.2.53–55)

That a man should be capable of feeling such sentiments, much less of intending to act upon them, must necessarily be beyond the comprehension of a Richard who is himself alone. Not that Hastings is an extraordinarily noble fellow. Insofar as he is characterized, it is by an intensely human delight in the destruction of his enemies. This portion of his humanity Richard can play upon for his own purposes, but Hastings's loyalty to those he loves is something Richard cannot manipulate, not, by any means, because it is too noble for manipulation, but because it is a kind of humanity that Richard cannot understand. The solution to Hastings therefore must be mere stupid brutality: "Chop off his Head: / Something wee will determine" (*RIII*.3.1.194–195). And that "something" turns out to be "Chop off his head." The subtlety with which Richard concealed his guilt for the murder of Clarence disappears completely when he destroys Hastings, causing the scrivener to comment: "Who is so grosse, that cannot see this palpable device? / Yet who so bold, but sayes he sees it not?" (*RIII*.3.6.11–12). Richard appears to believe that the achievement of power marks the end of any need for the concealment of villainy, that so long as men can be frightened into acquiescence no more is necessary. But, of course, Richard does not really understand fear either, does not see that it can inspire men to destroy him as well as obey him.

A miscalculation of the effects of both pity and fear causes Richard to turn Buckingham from an essential supporter to an active enemy. The loss of power entailed is entirely preventable and again the result of Richard's inability to foresee the reactions of "men like one another." Earlier in the play Richard flattered Buckingham by calling him "My other selfe." When the time comes to kill the little princes, Richard appears to have convinced himself of the truth of the epithet, forgetting that he is himself alone and that Buckingham is subject to the inconvenient emotions and inefficient moral hesitations of other men. When Buckingham fails or refuses to understand Richard's coy hints ("Young *Edward* lives, thinke now what I would speake"), Richard, instead of dropping the matter, loses his temper: "Cousin, thou wast not wont to be so dull. / Shall I be plaine? I wish the Bastards dead" (*RIII*.4.2.17–18). It is not Richard's business to be plain, even with Buckingham. The duke's recoil from the proposed murders is evidence only of a greater moral sensitivity than Richard's—greater, that is to say, than none at all. Buckingham soon returns to claim the reward promised for his connivance in the judicial murder of Hastings. It is not clear whether he wishes Richard to understand that, as DeFlores puts it in *The Changeling*, "The last is not yet paid for" and that he will proceed to new villainy only when he has been rewarded for old, or whether he wants to collect what is coming to him before he clears out. Richard does not bother to discover. He insults Buckingham and leaves him terrified:

> BUCK. O let me thinke on *Hastings*, and be gone
> To Brecnock, while my fearefull Head is on.
> ($RIII.4.2.102–103$)

Richard's disaffecting of Buckingham is the gross stupidity of an extremely intelligent man. The destruction of Hastings would probably have eventually become a necessity for Richard. Properly managed, Buckingham could have been his creature forever. But Richard is a Machiavel and a Machiavel can be most succinctly defined as an incompetent Machiavellian. With the great and significant exception of Claudius, the true, competent Machiavellians (Bolingbroke, Tiberius, Octavius) of the Elizabethan drama survive. The Machiavels (Barrabas, Richard III, Sejanus, Iago) destroy themselves. The source of Richard's self-destructive incompetence as a politician is the source of his strength as a destructive force—his inability to share in and hence to understand and to predict the emotions of other men.

In creating a Richard to inhabit the world of second causes, Shakespeare has imagined a self-created self. He has given us a Richard who responds to the threat of a loveless, hate-filled and destructive nature by devising a persona which can successfully direct outward the hatred and destructiveness that would otherwise destroy their owner. But, of course, in the end they do destroy their owner, first because they force the men and women against whom Richard directs his destructive instincts to unite in hatred against him and to destroy him in order to preserve themselves. But also there is within Richard's nature none of the love that sometimes moves men, however minimally, in their dealings with one another. Because he cannot understand what he does not possess,

Richard is unable to predict and control the actions of men moved by love and pity. The absence of love is essential to the efficient functioning of the murderous Machiavel, but it is also the flaw which results in his destruction. In order to preserve himself, Richard creates a destructive self, but the self he creates turns out to be as self-destructive as the desperate man who called him into being.

The question remains, to what degree does Shakespeare present this ultimately self-destructive act of self-creation as the free choice of a free will? Within the context of human causes a minimal freedom is present, I think. Richard boasts of choosing to be what he is: "Let Hell make crook'd my Minde." "I am determined to prove a Villaine." But these melodramatic proclamations of free choice are expressed in a context that limits their freedom almost to the point of making it disappear:

> Then since the Heavens have shap'd my Body so,
> Let Hell make crook'd my Minde to answer it.
> (*3H6.* 5.6.78–79)

> And therefore, since I cannot prove a Lover,
> To entertaine these faire well spoken dayes,
> I am determined to prove a Villaine,
> And hate the idle pleasures of these dayes.
> (*RIII.*1.1.28–31)

In fact Richard's choice of self is severely limited by the nature from which he can form that self and in his first soliloquy the only apparent alternative to the murderous Machiavel is a desperate thug, a hewer with a bloody ax. Which brings us to the question of what has so limited Richard's nature, the question of the first cause.

"Nature," says Hamlet, thinking socially, "cannot choose his origin." Richard's unchosen origin is, like everyone else's, his mother's womb and he believes that it was there that love forswore him. He is thinking consciously in the first soliloquy of human, venereal love. It is important that our thoughts should not be so limited as Richard's, for here Shakespeare is having him tell us more than he knows, or more, at least, than he is conscious of knowing. For Richard, his abandonment by love in the womb resulted in his deformity:

And for I should not deale in her soft Lawes,
Shee did corrupt frayle Nature with some Bribe,
To shrinke mine Arme up like a wither'd Shrub.
(*3H6*.3.2.154–156)

The other characters in the play see the deformity as significant of something more than the corruption of nature. Margaret makes the point with her usual force:

Qu. But thou art neyther like thy Sire nor Damme,
But like a foule mishapen Stygmaticke,
Mark'd by the Destinies to be avoided,
As venome Toades, or Lizards dreadfull stings.
(*3H6*.2.2.135–138)

The epithet "foul stigmatic" has already been applied to Richard by young Clifford in *Henry VI, Part II*. Its implications are at least triple. According to the *O.E.D.* it was a fairly common literaryism for a deformed person. But it derives from Greek through Latin. In classical antiquity a man might be stigmatized—that is have his flesh branded—either because he was a criminal or because he was a slave. (The custom of branding criminals was, of course, current in Shakespeare's time.) Richard qualifies on both counts. His criminality is obvious and his slavery is characterized, again by Margaret in *Richard III*, where, rising to an eloquence unusual even for her, she addresses him as

Thou elvish mark'd, abortive rooting Hogge,
Thou that wast seal'd in thy Nativitie
The slave of Nature, and the Sonne of Hell.
(*RIII*.1.3.228–230)

But if Richard is a slave, who has enslaved him? Or to pass to Margaret's contention that he has been "Mark'd by the Destinies," if Richard's deformity is a sort of skull-and-crossbones label, where did the poison come from?

To arrive at an answer, we must combine the insights of Richard's enemies with the results of his own self-analysis in both the soliloquies of *Henry VI, Part Three.* For Margaret, Richard's deformity is a mark set upon him by "destiny" to warn his fellow men of his fatal nature. For Richard, it is the result of love's abandonment of him. In the second soliloquy Richard defines that love in a way that reconciles the two explanations for his deformity:

> And this word [Love] which Gray-beards call Divine,
> Be resident in men like one another,
> And not in me: I am my selfe alone.
>
> (*3H6*.5.6.81–83)

If it was divine love that forsook Richard at his conception, the results are precisely what we might expect. The consequence of the withdrawal of the ordering force of God's love would be: "To dis-proportion me in every part: / Like to a Chaos, or an unlick'd Beare-whelpe" (*3H6*.3.2.160–161). Created order is the result of the imposition upon elemental chaos of God's love. If God, in his just anger, withdraws that love, the result is a return to, or toward, chaos. Richard is the result of such a withdrawal of divine love and his deformity is the sign of it.

These lofty Empedoclean suggestions, concepts basic to Shakespeare's highest art, are, with a self-directed irony typical of Richard, and a willingness to attempt any juxtaposition typical of Shakespeare, set against the grotesque unnatural natural history of the "unlick'd Beare-whelpe." The Arden edition elucidates by quoting Golding's Ovid: "The Bear whelp . . . like an evill favored lump of flesh alyve dooth lye. / The dam by licking shapeth out his members orderly."[10] Anne, in the scene of their courtship, will confirm her future husband in this view of himself by calling him a "lumpe of fowle Deformitie." But Young Clifford has, in fact, already drawn Richard's attention to the resemblance: "Hence heape of wrath, foule indigested lumpe / As crooked in thy manners, as thy shape" (*2H6*.5.1.157–158). The "stygmaticke" is a creature enslaved by nature, the "chaos" is a creature deprived of God's love. The "lumpe," absurdly enough, is the most suggestive of the three:

> But, O man who art thou which pleadest against God? shal the thing formed say to him that formed it, Why hast thou made me

thus? Hath not the potter power of the claie to make of the same lompe one vessell to honour, and another unto dishonour?

What and if God wolde, to shewe his wrath, and to make his power knowen, suffre with long pacience the vessels of wrath, prepared to destruction? (Romans 9 : 20–22)

Romans 9 is, I think, the fundamental gloss on Richard's nature and significance. Shakespeare has imagined the coming into being and the destruction of a vessel of wrath. Like Robert le Dyable, Richard has, from the womb, been a creature of evil, but Robert inhabited a semi-Pelagian universe ruled by a benevolent God. Robert's will was free enough and strong enough to accept the grace offered to him. Richard, like Robert (some versions of him at least), is born with teeth "which plainly signified, / That I should snarle, and bite, and play the dogge" (*3H6*.5.6.76–77). Richard and Robert are born to do evil. Robert chooses to stop doing evil, but like Faustus, Richard chooses to do evil. Yet both Richard and Faustus can, I maintain, be seen as "choosing" out of necessity, in response to the will of a predestinating God who has determined from eternity that they are to be numbered among the reprobate. But neither Richard nor Faustus *must* be seen in this way. The terrible possibility exists as a device for increasing the intensity of the terror with which an audience responds to these tragedies. It may, of course, also cause the more intelligent and informed members of such an audience to think about the relationship of these created Gods and worlds to the reality they imitate.

Marlowe emphasizes the possibility of Faustus's lack of freedom by having him try unsuccessfully to obtain grace through repentance. In Shakespeare the same purpose is served by the insistence on providential design. Faustus may be trapped in a world created by an omnipotent being who refuses to listen to his pleas for grace. Richard may be the uncomprehending instrument of a power who has decided to use him in working out a plan that requires his (possibly eternal) destruction. Richard's becoming the murderous Machiavel of the first soliloquy is an act of self-creation, but it is also, of course, a transformation into the instrument required by God's plan, and so we may be watching the process by which the potter fashions a vessel of his wrath.

The deterministic possibility gets its strongest single emphasis at the moment of Henry VI's murder. Richard stabs the king at the end of a speech in which Henry prophesies the horror which Richard will create, and asserts that he was born to this end:

> Thy Mother felt more then a Mothers paine,
> And yet brought forth lesse then a Mothers hope,
> To wit, an indigested and deformed lumpe,
> Not like the fruit of such a goodly Tree.
> Teeth had'st thou in thy head, when thou was't borne,
> To signifie, thou cam'st to bite the world:
> And if the rest be true, which I have heard,
> Thou cam'st—

RICH.   Ile heare no more:
> Dye Prophet in thy speech,   *Stabbes him.*
> For this (among'st the rest) was I ordain'd.
> (*3H6*.5.6.49–58)

The theatricality of the moment does not detract from its sincerity. Richard, as the Arden editor says, "adopts the fate of which he is the instrument and the victim."[11] But the adoption is not eager, or even necessarily willing. In some part, Richard kills Henry in order to make him stop talking—stop telling Richard that he is, indeed, predestined to evil, a creature without freedom. Richard's "Let Hell make crook'd my Minde" is partly bravado, an attempt to assert a freedom of choice which he knows or fears is not really his. The knowledge or fear is something we must share, for it is basic to the experience and understanding of Shakespeare's art in the creation of this protagonist.

The catastrophe of Richard's tragedy is accompanied by the same mystery as to its significance that surrounds the soliloquies of self-creation and self-analysis in *Henry VI, Part Three*. The physical destruction, the defeat at Bosworth, is assigned by the providential pieties of Richmond to the will of God as first cause. It is quite possible to accept this explanation and to see that will working through second causes— through the unifying effect upon England of Richard's destructive ambition and through the inherent incompetence that is the necessary concomitant of Richard's brilliance as a political animal. But mysteries remain despite such explanations and the questions they raise are the most important sources for whatever terror and pity are aroused in us by the spectacle of Richard's destruction. Again the inspiration for these emotions is our sense of the relationship of the creator to his creation, of the potter to the vessel of his wrath.

Richard's first soliloquy dramatized the creation of a self; his last presents us with that self's threatened disintegration:

> Cold fearefull drops stand on my trembling flesh.
> What? do I feare my Selfe? There's none else by,
> *Richard* loves *Richard*, that is, I am I.
> Is there a Murtherer heere? No; Yes, I am:
> Then flye; What from my Selfe? Great reason: why?
> Lest I Revenge. What? my Selfe upon my Selfe?
> Alacke, I love my Selfe. Wherefore? For any good
> That I my Selfe, have done unto my Selfe?
> O no. Alas, I rather hate my Selfe,
> For hatefull Deeds committed by my Selfe.
> I am a Villaine. . . .
> I shall dispaire, there is no Creature loves me;
> And if I die, no soule shall pittie me.
> Nay, wherefore should they? Since that I my Selfe,
> Finde in my Selfe, no pittie to my Selfe.
>
> (*RIII*.5.3.181–203)

Here Richard approaches his own meaning and it is possible, I think, for us to come closer to that mystery than he does. Richard faces, at the end, the truth that we have suspected about him from the beginning: he hates himself. And we can see more clearly than he can that the hateful deeds for which he hates himself have brought him to his destruction. His fear of himself is justified. He *is* revenging himself upon himself. He is in the presence of his own murderer and he cannot escape. But we can understand, as he cannot, the origin of this psychic paradox: "*Richard* loves *Richard*, that is, I am I." Identity, he soon admits, is no guarantee of love. But his phrase for identity suggests another. God, when asked by Moses to name himself, obliges with "I am that I am." Richard, in the presence of himself, is, in a double sense, in the presence of his creator and destroyer. Richard, the self-creator, is here supremely himself alone, but there is one else by. The creator of the self from which Richard creates himself is God and it is to that first creator's decision to withhold love from his creature that Richard's tragedy owes both its beginning and its end. A human being without love is a being of universal hate and though the desire for self-preservation may inspire the self to take forms which will direct that destructive hatred outward, in the end the destruction will include the self, and the full process is seen to have its source in the will of the creating God. The terrifying meaning of evil in a providentially ordered universe is fully dramatized in the nature, crimes, and destruction of Richard III, but a mystery remains in the questions of whether grace may not be offered even to this apparently reprobate creature.

Richard cannot pity, love, nor fear other men; he cannot pity nor love himself. But why should not the paradigm hold for fear? The answer is to be found in the fear's origin.

> Give me another Horse, bind up my Wounds:
> Have mercy Jesu. Soft, I did but dreame.
> O coward Conscience! how dost thou afflict me?
>
> (*RIII*.5.3.177–179)

Lady Anne has prepared us for the spectacle of these afflictions:

> For never yet one howre in his Bed
> Did I enjoy the golden deaw of sleepe,
> But with his timorous Dreames was still awak'd.
>
> (*RIII*.4.1.83–85)

Conscience, the origin of Richard's fear, can exercise its power over him only in sleep. When the will relaxes its control, timorous dreams take over the self-tormenting function of those fantasies of power, dreams of sovereignty, with which Richard tortured himself before his rise to the throne. But it will not do simply to modernize Richard's conscience into an equivalent for the diseased superego of a psychic masochist. The Shakespearean meaning of Richard's conscience lies in the fact that though it is a part of his consciousness, it is not simply a part of his self. It is the voice of God within him and consequently

Richard can fear it as he can fear nothing human, either self or other. But this raises a question. If Richard is capable of fearing the voice of God, is he also capable of loving it? When Robert le Dyable reaches an equivalent moment in his spiritual career he is impelled to contrition and to the love of God by fear of damnation. Why does this not happen to Richard?

The answer lies hidden in the mystery of God's judgments. The freedom of Richard's will is either real or apparent. In either case its strength is beyond question. What we see in Richard's final soliloquy is a human self threatened with disintegration as a result of pressure from divine power. But Richard's human will successfully resists that pressure and reintegrates the threatened self:

> Let not our babling Dreames affright our soules:
> For Conscience is a word that Cowards use,
> Devis'd at first to keepe the strong in awe,
> Our strong armes be our Conscience, Swords our Laws.
> March on, joyne bravely, let us too't pell mell,
> If not to heaven, then hand in hand to Hell.
>
> (*RIII*.5.3.308–313)

The irony of this sardonic bravado lies in the fact that Richard's successful preservation of his psychological self invites the destruction of his spiritual self. Shakespeare never pronounces on the eternal fate of his characters, but he frequently demands that we consider the possibilities. He is doing so here and we can only conclude that Richard has not found grace before he goes into battle. Since at Bosworth Field he notoriously did not have even the space between the stirrup and the ground to seek for mercy in, the play forces us to confront the possibility that hell is Richard's destination.

The play does not tell us if Richard's will is free to seek grace nor does it tell us if grace is available were he to seek it. But the absence of answers is not the same thing as the absence of questions. The terrible dreams that affright Richard, the products of God's voice within him, embody a question in the form of two possibilities. Viewed Calvinistically these pangs of conscience can be a deserved, divinely inflicted punishment upon a reprobate sinner. But if we grant the possibility that Richard's will is free, then these torments may be grace itself, battering Richard's heart, attempting to bring him to contrition. When Richard tries to talk Queen Elizabeth into granting him the hand of her daughter despite his murder of her sons, he makes an obviously hypocritical appeal to determinism: "All unavoyded is the doome of Destiny" (*RIII*.4.4.218). Elizabeth, in reply, appeals to grace in a way that affirms its mysterious nature:

> True: when avoyded grace makes Destiny.
> My Babes were destin'd to a fairer death,
> If grace had blest thee with a fairer life.
> (*RIII*.4.4.219–221)

Does Richard avoid grace or does grace refuse to bless him? Or, to focus upon the final moment of the failure of grace, when Richard says "Have mercy Jesu," and then continues, "Soft, I did but dreame," is the failure to complete the impulse toward contrition the result of Richard's freely willed avoidance of grace, or of God's refusal to bless the appeal? The play does not tell us, but it certainly asks us. We may answer as we choose, but we must not attribute our answer to the play, for the play's primary meaning resides in its refusal to provide *a* meaning and its confrontation of ignorance is a source of its tragic power.

In *Richard III* Shakespeare first explores the tragic implications of a belief in providence. These implications had, of course, been explored and agonized over by theologians for centuries. In the Old Testament we learn that "The King's heart is in the hand of the Lord, as the rivers of waters: he turneth it whethersoever it pleaseth him" (*Proverbs* 21 : 1). Augustine assures us that providence permits the rule of evil emperors in order that justice may be served: evil princes are a punishment for evil people.[12] And this is a sentiment heartily and regularly endorsed by the Tudor establishment through the *Book of Homilies*.[13] But there is a cause for fear and trembling in this orthodoxy and Calvin expresses it by quoting Augustine:

> If any be more combered with this that we nowe say, that there is no consent of God with man, where man by the righteous moving of God doeth that which is not lawfull, let them remember that

which Augustine saith in another place: Who shall not tremble at these judgements, where God worketh even in the hearts of evil men whatsoever he will, and yet rendreth to them according to their deservings?[14]

Chance does not exist in the providentially controlled world which is suggested as a possibility in *Richard III*. Richard begins his last speech with the lines: "Slave, I have set my life upon a cast, / And I will stand the hazard of the Dye" (5.4.9–10). The play answers Richard with Einstein's reply to Bohr: "Der Herr Gott würfelt nicht." The Lord God does not throw dice. The concept of providence explains away the injustice that is inherent in accident, but Shakespeare's examination of providence raises the question of whether justice can exist in a world where accident does not.

CHAPTER 5

Hamlet

AFTER *Richard III* Shakespeare abandons for a time the mystery of God's judgments as an important instrument for achieving his tragic effects. Friar Lawrence indicates the presence of a struggle between grace and rude will in *Romeo and Juliet*, but trying to turn his vegetable metaphors into a central concern of the play brings one to end up tut-tutting at the star-crossed lovers in a manner bound to interfere with a humane participation in the spectacle of the passionate love of the young destroyed by bad luck and by the passionate stupidity of the old. A pattern formed by the demands of divine providence and justice is more legitimately discernible in *Richard II*. There John of Gaunt tells the duchess of Gloucester that the punishment of Richard for the murder of her husband and his brother, Thomas of Woodstock, is the business of God, not man:

> Gods is the quarrell for Gods substitute,
> His deputy annointed in his sight,
> Hath causd his death, the which if wrongfully,
> Let heaven revenge, for I may never lift
> An angry arme against his minister.
> ($Q_1.RII.$1.2.37–41)

In act 5 the duke of York suggests to his duchess that God has worked his will by turning the hearts of Richard's subjects against him:

> . . . had not God (for some strong purpose) steel'd
> The hearts of men, they must perforce have melted
> And Barbarisme it selfe have pittied him.
> But heaven hath a hand in these events,
> To whose high will we bound our calme contents.
> (*RII*.5.2.34–38)

This "amen" to the spectacle of God's will being done on earth is an instructive example of the proper Christian method for coping with

101

what puzzles us, but in fact what puzzles and fascinates us in *Richard II* is not the will of God at all, but the wills, strengths, and weaknesses of men interacting in the struggle for power. So absorbing is this interest in the world of second causes that any reference by the play to first and final causes is perfunctory at best.

It is hardly even perfunctory in the remaining plays of the second tetralogy. In the second part of *Henry IV*, the king wonders how Richard could so accurately have prophesied Northumberland's treachery. Warwick tells him:

> There is a Historie in all mens Lives,
> Figuring the nature of the Times deceas'd:
> The which observ'd, a man may prophecie
> With a neere ayme, of the maine chance of things,
> As yet not come to Life, which in their Seedes
> And weake beginnings lye entreasured:
> Such things become the Hatch and Brood of Time;
> And by the necessarie forme of this,
> King *Richard* might create a perfect guesse,
> That great *Northumberland*, then false to him,
> Would of that Seed, grow to a greater falsenesse,
> Which should not finde a ground to roote upon,
> Unlesse on you.   (*2HIV*.3.1.80–92)

The determinism here proposed is entirely naturalistic. Queen Margaret's skill in prophecy was the result of her ability to perceive that pattern formed by God's visitation of iniquities. Richard II's accuracy is based on a knowledge and experience of men. And yet Richard, as much as Margaret, perceives necessities, and Henry IV must accept them for what they are:

> KING.   Are these things then Necessities?
> Then let us meete them like Necessities.
>   (*2HIV*.3.1.92–93)

In these later histories we watch men coming to a knowledge of their necessary forms and facing their necessities as best they can. That the will, as above all in Hal's case, contributes to the creations of those

forms and necessities does not alter their nature as necessities and from
the unlikely figure of Francis Feeble we learn how we should meet
them:

> By my troth, I care not, a man can die but once, we owe God a
> death, Ile ne'er bear a base mind, and't be my destiny: so, and't
> be not, so, no man is too good to serve's prince, and let it go which
> way it will, he that dies this yeere is quit for the next.
>
> (Q.*2HIV*.3.2.251–255)

Hamlet, who is born to set right the time, is preeminently a man who
discovers his necessary form and faces his necessities. But in his play,
the hero tells us, there's a divinity that shapes our ends and a special
providence in the fall of a sparrow. Heaven most certainly has a hand
in the events of this tragic action, but it turns out that binding one's
content to the high will of heaven is a less calm business than York's
rather complacent piety would suggest. The will of Hamlet's God is
mysterious and his purposes are incomprehensible. To set right the time,
Hamlet, it seems, must kill the murderer of his father, something that
he wants to do but cannot do, first because he is afraid that Claudius
may not be guilty. If he is not, then the ghost is a diabolical illusion and
Hamlet would not be justified in killing the man whom he detests.
Hamlet fears that the ghost is the bait on a Satanic hook:

> The Spirit that I have seene
> May be the Divell, and the Divel hath power
> T' assume a pleasing shape, yea and perhaps
> Out of my Weaknesse, and my Melancholly,
> As he is very potent with such Spirits,
> Abuses me to damne me.   (2.2.618–623)[1]

Hamlet's fears are justifiable and not the rationalizations of a born
shilly-shallier. Indeed it can be argued that his suspicions are correct
and the mere fact that the ghost tells the truth about Claudius proves
nothing:

> . . . oftentimes, to winne us to our harme,
> The Instruments of Darknesse tell us Truths,

103

Winne us with honest Trifles, to betray's
In deepest consequence. (*Mac.*1.3.123–126)

The ghost of old Hamlet may be the equivalent of the Witches in *Macbeth* and Hamlet the equivalent of Macbeth himself. This viewpoint can be buttressed by the citation of Renaissance treatises on ghosts which maintain that, unlike old Hamlet, "real" spirits from purgatory are characterized by dignified forbearance, do not go about bellowing for revenge, and refrain from starting like guilty things when they hear a cock crow.[2]

One wonders how Renaissance ghost experts acquired their expertise —and, of course, one knows. Convinced of the existence of nonexistent things, they imagined forms for aery nothingness that would fit comfortably into the intellectual constructs which they called truth. The Catholic who contemplated the notion of ghosts found one explanation for it in the notion of purgatory, so for him ghosts might be the spirits of the dead released from purgatory. The Protestant who had banished the notion of purgatory from his truth had also to banish the notion of purgatorial ghosts. A ghost could only be a devil who had taken on the form of a dead man. Shakespeare called his constructs art rather than truth, thus releasing his imagination to invent forms whose end is to contribute to the creation of a new construct rather than to conform to a preexisting one. The ghost in *Hamlet* is put there not to define ghosts but to help to define *Hamlet*. He comes from purgatory and to that degree is Catholic, but his behavior is distinctly nonpurgatorial. He is possessed by a hatred for his brother that leads him to demand a retributive killing from his son—a demand that suits the Protestant imagined form much better than the Catholic. Old Hamlet's ghost is hybrid for a purpose, and is an excellent, if rather simple, example of the work of Shakespeare as intellectual *bricoleur*, for he has created the form he needed out of handy bits of Catholicism, Protestantism, and Senecan classicism, but the result is art and we are only dimly if at all aware of *bricolage*. We experience the whole and not its parts. The fact that the ghost satisfies no single orthodoxy does not prevent our emotional acceptance of its "honesty" when we experience it, but does serve to validate Hamlet's rational suspicions when the immediate experience is over. When these suspicions are in turn dispelled, we accept the ghost rationally, too, unless we are possessed by a strong streak of intellectual perversity, for since Shakespeare has created the ghost partly to define the world of his play he has made the nature of this defining ghost as clear as possible. This does not mean, of course, that as a result everything is perfectly clear, for one function of the ghost's clarity is to indicate the existence of a mystery. The world which Shakespeare creates in *Hamlet* includes a God, and the ghost is the first and most striking indication of His existence and nature. The ghost tells us that he has been

> Doom'd for a certaine terme to walke the night;
> And for the day confin'd to fast in Fiers,
> Till the foule crimes done in my dayes of Nature
> Are burnt and purg'd away.   (1.5.10–13)

There is only one possible answer to the question, "Who has doomed him?" The ghost walks the night because the God of the play required him to do so and the facts which he discloses to his son are revealed either by that God's will or permission.

Hamlet concludes, at the end of the play, that heaven has been ordinant in the smallest details of his life and when he observes that there is a special providence in the fall of a sparrow, he is telling us that in *Hamlet* there is no such thing as *special* providence. Providence has been at work always and in everything. Nothing could be more orthodox than such a belief and no belief could be potentially more disturbing in tragedy, for if heaven is ordinant in all things, then it must be ordinant in the causes and effects, the undeniable suffering and apparent injustice of the tragic action. This is one of the mysteries that *Hamlet* explores and the exploration is carried out, I think, in detachment from any commitment to a specific Christian orthodoxy. Shakespeare is not treating us to an imaginative presentation of theology. He is testing theology with his imagination and using theology for his artistic purpose.

Through the instrument of the ghost, the God of the play intervenes in the world of *Hamlet* to set the tragic action going. Without such supernatural intervention there would have been no tragedy, which is to say there would have been no punishment for crime. In creating Claudius Shakespeare has fashioned what is, for him, a unique villain—one who is a competent Machiavellian rather than a self-destructive Machiavel. He has committed a perfect crime and without supernatural intervention he would die in his bed, full of years and honors. Ultimately it is God who does not permit him to do so. Far too much has been made of *Hamlet* as a play about revenge. It is also, and I think more importantly, a play about the divine retributive justice that is the first and final cause of that revenge, and Hamlet, though he seeks revenge and not justice, is the agent of divinity. His vengeance achieves God's justice and a far more comprehensible justice than that which destroyed the innocent "unto the third and fourth generation" in *Richard III*. And yet Hamlet's function in the providential pattern which is worked out in the later tragedy is that of the villain of the Histories. Hamlet like Richard is the scourge of heaven and he knows it. In *Richard III* Shakespeare imagines an evil and probably damned instrument of God's just purpose. But the job (one of many) that Shakespeare sets himself in *Hamlet* is to investigate the question: "Can a man serve as the scourge of heaven without being destroyed morally and spiritually?" Can Hamlet both kill Claudius and save his own soul? The investigation is made primarily in terms of providence. The attendant mysteries of grace and free will, predestination, election and reprobation exist by implication.

The ghost, as supernatural agent of divinity, reveals to Hamlet that Claudius has seduced his mother and murdered his father. Hamlet's reaction to the news is straightforwardly human: he wants to kill Claudius. This is a deplorable desire, to be sure. If Hamlet were perfect in every way he would forgive Claudius his trespasses, go to his erring uncle, and suggest that they kneel together and pray for Claudius's limed soul. But Hamlet is not perfect in every way. He is a fallen man like the rest of us and those who cannot sympathize with his determination to kill his uncle should be content with their moral superiority and not try to understand Shakespeare's tragedy. We can, of course, see that Hamlet's desire to kill is wrong—evil, indeed—but it is important to see also that this evil serves the providential purposes of the God of this play. Calvin says of the methods of providence that "whatsoever we conceive in minde, is by the secret inspiration of God directed to this ende."[3] Hamlet has come to understand precisely this when he says to

Horatio, toward the end of the play: "There's a Divinity that shapes our ends, / Rough-hew them how we will" (5.2.10–11). Before he arrives at this conclusion, Hamlet necessarily seems to the pious to show, in Claudius's pious phrase, "a will most incorrect to Heaven," but that will is always directed to Heaven's ends and Hamlet, when the ghost has left him, senses, rebels against, and accepts his predestined role:

> The time is out of joynt: Oh cursed spight,
> That ever I was borne to set it right.
> Nay, come let's goe together. (1.5.189–191)

An exchange between Horatio and Marcellus has already defined the relationship between the sense of God's control and the necessity for human action:

> HOR. . . . to what issue will this come?
> MAR. Something is rotten in the State of Denmarke.
> HOR. Heaven will direct it.
> MAR. Nay, let's follow him.   (1.4.64–67)

God has willed that the time be set right and the rottenness destroyed, but the men who are God's instruments must come and go, the creatures of their business and desires, though directed by the will of Heaven.

Hamlet is brought to his sense of a shaping divinity by the "odd coincidences" that occur on his interrupted voyage to England, but he is apparently unaware that the most striking demonstration of providential control comes in his springing of "The Mousetrap" and the events that follow it. What Hamlet conceives in his mind is a plan for testing Claudius's guilt and the ghost's honesty. His human motives in this case are not evil. He wants to make sure that in killing Claudius he is not being diabolically tempted to perform a damnable action. But again his human motives serve, but are different from, the purposes of providence. Hamlet wants to catch the conscience of Claudius in order to free his own. He hopes that the play will so work upon the king that he will proclaim his guilt. If Claudius had done so loudly enough, the time would have been set right and the rottenness destroyed without the necessity of killing. Claudius's superb self-control sees to it that the proclamation of guilt is perceptible only to Hamlet and Horatio, but Hamlet can now act secure in the knowledge that Claudius deserves the death he proposes to give him.

Heaven does not announce its purposes but they are to some degree made known by the event. Hamlet confronts Claudius with the image of his crime. As a result the king is "struck to the soul," forced to confront the knowledge of his guilt and its eternal consequences, and as a result of that confrontation his will is confronted with a choice of alternatives: he may repent and confess his crime and accept the temporal consequences of it, or he may attempt to avoid those consequences by concealing the crime and trying to deal with Hamlet, who has somehow learned of it. But the choice of ends is only apparent. In fact Claudius is being given a choice of means to a predetermined end. Heaven has willed the temporal punishment of Claudius and, for all of his rough-hewing, either choice will lead him to his earthly destruction, and yet the choice is far from meaningless, for it may also be a choice between eternal salvation or damnation and Claudius knows it.

Claudius is an apparently anomalous but perhaps not uncommon figure: a Machiavellian Christian. The alternative of repentance presented to the Christian Claudius is balanced by that of political action presented to the Machiavellian. The mousetrap reveals that Hamlet knows of Claudius's crime and is determined to punish it. But since "The Murder of Gonzago" can be interpreted as Hamlet's mad threat to play "one *Lucianus* nephew to the King" with respect to his uncle, Claudius has now acquired an excellent public reason for hustling Hamlet out of the country, and he takes it. Whether he has decided at this point to have Hamlet killed in England is neither clear nor terribly important. If he has not, the decision to do so follows upon his failure to repent; if he has, the failure to repent means that the decision goes unrevoked. As a politician Claudius acts first and agonizes afterward— that is, he sets a train of events in motion and then ponders the moral question which may cause him to put a stop to it while there is still time. Thus his first reaction to "The Mousetrap" is Machiavellian. He arranges with Rosencrantz and Guildenstern for Hamlet's banishment. Only then does he turn to the Christian alternative:

> what if this cursed hand
> Were thicker then it selfe with Brothers blood,
> Is there not Raine enough in the sweet Heavens
> To wash it white as Snow? Whereto serves mercy,
> But to confront the visage of Offence?
> And what's in Prayer, but this two-fold force,
> To be fore-stalled ere we come to fall,
> Or pardon'd being downe? Then Ile looke up,
> My fault is past.   (3.3.43–51)

But he is Christian, intelligent, and honest enough to know that the psychological state into which he has been thrown by the dramatization of his murder of old Hamlet cannot be dignified with the name of repentance so long as it remains merely a psychological state. As a man of action he knows that his emotions, if they are of value, will have consequences in action:

> But oh, what forme of Prayer
> Can serve my turne? Forgive me my foule Murther:
> That cannot be, since I am still possest
> Of those effects for which I did the Murther.
> My Crowne, mine owne Ambition, and my Queene:
> May one be pardon'd, and retaine th' offence?
>   (3.3.51–56)

His inability to confess and make satisfaction is to him proof positive of the inefficacy of his contrition. He is trapped and he knows it, though he continues to struggle:

> What then? What rests?
> Try what Repentance can. What can it not?
> Yet what can it, when one cannot repent?
> Oh wretched state! Oh bosome, blacke as death!
> Oh limed soule, that strugling to be free,
> Art more ingag'd: Helpe Angels, make assay:
> Bow stubborne knees, and heart with strings of Steele,
> Be soft as sinewes of the new-borne Babe,
> All may be well.   (3.3.64–72)

Claudius's failure to achieve true repentance is, for me, the most moving and terrifying event of the play and I find it essential to my understanding of the tragedy to ask why he does not succeed. Roy Battenhouse is very helpful here. He points out that "the birdlime image occurs in several memorable passages in St. Augustine's *Confessions*." There it is associated precisely with the kind of spiritual struggle toward regeneration—Augustine's own struggle—that Claudius is undergoing here and the birdlime symbolizes the things of the world that prevent regeneration—"honours, gains, marriage" for Augustine, "Crowne, Ambition, Queene" for Claudius. Battenhouse goes on:

> For Augustine, escape from this soul-sickness was possible only as he succeeded in achieving a complete humility, aided from the outside by the ministry of friends and the voice of a child. This is a direction in which we see Claudius looking: "Help, angels! Make assay! / Bow, stubborn knees, and heart . . . / Be soft as sinews of the newborn babe!"
>
> Why does this noble effort not succeed? Unlike Augustine, Claudius lacks neighbors to lend him spiritual aid. Hamlet, at this moment, lurks in the background as a Black angel. Claudius, left unassisted, finds his thoughts unable to ascend with his words:
>
> > My words fly up, my thoughts remain below.
> > Words without thoughts never to Heaven go.
>
> One further reason for the failure is that Claudius has not ordered quite aright his attempt to pray. . . . Perhaps, on a second attempt, he might have done better.[4]

All this is highly illuminating, but surely the reasons advanced for Claudius's failure (and Augustine's success), excellent so far as they go, must also include what Augustine saw as the essential—grace itself, prevenient grace: "subsequent grace indeed assists man's good purpose, but the purpose would not exist if grace did not precede."[5] Simply to assume that such grace is present and that Claudius has rejected it is to assume more than the scene gives us intellectual or emotional warrant for. The possibility is double here and must be felt as double if the play is to have its full effect and significance. The God of the play may be using Hamlet's mousetrap precisely as an instrument of grace with regard to Claudius. That is, he may be leading Claudius into a psychological condition where he will wish to attempt to repent and will be capable of freely choosing God's proffered grace, but where ultimately his will, though free, will prove too weak and corrupt to make the proper choice. This would be the action of Augustine's God at least in his (and Augustine's) more benevolent moments:

> To yield our consent, indeed, to God's summons, or to withold it, is (as I have said) the function of our own will. And this not only does not invalidate what is said, "For what hast thou that thou didst not receive?" (I Cor.iv.7) but it really confirms it. For the soul cannot receive and possess these gifts, which are here referred to, except by yielding its consent.[6]

If the God of the play is Augustine's God, he has foreseen that Claudius will be unable to yield his consent to God's summons, but the failure is of Claudius's will, and God's justice working through Hamlet presents Claudius with this opportunity to exercise his free will. However, this mysterious but comparatively benevolent deity is not insisted on by the play. It is simultaneously and equally possible to interpret Claudius's failure to repent as evidence that the God of the play is Calvin's God, who has willed the reprobation of Claudius, willed his attempt to repent and its failure, withheld from eternity the grace that Claudius vainly seeks. We have seen that the reprobate are capable of "a certain penitencie." They are also capable of a certain faith:

> experience sheweth that the reprobate are somtime moved with the same feeling that the elect are, so that in their owne judgement they nothing differ from the elect. Wherefore it is no absurdity, that the Apostle ascribeth to them the tast of the heavenly giftes, that Christ ascribeth to them a faith for a time: not that they soundely perceive the spiritual force of grace and assured light of faith: but because the Lorde, the more to condemne them and make them inexcusable, conveyeth himselfe into their mindes so farre forth, as his goodnesse may be tasted without the spirite of adoption.[7]

From the Calvinist perspective, Claudius is given a taste of divine good-ness, a temporary faith that moves him to an unsuccessful try at con-trition. The motive which Calvin ascribes to his God must be strongly emphasized. Men like Claudius are allowed to fail at repentance not, or not entirely, in order to torment them, but "the more to condemne them and make them inexcusable." Again, it is God's justice that is being demonstrated and insured here. The reprobate, having failed to achieve contrition, will have no cause for complaint when they are damned. God sends his word to the elect so that they may be regenerated.

> When hee sendeth the same worde to the reprobate, though not for their amendement, yet he maketh it to serve for an other use: that both for the present time they may be pressed with witnesse of conscience, and may against the day of judgement be made more inexcusable.[8]

Augustine's God extends grace to Claudius knowing that he will fail to attain it although he is free to accept it. This is a terrifying mystery. Calvin's God has withheld grace from Claudius from eternity, but al-lows him to go through the motions of attempting to attain it, though he has willed Claudius's failure. This is less mysterious and more terri-fying. Out of theological mysteries and terrors Shakespeare makes a part of his tragic drama and the availability of such mystery and terror with-in himself and his audience partially explains, I think, why tragedy was a possible form for Shakespeare and his contemporaries. In *Richard III* the reprobate protagonist never attempts to attain grace. His mystery is that of the nature of the evil instrument of God's providence—the scourge of God—and Hamlet's mystery is in part a version of that. Claudius's mystery is closer to Faustus's—that of a damned soul who cannot repent—and as with Faustus, it is this failure which causes the tragic catastrophe. Had Claudius been strong enough or free enough to confess his sin and accept its earthly consequences, there would be no *Tragedy of Hamlet*. Claudius's failure to repent is, in my opinion, the peripeteia of the play and the stage picture at this point is remarkably like the one devised by Marlowe for the peripeteia of *Dr. Faustus*. There Faustus also sinks to his knees and prays "O Christ my Saviour, my Saviour / Helpe to save distressed *Faustus* soule." Just as Faustus's

appeal evokes the stage direction *Enter Lucifer Belzebub and Mephisto-
philis*, so Claudius's "Helpe Angels . . ." is soon followed by *Enter
Hamlet* and Hamlet like Lucifer is bent on securing his victim's damnation. Lucifer's course is to interrupt Faustus's attempt. Hamlet allows
Claudius to continue, but Hamlet's projected interruption would have
been final and he fears that by killing Claudius at prayer, he might be
killing him when he is in a state of grace and he wants to damn Claudius as well as kill him. The desire is both evil and absurd, for Hamlet is
proposing to usurp the powers of God at the Last Judgment. This is a
striking example of hubris but the consequences of it must be examined
closely and carefully, for they are not precisely what standard descrip-
tions of tragedy might lead us to expect.

Like Claudius, Hamlet, at this moment, is being presented alternative
choices, for the play's peripeteia is double. The tragic catastrophe is the
result of Claudius's failure or inability to repent, but it is simultaneously
the result of Hamlet's failure to kill Claudius. The unguarded, unsuspecting king is Hamlet's dilemma made flesh and set before him. He
must either kill Claudius or spare him. He elects to spare him and the
result is the death-filled scenes that follow. Are we supposed to believe
that Hamlet should therefore have killed the king at prayer, as we are
clearly meant to believe that Claudius should have repented and confessed the murder? I do not think so. I am maintaining that one of the
basic questions of the play is "Can Hamlet serve as the instrument of
divine justice and save his own soul?" If he were to kill Claudius here
the answer would have to be "no." To stab a kneeling, defenceless man
while he is trying to purge his soul of sin is as damnable an action as it
is possible to devise and surely Shakespeare has so devised it in order
to make Hamlet's refraining from it meaningful. But again, the meaning is not quite what we might expect. The motives that prevent Hamlet's committing a damnable act are themselves damnable. Hamlet's
goodness and nobility—of which, after all, he has a large supply—do
not stop him from murdering a man at prayer. His evil and ignobility
do, and when we see human evil result in good, we may justifiably suspect that we are being shown an example of providence at work. The
good is double: Hamlet does not commit a damnable act and Claudius
is able to seek his salvation. Hamlet's evil desire to damn Claudius re-

sults in the good of his sparing him. But hallelujahs would be premature, for disaster is also the result of sparing Claudius. Polonius, Ophelia, Rosencrantz, Guildenstern, Laertes, Gertrude, and Hamlet die because of it. Good comes of evil, but evil comes of that good. Because Claudius does not find grace, seven people die and, as we have seen, Shakespeare leaves the causes of Claudius's failure frighteningly mysterious. Incomprehensible ironies are the result of providential control and the final evidence of what I shall unsatisfactorily call Hamlet's election is, I think, his recognition and acceptance of that incomprehensibility.

Hamlet's evil impulses are directed by providence to a good end. Claudius's good impulses fail of their object and that failure is the cause of even greater evil than the sin which set the tragic action in motion. I would like to suggest that in the prayer scene Shakespeare is defining the action of the play as the mutual destruction of an elect protagonist and a reprobate antagonist and I hope that the substitution of the theological terms for the usual "good" and "evil" will disinfect the play of a prim morality that is foreign to it. But there is also a danger that the substitution will suggest a meretricious clarity and one must keep in mind that in any theology election and reprobation are finally absolutely mysterious concepts. Beyond that, however, it is important to recognize that the moral and psychological state which Shakespeare has imagined in Hamlet at the end of the play is quite different from grace as dreamt of in any orthodox theology. But before we turn to that central and difficult problem, we should look at the spectacle of Claudius's reprobation.

The first effect of Hamlet's forbearance is to permit Claudius to complete the unsuccessful search for grace that he has been inspired to undertake by the operation on his conscience of "The Mousetrap." Hamlet's determination to damn Claudius is thus ironically employed to permit his enemy to seek salvation. But, of course, that irony doubles back on itself. By failing in his search, Claudius further damns himself—or his prior damnation by God is further justified. Hamlet leaves Claudius to work out his own damnation, and Claudius does precisely that. I have said that "The Mousetrap" presents Claudius with alternatives—the Christian and the Machiavellian. He proves incapable of the Christian, either because he rejects it or it rejects him. He is superbly capable of the Machiavellian, however.

The Machiavellian trap is baited with the blood of Hamlet. The revelation and threat contained in "The Murder of Gonzago" make Hamlet's destruction Claudius's only viable course of action other than repentance. But by turning to it Claudius begins the process of turning himself into a self-destroying Machiavel. The process is slow, however, and his first moves are brilliant enough. The plan to send Hamlet to England and have him killed there has only one weakness—it necessarily removes Hamlet from Claudius's immediate control and Claudius's sense of the danger of that is already hinted at in the play's second scene when he refuses Hamlet permission to return to Wittenberg. This weakness in the end proves fatal but Claudius's reasons for risking it are made clear when he answers Laertes' demand for an explanation of why he has not proceeded directly against "feates, / So crimefull, and so Capitall in Nature":

> The Queen his Mother,
> Lives almost by his lookes: and for my selfe,
> My Vertue or my Plague, be it either which,
> She's so conjunctive to my life and soule,
> That as the Starre moves not but in his Sphere,
> I could not but by her. The other Motive,
> Why to a publike count I might not go,
> Is the great love the generall gender beare him.
> (4.7.12–19)

Here is a demonstration of the "poetic" element in divine justice. Love of Gertrude, Claudius's motive for murder, effectively prevents his success as a Machiavellian just as it frustrated his attempt at contrition. And if we accept his estimation of Hamlet's popularity as sincere rather than an improvised substitute for his true fear—the revelations Hamlet might be able to make about Claudius's crimes—then we see that the necessity for keeping power effectively frustrates its keeping. He would endanger his power by proceeding directly against Hamlet, the major threat to his power. His crown, his own ambition, and his queen—the effects for which he did the murder—prevent Claudius from acting with the necessary ruthlessness of the true and successful Machiavellian. Instead he enters on a course of elaborate deceit which results in his own death as well as that of Gertrude, Laertes and Hamlet, Rosencrantz and Guildenstern.

The final effect of "The Mousetrap" is to lure Claudius into working out both his earthly destruction and his possibly predestined damnation. But in assuming that Claudius is reprobate in the sense of a man who will go to hell I am assuming more than I can possibly know. There must necessarily be doubt about the eternal destination of all the Shakespearean villains and heroes we consider, for unlike Marlowe's, Shakespeare's artifices do not include visible damnations. Even Richard, Iago, and Macbeth may not be damned, unlikely though it seems, and Claudius's chances of salvation, though still slight, are definitely better than theirs. But the eternal fates of Hamlet and Othello are far more mysterious, and that mystery is an indispensable element in these works of art. One must substitute neither certainty nor indifference for it. Thus the question of Hamlet's eternal destination cannot be given a definitive answer. The evidence is necessarily insufficient and, in any case, only the mind of God would be capable of evaluating it if it were complete. Nevertheless, I shall maintain that Hamlet is in a state of grace at the end of the play. I am well aware, however, of the difficulties of supporting such a statement and I recognize that finally I shall define a state of grace as that state which Hamlet is in at the end of the play. And certainly that state bears little relationship to the psychological condition of the elect as it is usually imagined in Christian theology. Repentance and faith, the two great clues to a Christian's spiritual condition, have almost nothing whatever to do with Hamlet. His single moment of repentance is formal and perfunctory and as for faith, he appears to die believing exactly and only one thing.

The absence of repentance cannot be explained by an absence of deeds to repent. Hamlet is directly responsible for three deaths and indirectly responsible for a fourth. But the deaths of Polonius, Rosencrantz, Guildenstern—even Ophelia—simply do not engage his conscience. Hamlet's superego reproaches him not for killing people, but for not killing them.

He responds to Laertes' grief for Ophelia and to the suggestion that he is responsible for that death with rage. Even Horatio's bemusement at learning that Rosencrantz and Guildenstern go to it makes Hamlet slightly testy. Much has been written about Hamlet's neurotic hypersensitivity but surely it is as much his tough-mindedness that sets him apart from "us," and makes us feel, as we do at such moments ("Ile lugge the Guts into the Neighbor roome"; "Why man, they did make love to this imployment") that we are in the presence of a prince out of our star.

Richard III's ruthlessness is the result of his lack of humanity. Hamlet's is both a cause and a result of a human greatness which is double— the extrinsic greatness of his position on Fortune's wheel and the intrinsic greatness of his mind. Being born doubly great makes it easy for him to detach himself from lesser humans and the resulting indifference is a necessity if he is to maintain his humanity against the assaults of what Claudius is and stands for. But if these were the only sources of his toughness, we would have to judge him as a properly formidable opponent for Claudius, but one who is neither morally nor spiritually better than the man he destroys—a superior sort of Renaissance fascist whose loss would leave us without a sense of loss. In fact Hamlet's toughness derives not from any conviction on his part of his own greatness, but rather from his strong sense of his own nescience. The play shows us the development and alteration of this sense from its beginning in adolescent rejection of the world and his own "too sallied flesh" to the mature prose acceptance of "Not a whit, we defy Augury," and this process is the heart of the play and of Hamlet's mystery. I wish to ask only one large and unanswerable question about it: is it the process of a man working out his salvation, the tragic process of an elect protagonist, destroyed by the divinely imposed necessity of destroying a reprobate antagonist? Hamlet, as we have seen, senses such a necessity from the beginning and curses the fact that he has been predestined to set right the time. By the time he has killed Polonius, he has become able to accept that necessity because he begins to understand the meaning of necessity—to understand that there is nothing to be done with necessities except, in Henry IV's phrase, to meet them as necessities. He begins to believe that the agonies of his self-reproach and the puzzlement of his will are parts of a process that will bring him inevitably to actions predetermined by a greater will:

For this same Lord,
I do repent: but heaven hath pleas'd it so,
To punish me with this, and this with me,
That I must be their Scourge and Minister.
I will bestow him, and will answer well
The death I gave him.   (3.4.172–177)

The contrition is perfunctory and when we remember the intensity of Claudius's desire to repent, we are tempted to dismiss Hamlet as morally callous or superficial by comparison. To do so is, I think, to miss the point. Hamlet does what Claudius cannot do. He accepts responsibility for what he has done and will do, but he does not accept the ultimate responsibility for it. He repents the killing of Polonius and he will answer for it because he has done it. But to say that he has done it is not to explain why it has happened. It has happened because he has done it, and because Polonius is a wretched, rash, intruding fool, and because Hamlet has rashly taken him for his better, but, above all and finally, because it has pleased heaven that it should happen. Hamlet does not suggest for a moment that the fact that he is heaven's instrument should excuse him from the consequences of his deeds, either temporal or eternal. He accepts responsibility but refuses guilt, thus giving evidence that his psychic state is the opposite of neurosis, that it is a condition for which there is no word since it is so rare that neither "normality" nor "health" will do. The source of Hamlet's (in my opinion) extraordinary reaction to the killing of Polonius lies in his justified conviction that he is the scourge and minister of God. He is a scourge because in destroying the rottenness in Denmark he is responsible for human suffering and must suffer in turn for inflicting it. He is a minister because in setting right the time he will restore the sanctity and health of the state. He is punished for the suffering he causes by that suffering and by its consequences. The murder of Polonius punishes the murderer by making him a murderer as well as by subjecting him to the revenge of the murdered man's son.

I would suggest that most of us, if we found ourselves in Hamlet's position and possessed of Hamlet's convictions, would react in one of two ways—or perhaps in both of two ways, simultaneously or alternately. We would suffer our customary agonies of remorse on the one hand while pitying ourselves for the injustice of being punished for doing what God has willed. And we would, of course, do our best to avoid the consequences of our action on the double grounds that we were very sorry we did it and in any case we weren't responsible. Hamlet, unlike "us," suffers no remorse, pities himself not a bit, and accepts his responsibility and the consequent necessity to answer for what he has done.

But we must reconcile this interpretation of Hamlet's determination to "answer well" the death of Polonius with the answer he, in fact, makes. The antic disposition with which he "answers" Claudius, Rosencrantz, and Guildenstern is not of much importance, but his self-justification to Laertes is. He explains losing his temper at Ophelia's graveside and his regret for having done so to Horatio:

> ... I am very sorry good *Horatio*,
> That to *Laertes* I forgot my selfe;
> For by the image of my Cause, I see
> The Portraiture of his; Ile court[9] his favours:
> But sure the bravery of his griefe did put me
> Into a Towring passion.   (5.2.76–81)

This is generous and human enough. In equating Laertes with himself, Hamlet is also equating himself with Claudius. But whereas Hamlet accepts the responsibility but not the guilt for the death of Polonius, Claudius accepts the guilt but attempts to avoid the consequences of the death of old Hamlet. The excuse Hamlet gives for his loss of control, though surely partial (he does not mention Laertes' veiled accusation of him), is completely comprehensible. Laertes' extravagant grief is an excellent example of the false expression of true emotion. The difficulty comes when Hamlet attempts to court Laertes' favors, for he does so as disingenuously as any other courtier:

> Give me your pardon Sir, I've done you wrong,
> But pardon't as you are a Gentleman.
> This presence knowes,
> And you must needs have heard how I am punisht
> With sore distraction? What I have done
> That might your nature honour, and exception

> Roughly awake, I heere proclaime was madness:
> Was't *Hamlet* wrong'd *Laertes?* Never *Hamlet*.
> If *Hamlet* from himselfe be tane away:
> And when he's not himselfe, do's wrong *Laertes*,
> Then *Hamlet* does it not, *Hamlet* denies it:
> Who does it then? His Madnesse? If't be so,
> *Hamlet* is of the Faction that is wrong'd,
> His madnesse is poore *Hamlets* Enemy.
>
> (5.2.173–186)

This is a lie. Hamlet is not mad, never has been mad, and certainly was not mad when he killed Polonius. Far from being his enemy, Hamlet's feigned madness, by releasing him from the necessity for rational conduct, has probably preserved his sanity. Hamlet is substituting a lie for an untellable truth: "I killed your father because I thought he was my uncle and I wanted to kill my uncle because I know he killed my father, though I can't prove it." But Hamlet is selecting a lie that tells a version of what he sees as the truth. He has killed Polonius, but he has not wronged Laertes. He is responsible for the death of Laertes' father, but he does not deserve to be killed by Laertes, though he intends to kill Claudius for a similar crime. He is not guilty in the sense that Claudius is guilty. Even so, there is a strain of sophistry or at least of overstatement in the speech, though it emerges finally into sincerity and truth:

> Sir, in this Audience,
> Let my disclaiming from a purpos'd evill,
> Free me so farre in your most generous thoughts,
> That I have shot mine Arrow o're the house,
> And hurt my brother.[10]   (5.2.187–191)

We should remember that Claudius is "in this audience," and it is by comparison with him that Hamlet is innocent of "a purpos'd evill." Hamlet's responsibility does not include such guilt and he is right to refuse it. The consequences of his action he must accept, however, and these include death, since the murder of Polonius turns Laertes into an instrument of Claudius, just as the murder of old Hamlet turns Hamlet into an instrument of God. The two sons kill and forgive each other:

LAER. Exchange forgivenesse with me, Noble *Hamlet*;
Mine and my Fathers death come not upon thee,
Nor thine on me.   *Dyes.*
HAM. Heaven make thee free of it, I follow thee.

(5.2.339–342)

At such moments in tragedy it is necessary to distinguish between guilt
and responsibility and even more necessary to distinguish between justice and consequences. What happens to Hamlet is an example of the latter, not the former. But so is what happens to Polonius and, perhaps,
even to Laertes, though he does not think so. The concept of providence
asserts that in fact justice and consequences coincide but, in a work like
Hamlet, we are not told how.

What is revealed about Hamlet by the killing of Polonius and his subsequent attitude toward it does not, I think, necessarily prevent our seeing him as the elect protagonist of a Christian tragedy. The deaths of
Rosencrantz and Guildenstern present us with a harder case. Polonius
and Laertes are caught in traps they have made for Hamlet, Laertes characterizing himself as:

> . . . a Woodcocke
> To mine owne[11] sprindge, *Osricke*,
> I am justly kill'd with mine own Treacherie.

(5.2.332–334)

Rosencrantz and Guildenstern are caught in a trap set for Hamlet but
Shakespeare has neglected to make it absolutely clear that they have
helped to set it or even that they are aware of its existence. Is this ambiguity deliberate on Shakespeare's part or is it the result of carelessness? I
think it is probably the former. If Shakespeare had made it absolutely
clear that Rosencrantz and Guildenstern were totally ignorant of Claudius's murderous intentions, our sympathy for Hamlet in act 5 would be
seriously endangered. If on the other hand he showed us Rosencrantz and
Guildenstern plotting Hamlet's murder with the king, he would transform them into villains of a quite different sort from the ones he has
been at pains to create.

Hamlet, at any rate, is convinced that they are guilty. He tells his mother that they deserve the destruction which he sees them arranging for themselves:

> Ther's letters seald, and my two Schoolefellowes,
> Whom I will trust as I will Adders fang'd,
> They beare the mandat, they must sweep my way
> And marshall me to knavery: let it worke,
> For tis the sport to have the enginer
> Hoist with his owne petar, an't shall goe hard
> But I will delve one yarde belowe their mines,
> And blowe them at the Moone: ô tis most sweete
> When in one line two crafts directly meete.[12]
>
> $$(Q_2.3.4.203-211)$$

It is at this point that Hamlet most obviously adumbrates Vindice, the lethal *farceur* of *The Revenger's Tragedy*, the practical joker whose exploding cigars blow your head off. The satisfaction that Hamlet takes in the ingenuity with which he destroys his former friends may be grim, but it is satisfaction nevertheless and it is a chilling quality:

> Hor. So *Guildensterne* and *Rosincrance*, go too't.
> Ham. Why man; they did make love to this imployment
> They are not neere my Conscience; their defeat[13]
> Doth by their owne insinuation grow:
> 'Tis dangerous, when the baser nature comes
> Betweene the passe, and fell incensed points
> Of mighty opposites. $(5.2.60-66)$

This refusal of guilt is not relieved, as it was in the case of Polonius's death, by even a perfunctory repentance, and yet Hamlet's ruthlessness does not, I would guess, repel most of us when we experience the play in the theater. This is not because most of us are insensitive and immoral, but because Shakespeare has taken care that we should not be deeply concerned by the destruction of this pair. The care he has taken is not, however, what we would expect to find when we look for it after the fact. He does not make Rosencrantz and Guildenstern obvious, oily, self-seeking villains. He makes them especially ordinary—standard, interchangeable, mass-produced—and he does this, above all, by making two of them:

> KING: Thankes *Rosincrance*, and gentle *Guildensterne*.
> QU. Thankes *Guildensterne* and gentle *Rosincrance*.
>
> (2.2.32–33)

Thanks Tweedledee and gentle Tweedledum. The result is that we find it easier than it should be to share Hamlet's view of them as "baser natures," but Shakespeare undercuts our comfortable appropriation of the heroic point of view by making the "baseness" in question consist precisely in the characters' resemblance to ourselves. Their sins are those of ordinary men: a betrayal of personal loyalties, an exaggerated regard for constituted authority, a dependence upon cliché as a basis for moral decision. Ordinarily these do not cost us our lives, but in a tragic world consequences are usually disastrous beyond the ordinary. Shakespeare is here demonstrating that if Everyman were used after his desert he would not 'scape whipping though if used justly he might, perhaps, hope to escape beheading.

Hamlet's indifference to Rosencrantz and Guildenstern is also made more excusable by the fact that he is becoming indifferent to his own dying of the death he has sent them to. The deaths that he has inflicted have made his own crisis dangerously imminent and his acceptance of that probable consequence makes our acceptance of his ruthlessness toward Rosencrantz and Guildenstern considerably easier. Horatio says, speaking of Claudius:

> HOR. It must be shortly knowne to him from England
>   What is the issue of the businesse there.
> HAM. It will be short,
>   The *interim's* mine, and a mans life's no more
>   Then to say one.[14]   (5.2.74–78)

Hamlet is speaking from experience. He has said "one" three times. We cannot tell whether the man whose life Hamlet has in mind is Hamlet or Claudius or both, but he is clearly not disposed to agonize more over any death, his own included, than he did over Polonius's or Rosencrantz's or Guildenstern's. Again, this toughness would be frighteningly inhuman if it were not for two facts: first, it is a state that Hamlet has arrived at only after a long and intensely painful process; second, it is the result of a profound belief in the existence of an "ordinant" God.

At the play's beginning, Hamlet does not set his life at a pin's fee. There is nothing he would more willingly part withal, and yet, as he tells us in the "To be or not to be" soliloquy, he fears death because he is ignorant of what may come after it. By the time of the gravedigger's scene he is able to meet the challenge that he sets the skull of Yorick—he makes us "laugh at that." And finally he concludes that his ignorance of the unknown is no greater than his ignorance of the known: "since no man of ought he leaves, knowes, what ist to leave betimes?"

But Hamlet does in fact, know one thing: "There's a Divinity that shapes our ends, / Rough-hew them how we will." (5.2.10–11). We must acquiesce in Horatio's "That is most certaine," as applying to the world Shakespeare has created for this play. We need not, of course, assume therefore that Shakespeare insists that it is equally true of the reality he did not create and which we share with him. He may have believed so, but that is another matter.

Above all, we need not—indeed, we must not—assume that Hamlet asserts that the existence of a shaping divinity makes the world a nice place. The fact that heaven is ordinant lessens none of the horror of what it orders and may, indeed, increase that horror considerably if we try to puzzle out the nature of the divinity that shapes what happens in *Hamlet*. God's existence does not even make what happens comprehensible. What Hamlet faces at the last is the fact that though he knows one thing, he does not understand anything. What he is asserting is that the incomprehensibility of his world does not make it meaningless. He accepts death and ignorance together in his greatest and plainest speech:

> HAM. . . . there's a speciall Providence in the fall of a sparrow.
> If it be now, 'tis not to come: if it bee not to come, it will bee now:
> if it bee not now; yet it will come; the readiness is all; since no man
> of ought he leaves, knowes, what ist to leave betimes? let be.[15]
>
> (5.2.166–171)

This has been called fatalism, but surely it is not. Fatalism—true Islamic,

Averroist fatalism—holds that God's will is subject to fate. Hamlet is facing necessity *as* necessity and he can do so because he is convinced that by so doing he is accepting an expression of divine will. Hamlet is saying "Thy will be done." Amen, *ainsi soit-il*, let be. Nothing is easier to say or harder to mean and Hamlet's ability to mean it is, for me, the final and indeed the only possible proof of what I must clumsily call his election.

The elect protagonist of a Christian tragedy need not be a nice man or even a good man any more than the world of Christian tragedy need be a nice or good world. Hamlet is neither so bad nor so good as Robert le Dyable. Like Robert he kills, but because he believes he kills as heaven's scourge and minister, he rejects the guilt that overwhelms Robert. Robert seeks to save himself through penance. Hamlet finds salvation and accepts it, or by accepting it, finds it. He does not seek it. "Is she to bee buried in Christian buriall, that willfully seekes her owne salvation?" (5.1.1–2). The gravedigger's question is, in the context of *Hamlet*, very much to be asked. Only, it would seem, if we drown ourselves in our own defense can we find Christian burial. Hamlet qualifies by taking up arms against a sea of troubles, but he does not go to the water and drown himself; he lets the water come to him and drown him. He accepts the end shaped for him by divinity and his ability to do so is a sign of an election which he does not deserve except insofar as he does not reject it: "It must ever in the election of saints be remembered, that to choose is an act *of God's good pleasure, which presupposeth in us sufficient cause to avert, but none to deserve it.*"[16] But election implies reprobation —the apparent fate of Claudius, the one character in the play who does willfully seek his own salvation. Calvin insists on the same cause for both: "Againe I aske: how came it to passe, that the fall of Adam did wrap up in eternall death so many nations with their children being infants without remedie, but because it so pleased God?"[17] The tragedy of *Hamlet* agrees, I think, in making God's pleasure the source of its events:

Enter Saylor

SAY. God blesse you Sir.

125

HOR. Let him blesse thee too.
SAY. He shall Sir, and't please him.

(4.6.6–8)

This, when thought about, is at least as frightening as it is comforting. Shakespeare is able to create art out of the comfort and terror which are both inherent in this concept of God. But he counters what I must finally call the horrors of theology by having his elect protagonist proclaim his total ignorance: "no man of ought he leaves, knowes." The insomnia of theological logic brings forth monsters, and Shakespeare's tragic art puts them to use as possible gods for the play. But art can encompass the monsters it evokes by pointing out that they are art—contrivances meant not as knowledge but as provisional replacements for our continuing ignorance.

Hamlet contains a mousetrap and its maker—Hamlet and his play. But the trope in turn indicates the presence of another contrivance— the process of the drama as an artifice constructed by its God for the purpose of catching consciences. Claudius's conscience is caught, finds itself guilty, and Claudius is destroyed in this world and perhaps damned in the next. But Hamlet's conscience too is caught, finds itself not guilty, and Hamlet is destroyed in this world but perhaps saved in the next. But the implied divinity of the play is Himself an artifice who necessitates a creator. Shakespeare, creating the implied God of his dramatic world out of the comforts and terrors of the beliefs of his time, also builds a mousetrap. His purpose is to catch the consciences of the guilty creatures who will sit at his play, to put them through a process whose therapeutic and aesthetic effects are highly beneficial to its victims. But what of intellectual effects? Is it possible that the play wishes to bring us, as it brings Hamlet, to a knowledge of our ignorance? If so, it is inevitably and necessarily impossible to understand. Like the world of *Hamlet*, *Hamlet* itself is incomprehensible but not meaningless.

CHAPTER 6
Othello

AT LINE 90 of scene 3 in act 3 of *Othello*, just before Iago begins his work of destruction, the Moor stands watching Desdemona leave the stage and says:

> Excellent wretch: Perdition catch my Soule
> But I do love thee: and when I love thee not,
> Chaos is come againe.

As prophecy the lines are ironically precise. Othello stops loving his wife, chaos comes again, and it seems likely that when he kills himself at the play's end, perdition catches his soul. But the lines are more than that point of dramatic irony on which the action of the tragedy is poised. They are also the play's clearest direct statement of the action's meaning, and like most such Shakespearean statements they ask more questions than they answer.

According to the lines, the health of a man's mind and soul depends upon his ability to sustain love—an unexceptionable statement whose truth is obviously demonstrated by the tragedy. But the particular language of the lines moves them beyond banality. As we have seen in *Richard III*[1] the juxtaposition of love and chaos evokes a conceptual view of the created universe, the view which sees matter as composed of elements that are by nature in contention and whose order is the result of the imposition upon them of divine love. This elemental view is basic to Shakespeare's art, where it coexists with and complements the hierarchical view of order so memorably presented by Ulysses in *Troilus and Cressida*. What the maintaining of degree is to hierarchical order, the maintaining of love is to elemental order. Othello's lines, then, suggest that the particular tragedy of this single man, his psychic and spiritual destruction, is more than personal, or even representatively human. The tragedy is a component of its universe, defining it and defined by it. The laws that destroy and damn Othello govern all men and all created things and express, we must assume, the nature of their creator.

The orthodox optimism of Shakespeare's time accepted, of course, the notion that the creation is an expression of the creator and saw the universal order which exists despite the chaos inherent in it as proof of God's goodness: "How could it be that the elements, so divers and contrary as they be among themselves, should yet agree and abide together in a concord, without destruction one of another to serve our use, if it came not onely of GODS goodnesse so to temper them?"[2] Chaos does not come again because God's goodness, his grace and his providence, will not let it. But that statement asks its own question: when chaos comes again, as it does for Othello, does it do so because God lets it? Does our ability to sustain love depend upon God's grace?

Othello, like the other Christian tragedies, asks that question but does not answer it and as usual the refusal (or inability) to answer finds its expression in a series of possible answers. In *Othello*, however, the series is presented to us according to a different order of emphasis from the one that obtains in the two Shakespearean tragedies I have examined so far. In *Richard III* and *Hamlet* there is a dominant possibility, namely that there is a special providence in the fall of a sparrow, a providence which is equally to be found in the falls of Richard, Claudius, and Hamlet himself. In these plays the paradoxical nature of the concepts of grace and providence is the source for an important part of the power with which these tragedies inspire pity and terror. The destruction of Richard and the triumph of Richmond are evidence for providential control. Even the mutual destruction of Hamlet and Claudius serves to purge Denmark of its rottenness. But the only good that comes of the tragic suffering in *Othello* is the punishment of those who are guilty of inflicting pain upon the innocent. There, the predominance of grace and providence as possible explanations for the action recedes and is replaced by the newly ascendant possibility that the tragedy is the result precisely of that receding. The *Othello* world is one from which God appears to have withdrawn, leaving its disposition to the freed wills of men. Or, to put it another way, in *Othello* the Pelagian possibility replaces the Augustinian possibility which largely directs our conceiving of the worlds of *Richard III* and *Hamlet*.

This receding of a sense of grace, providence, and consequently, of predestination as forces operating to determine the action of the play is a part of Shakespeare's larger artistic strategy in *Othello*. In this play he limits himself conceptually just as he narrows his usual range in time, place, and action, and all these efforts of limitation are directed toward the achieving of an emotional intensity that derives from our sense of participating in the mutually destructive interaction of brilliantly imagined human minds. Too strong a suggestion that this conflict is the expression of a divine will rather than the human wills that so thoroughly engage us would distract us from our absorption in the psychological struggle that is this play's great achievement. And so the potentially intrusive concepts are replaced by others that will contribute to the drama's great effect. As always in Shakespeare the conceptual is a means to art and not its end. And yet, among the purposes or inevitable results of Shakespeare's art is the imaginative examination of concepts. *Othello* is, among other things, Shakespeare's way of thinking about the possibility that the universe is not providentially ordered.

According to the *Homilies*, "it is not to be thought, that GOD hath created all this whole universall world as it is, and thus once made, hath given it up to be ruled and used after our owne wits and device."[3] It is not to be thought, but of course it *is* thought and the homilist himself has thought it. *Othello*, I shall maintain, is Shakespeare's way of thinking it and of enabling his audience to think it, but to think it only as a possibility and a possibility in two successive ways. The *Othello* world, apparently deprived of providential control, is first of all an artifact which does not claim to be more than a possible version of reality. "Tush . . . what stande we here upon? it is a Poesie and no divinitye, and it is lawfull for poetes to fayne what they lyst, so it be appertinent to the matter."[4] In the second place *Othello* can, but need not, be taken as occurring in a Pelagian world. If we choose to assume that the play is taking place in an Augustinian or Calvinist world of second causes and that the action we experience is a more than usually opaque manifestation of divine will, we may do so. Nothing in the play contradicts such an interpretation. But in the overtly providential plays our minds are directed toward this way of understanding the action. In *Othello* they are not. The tragedy is entirely without a supernatural dimension and the only event in it that could possibly be taken as evidence of providential control—the destruction of the Turkish fleet by the storm—is not, in fact, attributed to heaven's intervention. If our minds move toward a providential view of the play, the motive power must come from within ourselves, particularly if we move all the way to the Calvinist end of the interpretive spectrum, for the sense that human will is free from superhuman influence is so strong in this play that only a determined desire to see the will as supernaturally bound would impel an interpreter to view it in such a way.

A more strictly Augustinian interpretation of the play would not need to be so entirely self-generated. Such a theology is suggested, I believe, in some lines from the last scene, where Gratiano says of Desdemona's dead father:

> Did he live now,
> This sight would make him do a desperate turne:
> Yea, curse his better Angell from his side,
> And fall to reprobation.[5]   (5.2.206–209)

This describes, by analogy, the destruction of Othello. The sight that first turns him desperate, though inspired by Iago's imagery, is wholly imaginary. He "sees" Desdemona "topped" by Cassio and curses her from his side: "O Devil, devil. . . . / Hence, avaunt!" (4.1.255, 271). Then he discovers that she has been his good angel, the living manifestation of God's grace to him. At this point the "sight" becomes the one Gratiano is talking about: Desdemona's corpse. Confronted by its reality, Othello repeats the process of self-damnation, deliberately turning to hell as a preferable alternative to any existence, temporal or eternal, which would include the knowledge of his murder of Desdemona:

> Whip me ye Divels,
> From the possession of this Heavenly sight:
> Blow me about in windes, roast me in Sulphure,
> Wash me in steepe-downe gulfes of Liquid fire.
>   (5.2.277–280)

To the Calvinist the reprobation to which Othello here falls has been his predestined fate from eternity, the somehow just and necessary result of God's terrible decree. The Augustinian, while recognizing that Othello could not have chosen well without prevenient grace, insists that the fall to reprobation is, in some way that is mysterious to human reason, the just result of wrong free choice, and he can further moralize the spectacle by pointing out that Othello's disaster derives from a fundamental misapprehension about the nature of his world and his relationship to it. The lines in which Othello sees his love for Desdemona as his bulwark against chaos and perdition may well be qualified by the mild irony a mature man feels on contemplating the emotional intensity of which he remains capable. Nonetheless, for the Augustinian, these lines betray a tendency in Othello toward a terrible error: it is not the love of man for woman that saves us from chaos and perdition, but the love of man for God, and of God for man. The value which Othello originally places upon Desdemona is, in this view, idolatrous and he suffers the fate of the idolator when his idol seems to fail him. Again, this way of understanding the tragedy is not contradicted by the play and can be supported from the text. It is a possible interpretation. It does not exclude another, however.

I would suggest that what Shakespeare proposes as the clearest possible truth about the *Othello* version of reality is precisely what Homiletic orthodoxy holds to be unthinkable: God has given up his creation to be ruled after our wits and device. In this view of the *Othello* world, man is at liberty. His mind is free of supernatural grace and his will is consequently free to choose its own destiny. This, of course, is precisely Iago's view of the matter:

'tis in our selves that we are thus, or thus. Our Bodies are our Gardens, to the which, our Wills are Gardiners. So that if we will plant Nettels, or sowe Lettice: Set Hisope, and weede up Time: Supplie it with one gender of Hearbes, or distract it with many: either to have it sterrill with idlenesse, or manured with Industry, why the power, and Corrigeable authoritie of this lies in our Wills. If the ballance[6] of our lives had not one Scale of Reason, to poize another of Sensualitie, the blood, and basenesse of our Natures would conduct us to most prepostrous Conclusions. But we have Reason to coole our raging Motions, our carnall Stings, our unbitted Lusts: whereof I take this, that you call Love, to be a Sect or Seyen.

(1.3.319–332)

As Roy Battenhouse and William Elton have pointed out, Iago, however unconsciously, is a Pelagian.[7] But is Iago, for that reason, wrong? I would say that he is abundantly wrong, but not necessarily for that reason. The world which Shakespeare has created for him to exist in may well be an ironically Pelagian world.

In any case the portrait of the mind given us through Iago's metaphors is Pelagian. Both the garden and the balance are Pelagian images for psychic processes and the poised scales, with the will free to tip the balance, is a precise icon for the Pelagian sense of the will's relationship to the whole mind of which it is a part. It is a view that leaves no room for grace—at least not for grace in any supernatural form. Grace in a Pelagian world may exist in forms exterior to men, but to admit internal, supernatural grace as a working component of the psyche is, to the Pelagian, to deny the freedom of the will. I would suggest that in the creation of the *Othello* world, Shakespeare puts forward this view as the most likely model for the minds of the characters he is creating. In the other Christian tragedies he gives artistic form to the tragic implications of the belief that divine grace is granted to or withheld from the mind of man. In *Othello* he imagines a world in which internal grace may not exist and the mind of man is free to make the choices that will result in the shaping of its own ends. The implications of man's freedom turn out to be at least as tragic as the implications of man's bondage.

But if Iago's Pelagian view of the mind is, in one very basic way, possibly accurate within the context of the play, it is also, in another very basic way, wrong. First of all Iago is very clearly wrong in a parochial sense. What he believes to be true of himself is proved by his actions and fate to be completely untrue. He is, in fact, conducted by the blood and baseness of his nature to the most preposterous of conclusions—death by torture. He does not see that the hatred for Othello which possesses and motivates him totally is as much a sect or scion of what he calls "unbitted lusts" as is Roderigo's love for Desdemona. But this error indicates, I believe, another even more basic than that.

Perhaps the best way of identifying that error is to return to his metaphor and examine the content of the scales. According to Iago, these contain reason and sensuality in equal quantities and the will is therefore free to make a rational choice that will promote its own good. In proper

Pelagianism the scales of our life, the components of our nature, consist in equal parts of good and evil, so that the will is enabled by the equilibrium to choose without constraint between sinning and not sinning. In the play, however, these qualities are rather different, though not different in the way Iago would have them. They are paganized or syncretized into the ultimately pre-Socratic principles of love and strife.

If Iago is right in his basic apprehension of the Pelagian freedom of his mind and universe, then Othello is right in his sense of what preserves mind and universe from destruction. It is neither human reason nor divine grace but human love. The balance of his life consists in a scale of hate poised against one of love and this perilous equilibrium is expressed in the structure of the play with its balancing of antagonist against antiantagonist, Iago against Desdemona. Othello holds and contains the scales and the play questions Pelagian optimism by asking, "Can the unaided force of human love balance the blood and baseness of our natures?" The play's answer, clearly, is "No."

This is an answer that does not flatter our humanity and our natural impulse to evade it leads us to misinterpret the play. Usually such impulses to misinterpretation move us in one of two directions. We may try to alleviate the play's pessimism by overemphasizing its tendency to allegory—a tactic that allows us to see the hatred embodied in Iago as abstract, more diabolical than human, and thus not a dangerously valid comment on the strength of our own ordinary evil. Or we may take an opposite tack and discover, in the realism with which the play characterizes Othello's greatness and his love for Desdemona, evidence for believing that that his love and greatness are more than usually flawed and thus not a dangerously valid comment on the weakness of our own ordinary good. Both tendencies are misguided, I think, but both are also in some degree justified by the text and I would like to examine each in turn.

The structural resemblance of *Othello* to allegorized psychomachy is obvious. An heroic everyman, the protagonist is presented with a choice between embodied Vice and Virtue. The text repeatedly draws our attention to the allegorical analogue and Othello sums up this view of the action at the play's end: "Will you, I pray, demand that demy-Divell / Why he hath thus ensnar'd my Soule and Body" (5.2.299–300). But it is wrong to take the diabolical metaphor too literally, and seriously wrong if it allows us to escape the painful implications of Iago's humanity, for Iago is painfully human and his soliloquies, his dialogues with Roderigo and Othello, are brilliantly accurate imitations of real states of mind. Coleridge's famous "motive-hunting of a motiveless malignity" is a precise description of Iago's favorite mental activity, but we understand it correctly only so long as we remember that human malignity is by definition motiveless. "Malignity" *is* motive—according to this play (and to Freud) one of the two instinctual drives that move us to our actions.[8] When Iago tells us, repeatedly, that he hates the Moor, it behooves us to believe him. When he tells us why, it behooves us to realize that the emotion precedes the "motives" for it. But to move from that insight to the conclusion that Iago and his hatred are literary conventions instead of profound comments on human reality is to miss—or rather to evade— the point of the characterization. Rational hatred is a possible and common emotion which Iago does not exemplify. Irrational hatred is equally possible and probably more common. For Iago hatred is a necessity. He must have an object for the destructive force that would otherwise destroy its possessor—and does, nonetheless, destroy its possessor. Motives for the choice of Othello as object of the emotion must exist—or rather motives for the particular intensity of the emotion, for hatred in some form is Iago's inevitable response to all human beings. Some of the reasons for the extreme form it takes with regard to Othello are clear. Othello is successful, powerful, noble, and black. That a paranoid should hate him is inevitable and Iago's paranoid tendencies have brought him to the brink of insanity. His soliloquies are a determined effort to convince himself and, thanks to theatrical convention, to convince us that he is sane.

Shakespeare's success in the simultaneous creation of an "allegorical" embodiment of the force of hatred and a convincingly human mind is, in my opinion, total. Iago is an imaginative rethinking back into the human reality from which it emerged of a primary concept, a basic truth about that reality. The result is one of those artifacts whose complexity makes it an apparently inexhaustible source of meaning.

Desdemona's complexity is of another order. Simple in essence, she is, as a result of her simplicity, problematically complex in meaning. Iago's nature partakes of and confirms the complexity of the dramatic world he inhabits. Love, in that world, exists, in Othello himself at least, as the result of the repression of hatred. The Freudian critics of the play have made a (to me) totally convincing case for Iago's hatred as a product of the repression of an inadmissible, unconscious homosexual love.[9] But this ascendant hatred not only represses that love, it simultaneously allows Iago to allow himself to feel love and express it by putting its expression into the admissible mode of deception. Because in his hatred he is deceiving Othello, Iago can kneel in mock-marriage ceremony with him and he can imagine and describe himself in bed with Cassio, being passionately kissed by him. But at the same time that the deception of Othello permits in Iago the expression of a repressed love, it releases in Othello the elemental hatred which has been repressed by his love for Desdemona. Both characters are thus microcosms of an Empedoclean universe in which love and hate coexist in a dynamic and shifting interrelationship.

Desdemona is not such a microcosm. Her simplicity stands in contrast to an otherwise universal doubleness and appears to contradict what would otherwise be a universal human enslavement to the necessity for hatred. There is no hatred in Desdemona's love. Shakespeare has responded to the plot necessity for her technical innocence of adultery by giving her an innocence so complete that it cannot credit the possibility that adultery is ever committed by anyone:

> Do'st thou in conscience thinke (tell me *Aemilia*)
> That there be women do abuse their husbands
> In such grosse kinde?
>
> .   .   .   .
>
> I do not thinke there is any such woman.
>
> (4.3.62–85)

This is wondrous pitiful, but once we have experienced the pity of it, what are we to make of it? Can we accept it as a human possibility in the way we accept its opposite in Iago? Only, I should say, by accepting it as a temporary possibility, an innocence that must perforce be soon destroyed by experience, Iago or no Iago. But what of the love for Othello that coexists with that innocence? It is not destroyed even by murder:

AEMIL. Oh who hath done this deed?
DES. No body: I my selfe, farewell:
Commend me to my kinde Lord: oh farewell.

(5.2.123–125)

Can we accept Desdemona as a human possibility in the way I, at least, can accept Iago? I cannot. Iago's passions, however basic, are complicated. Desdemona's are impossibly simple, but this impossible simplicity does not prevent the character from functioning effectively within the work of art. So far as our emotional responses are concerned, her effectiveness is perfectly apparent, but she serves to direct our minds as well.

Shakespeare is testing with his imagination the possible validity of the optimism of a Pelagian world view and in doing so, he appears to have given the Pelagian possibility advantageous odds. He has imagined a heroine who is not only capable of goodness, but incapable of anything else. Desdemona has no need of supernatural grace. She is saved by being what she is—a natural embodiment of grace apparently untainted by original sin. And yet the tragedy occurs despite that grace and innocence. The first meaning of Desdemona's perfection seems to be that the unaided force of human love cannot balance the blood and baseness of our natures, as embodied in Othello, even when the object of that love is perfect. At the same time, this pessimism is qualified (whether to its mitigation or intensification I am not sure) by the sense we have that the tragedy is in part the result of that perfection. Because Desdemona's love is simple, it can answer Othello's hate only with love. So when he strikes her or calls her whore she can only be "obedient, very obedient." If her love were more fully human, if she were innocent of adultery but capable of it, she might understand Othello's jealous rage and answer it with a self-preserving fury of her own.

Shakespeare does not, however, want us to equate the absence of hatred in Desdemona's nature with an absence of all passion. There is a large admixture of frank physicality in her emotions as she describes them to the Venetian Senators and there is also operating in the text a subliminal association of Desdemona with the goddess of love herself. Desdemona is Venus in something of the same way that Iago is Satan—though the equation is a lot less obvious. The association is most clearly made at the beginning of act 2, which opens on the shore in Cyprus, where a terrible storm is in progress:

> The chidden Billow seemes to pelt the Clowds,
> The winde-shak'd Surge, with high & monstrous Maine
> Seemes to cast water on the burning Beare,
> And quench the Guards of th' ever-fixed Pole:
> I never did like mollestation view
> On the enchafed Flood.   (2.1.12–17)

The elements in contention seem to threaten the return of primal chaos, but what emerges from them are visions of love and the fact of peace.

Cassio is the herald and presenter of these visions and the main subject of his eloquence is Desdemona,

> a Maid
> That paragons description, and wilde Fame:
> One that excels the quirkes of Blazoning pens,
> And in th' essentiall Vesture of Creation,
> Do's tyre the Ingeniuer.[10]   (2.1.61–65)

Cassio's hyperbole proves its point: Desdemona is indescribable, particularly if one imagines her "in th' essentiall Vesture of Creation," "as God made her,"[11] naked as Eve. Or naked as Venus, which is a more appropriate association of ideas at the moment, since Venus was created, not from the side of Adam, but from a stormy sea, out of which she emerged to come ashore at Cyprus:

> Tempests themselves, high Seas, and howling windes,
> The gutter'd-Rockes, and Congregated Sands,
> Traitors ensteep'd, to enclogge the guiltlesse Keele,
> As having sence of Beautie, do omit
> Their mortall Natures letting go safely by
> The Divine *Desdemona.*   (2.1.68–73)

The divinity of Desdemona, *Venus Anadyomene*, a human goddess of Love and Beauty, is here made explicit and its further symbolic significance begins to be suggested, for she is *Venus Armata* as well: "Our great Captains Captaine." Cassio prays, with appropriate classicism:

137

> Great Jove, *Othello* guard,
> And swell his Saile with thine owne powrefull breath,
> That he may blesse this Bay with his tall Ship,
> Make loves quicke pants in *Desdemonaes* Armes,
> Give renew'd fire to our extincted Spirits.
>
> (2.1.77–81)

Othello, bringer of blessings and renewal, is godlike, too, and his conjunction with Venus/Desdemona would indicate his identity even if it were not obvious. Cassio's extravagance is presenting us with a vision of Venus in the act of love with Mars. This is followed by the entrance of Desdemona herself, to the accompaniment of Cassio's highest flight of rhetoric:

> Oh behold,
> The Riches of the Ship is come on shore:
> You men of Cyprus, let her have your knees.
> Haile to thee Ladie: and the grace of Heaven,
> Before, behinde thee, and on every hand
> Enwheele thee round.   (2.1.82–87)

Ave Desdemona, gratia plena. . . . But the extravagance is syncretic, for Cassio's "grace," enwheeling Desdemona round, suggests the Three Graces whose dancing forms accompany Venus, and the image, if it occurs to us, finally punctures Cassio's hyperbole, for with Desdemona enter in fact Iago, Roderigo, and Emilia, the Venus/Desdemona reality accompanied by far scruffier realities.

This reductive "realism" continues with Iago's improvisations on his own misogyny. These culminate with his version of Cassio's hyperbole, woman viewed as perfect in her self-denying nullity, swallowing her wrongs and not expressing her thoughts, and so supremely fitted for her *Kinder* and *Küche* roles, "To suckle fools and chronicle small beer." With the entrance of Othello, however, the verse returns to its exploration of the Venus/Mars icon, for Cassio's extravagance is not merely decorative Renaissance rhetoric. Its imagery is central to the meaning of the play.

Othello greets his wife with "O, my faire Warriour," and comments on their kisses: "And this, and this the greatest discords be / That ere our hearts shall make." (2.1.200–201). To which Iago adds, aside: "Oh you are well tun'd now: But Ile set down / the peggs that make this Musicke, as honest as I am." (2.1.202–203). Harmony is the daughter of Venus and Mars and the sexual union of the god and goddess is a primary image of the principle of *discordia concors*.[12] The union of Empedoclean Love and Empedoclean Strife, the origin of all forms and all order, is symbolized here. Lucretius's *De Rerum Natura* opens with an invocation to Venus which concludes with the vision of her domination of the god of war:

> For thou alone canst make men glad with tranquil peace; since Mars, the lord of arms, who rules the fierce pursuits of war, sinks oft upon thy bosom, overcome with love's eternal pain: so, looking up, with rounded neck bent back, he feeds his greedy sight on love, wide-opening his eyes on thee, thou glorious goddess, and his breath, as he reclines face upward, hangs upon thy lips. While he thus lies, and with thy sacred body thou enfoldest him above, pour forth sweet converse from thy mouth, requesting for the Romans placid peace.[13]

If we feel the need of a significant mythological justification for the image of Othello making "love's quick pants in Desdemona's arms," Lucretius is the place to find it. And the image was understandably a popular one with the Neoplatonic philosophers of the Renaissance. Edgar Wind quotes Pico della Mirandola:

> since in the constitution of created things it is necessary that the union overcomes the strife (otherwise the thing would perish because its elements would fall apart)—for this reason is it said by the poets that Venus loves Mars, because Beauty, which we call Venus, cannot subsist without contrariety; and that Venus tames and mitigates Mars, because the tempering power restrains and overcomes the strife and hate which persist between the contrary elements . . . if Mars were always subordinated to Venus, that is, the contrariety of the component elements to their due proportion, nothing would ever perish.[14]

The Mars and Venus icon returns us to our starting place and indicates its fuller meaning. When Othello fears the coming again of chaos, he does so as a human being who is both amused by and in awe of the destructive potential of his most constructive emotions. But Shakespeare has also given this very human voice the overtones of a symbolism that links his speech and the play to a Renaissance view of the nature of things and of man's place among them that is in some ways diametrically opposed to the Reformation view that is our main concern elsewhere. Christian Humanism, in its Neoplatonic moments (for even Calvin is a Humanist, though his moments are seldom Neoplatonic) saw man as free, thanks to God's goodness, to become and remain good as a result of his own efforts in response to God's love. Cassirer defines the contrast between this vision of man and the Augustinian:

> To question the Idea of the good, or to limit it by an ostensibly higher norm, would mean for Plato the dissolution of being itself and the sacrifice of all human as well as all divine order for chaos. Plato's theology is thus based on self-reliance and on the self-sufficiency of the moral life. In so far as this self-sufficiency has its foundation in the will, there can be no absolute depravity of the will for Plato. The power of Eros constantly works against the doctrine of original evil and triumphs over it. The fundamental assumption of Augustine's doctrine of grace was that the human will, once fallen from God, can never by its own agency find the power to return. For it is henceforth deprived of all ethical principles and of all independent initiative. The core of the Pelagian heresy, according to Augustine, consists in that arrogance of reason by which this faculty still clings to some form of independence and some possibility of self-activity. This capacity has been completely lost. Reason can no longer be directed towards the good except as it receives its direction from without through the medium of "*gratia praeveniens.*" In so far as the human will cooperates in regaining grace, this will itself is after all a work of God.[15]

A semi-Pelagian theology accompanies a Neoplatonic philosophy. Iago's view of man's freedom is not so different from Pico's, who imagines God as saying to man:

"Thou . . . art the molder and maker of thyself; thou mayest sculpt thyself into whatever shape thou dost prefer. . . ." O great liberality of God the Father! O great and wonderful happiness of man! It is given him to have that which he chooses and to be that which he wills. . . . At man's birth the Father placed in him every sort of seed and sprouts of every kind of life. The seeds that each man cultivates will grow and bear their fruit in him.[16]

Othello explores the tragic horror inherent in this "great and wonderful happiness."

The field of exploration is Othello himself. Shakespeare imagines a maker of choices who is a great man, one who is born great and has also achieved greatness, despite his foreignness and blackness, in the power structure of Renaissance Venice. His nobility, courage, and competence are described and demonstrated repeatedly in the course of the first two acts. The envy of Iago and Roderigo and the irrationality of Brabantio emphasize the superiority of the man who inspires their emotions while simultaneously making us begin to fear for a hero whose greatness can arouse so much malignity. The extreme complexity of the results, in terms of our reactions, of Shakespeare's choice of a black hero is well beyond my powers of analysis. Shakespeare is manipulating the racism of his time and that was clearly to some extent different from our own. But several of the more obvious effects of the contrast in pigmentation as opposed to race need to be recognized. The first of these is visibility. Othello's color helps him dominate the stage whenever he is on it. It is to him that our eyes are naturally drawn. The second effect is a function of the first: contrast. Othello is physically apart and this makes the impact of conjunction—particularly sexual conjunction with Desdemona—all the more striking. When Cassio imagines Othello making "love's quick pants in Desdemona's arms," we remember Iago's old black ram tupping a white ewe and the symbolic reconciliation of opposites in this act of love becomes the clearer for being black and white.

But perhaps a more important effect of the visible contrast of Othello's blackness is the paradoxical emphasis which it gives to his freedom. Othello, once a black slave, is now supremely at liberty. An extravagant and wheeling stranger, he is socially and racially detached from the world of the play. He can choose to serve or not serve and to love or not love. His decision to marry Desdemona is very carefully presented as an act of free choice. He notices her attraction to him, plays upon it, and finally brings her to a "hint" that is a declaration of love and of will-ingness to marry. His will rather than hers is presented with the final decision, and it is a decision motivated entirely by love. Despite Iago's claims to the contrary, no worldly advantage comes to Othello from his elopement—only the enmity of Desdemona's powerful father. Othello's subjection to love is deliberate, voluntary, and disinterested:

> But that I love the gentle *Desdemona*,
> I would not my unhoused free condition
> Put into Circumscription, and Confine,
> For the Seas worth.   (1.2.25–28)

In his speech to the senators, in fact, he appears to go so far as to claim that his love for Desdemona is not seriously affected even by sexual passion. When Desdemona asks that she be allowed to accompany him because she wants to live with him, because, in the Quarto version of the line, her heart's subdued "even to the utmost pleasure" of her lord, because if she is left behind "The Rites for why I love him, are bereft me," Othello seconds her but qualifies the physicality of her motives:

> I therefore beg it not
> To please the pallate of my Appetite:
> Nor to comply with heat the yong affects
> In my defunct, and proper satisfaction.
> But to be free, and bounteous to her minde:
> And Heaven defend your good soules, that you thinke
> I will your serious and great businesse scant
> When she is with me. No, when light wing'd Toyes
> Of feather'd *Cupid*, seele with wanton dulnesse
> My speculative, and offic'd Instrument:
> That my Disports corrupt, and taint my businesse:
> Let House-wives make a Skillet of my Helme,

And all indigne, and base adversities,
Make head against my Estimation.

(1.3.262–275)

Othello here underestimates the powers of the force he has subjected himself to. His imagery recalls again the theme of the domination of Mars by Venus, in such examples as Botticelli's *Mars and Venus* where Mars, who appears recently to have complied his young affects with heat, is dead to the world, while little fauns make a plaything of his helm.[17]

Othello's overconfidence in his ability to maintain his martial identity against the power of Eros is at least doubly ironic. His social function is to defend Venice from its Moslem enemies, but an Othello in bondage to Eros would not be of much use against the Turk and so Othello protests that he will be able to keep the two scales of his double nature in balance, enabling Mars to function in spite of Venus. Thus apparently obvious good, the control of strife by love, is shown to have potential danger inherent in it. But this irony is complicated by the "providential" destruction of the Turkish fleet, by the consequent evaporation of the need to meet strife with strife, and finally by our suspicion that precisely this loss of function leaves the destructive force in Othello free to destroy the love which should control it. So in the end it is not Venus who foils the speculative and offic'd instruments of Mars, but Mars himself. With Iago's help, of course. Iago, Vulcan-like, weaves the net that entraps them all, his magical web constructed from his victim's imagination. Othello's credulity enables Iago to create within Othello's mind a vision of cuckoldry as vivid as that which Vulcan supplied for himself and the amusement of the gods. Thus he transforms Othello/Mars into a murderous, preposterous version of Iago/Vulcan.

It is tempting to overemphasize the importance of Othello's credulity as a cause of the tragic action. By doing so we can conceal from ourselves the harsher implications about human nature in general that the play contains, taking refuge from them behind an apparently special weakness of the tragic hero. To do so we must, of course, make the assumption, tacit or not, that "we" would not be taken in by Iago, thereby overestimating our own acuity and underestimating Iago's brilliance. That Othello should believe Iago's lies about his wife is a venial sin. That he should kill her is a mortal one. He believes the lies because they are brilliantly told and he kills his wife because he believes the lies. Neither necessary cause is a sufficient one, but the credulity that is the necessary accompaniment to the hero's trust in the villain is far more forgivable than the hatred which converts his mistaken belief into murderous action. The villain, in other words, is largely responsible for the destruction of Othello's love, but Othello is the source of the fatal hatred which replaces that love.

Shakespeare marks the moment of love's departure with one of the finest images in the play:

> If I do prove her Haggard,
> Though that her Jesses were my deere heart-strings,
> I'ld whistle her off, and let her downe the winde
> To prey at Fortune. (3.3.260–263)

This image of a released hawk, one that has been taken wild and proved untamable, and Othello's equation of himself with the falconer who must finally free it, is a perfect equivalent for that state of mind which should be the result of a great, good, and noble man's discovery that the wife he loves has betrayed him. Othello is able to sustain the emotion for exactly as long as it takes him to express it, but that he should be capable of the emotion at all, for however brief a moment, marks him as an extraordinary man. Shakespeare gives no such moments to Posthumus or Leontes, his other serious characterizations of murderous jealousy. Once they are convinced or have convinced themselves that their wives have betrayed them, they move without transition to hatred and attempts at violent revenge, but because they inhabit the world of romance, their intentions are thwarted by a benevolent providence. A good and honest servant or the oracle of Delphi prevents evil plans from coming to complete fruition and out of hatred emerges the multiple good of contrition, forgiveness, regeneration, and reconciliation. But in the Pelagian world of *Othello*, the emergence of good must depend entirely upon man's unaided ability to sustain the good of which he may be momentarily capable. Othello, though a more than ordinarily good man, does not have a rational will sufficiently strong to keep his hatred in check without the help of love. Once he loses faith in the existence of Desdemona's love for him, the scales of his life swing wildly out of balance and hatred becomes the inevitable alternative to lost love: "Shee's gone. I am abus'd, and my releefe / Must be to loath her" (3.3.267–268).

As a result chaos comes again within the mind of Othello, and its reign is most vividly dramatized in act 4, scene 1 where the fall of the great man is literalized into an epileptic fit. Before his seizure Othello has a speech which conveys this psychic chaos. Iago has just assured him that Cassio has admitted his affair with Desdemona:

> OTH. What hath he said?
> IAGO Why, that he did: I know not what he did.
> OTH. What? What?
> IAGO Lye.
> OTH. With her?
> IAGO With her? On her: what you will.
> OTH. Lye with her? lye on her? We say lye on her, when they
> be-lye-her. Lye with her: that's fullsome: Handkerchiefe: Confessions: Handkerchiefe. To confesse, and be hang'd for his labour. First, to be hang'd, and then to confesse: I tremble at it. Nature would not invest her selfe in such shadowing passion, without some Instruction. It is not words that shakes me thus, (pish) Noses, Eares, and Lippes: is't possible. Confesse? Handkerchiefe? O divell. *Falls in a Traunce.*
> (4.1.31–43)

Othello's mind, presented with the image of Cassio lying on Desdemona is led by the ambiguities of the language to realize that the image may be a lie. But then he confronts the evidence for its truth: "Handkerchief" suggests hanged, the proper fate for the labour of love to which Cassio has confessed. But, in fact, confession is the act. *Con* in French means, as Cotgrave puts it, "A woman's &c." and *Fesse* is "A buttocke." As for hanged, it means equipped with male sex organs: "*Couillatris:* . . . well hangd (betweene the legs)."[18] And so, contrary to all proper rules of evidence, a man must be hanged before he can con-fesse. And the speech ends with the whirling anatomies of "Noses, Eares, and Lippes: is't possible. Confesse?"

In the midst of this psychic disintegration Shakespeare gives Othello a desperate assertion of sanity: "Nature would not invest her selfe in such shadowing passion, without some Instruction. It is not words that shakes me thus." The precision with which he is wrong indicates very clearly the source and process of his madness. Iago's words have created images and these have so unbalanced the scales of Othello's mind that his own words, breaking from the control of reason, cease to function as a means to the truth and begin to bring forth monsters without Iago's help. Othello's nature, like Iago's, is becoming a closed system capable of producing its passionate hatred without instruction—orders or knowledge—from outside. The chaos which comes again in *Othello* seems to have no other origin than the human minds of the play's characters and the destructive process which is set in motion by minds in interaction finally can proceed to its catastrophe without the necessity for such interaction, kept going by the force of the hatred released within Othello's mind alone. No supernatural power intervenes to prevent the catastrophe, and we are made aware of no divinity that shapes the ends to which the characters come. We suspect that the psychomachies of Faustus, Richard, Hamlet, and Macbeth are sciamachies because we sense that the outcome of each man's battle may have been predetermined by the will of God. What Coleridge called the civil war in Othello's heart is also a battle of shadows, but of a different kind.

The other tragic protagonists we consider do battle for and against real things. The crowns that Richard and Macbeth fight for are real and so are the obstacles to their attainment. Hamlet's father really was murdered by Claudius. Our sense of the unreality of their mental struggles comes at the end of their plays, accompanying our suspicion that the outcome has been predetermined by God, that their battles were lost and won before they were fought. In *Othello* the deterministic possibility is quite different and more familiar. What conducts Othello to his preposterous conclusion appears not to be divine will, but the blood and baseness of his own nature. That nature is far less base and bloody than Richard's or Macbeth's, less even, I think, than Hamlet's, but the tragedy is no less horrible as a result. *Richard III*, *Hamlet*, and *Macbeth* are tragic both in spite of and because of our sense that the events of these plays are providentially directed. *Othello* is tragic in spite of and because of our sense that the events are the result of the working of the free nature of the protagonist. In spite of the nobility of that free nature, the horrors occur; because of the freedom of that nature, human nature, even when noble, is revealed as cruel and unjust, the source of tragic horror. In the providential tragedies we may retain our piety in the face of God's apparent cruelty and injustice, by telling ourselves that the appearance conceals a justice and beneficence which we cannot see by the lights of nature and grace because we do not share in divine omniscience. If we wish to retain an optimistic, Pelagian, Neoplatonic humanism in the face of Othello's apparent cruelty and injustice, we can tell ourselves that the appearance is similarly only appearance. Othello, we can tell ourselves, is not "really" cruel and unjust. He only seems so because he is deceived. But in so excusing Othello, we deceive ourselves. The sciamachy that Othello fights and loses is not just a battle with the shadows brought into being by Iago's lies. It is a struggle between the component parts of Othello's mind and the forces that move him to destruction derive their power from the mind itself, from the "shadowing passion" that emerges out of the unconscious.

In *Othello* Shakespeare creates his tragic world out of a provisional acceptance of the possible truth of some commonplaces of Pelagian/ Humanist optimism. Human minds, in this world, may be subject to no other than human masters and, like the rest of the created universe, those minds are constructs of the forces of Love and Strife. As a result, in *Othello*, chaos comes again. Man's ability to choose the good is effectively weakened by his tendency to mistake good for evil and evil for good. Even worse, he compounds error with crime, because error so upsets the proper balance between love and strife that the mind becomes possessed with a lust for destruction, a desire to destroy love itself.

The destruction of Othello's love is the destruction of his greatness. The two are inextricable. The world of *Othello* is so conceived that greatness must sustain love and love must sustain greatness. When Othello cannot sustain the noble resolve to release Desdemona like an untamed hawk, what has failed him, love or greatness? The question makes a distinction that the play rejects. But just as we wish to believe that Othello ceases to be great because he has never been great, so we would like to believe that Othello ceases to love because he has never really loved. But Shakespeare has given Othello a speech that makes so comforting an opinion quite untenable:

> Had it pleas'd Heaven,
> To try me with Affliction, had they rain'd
> All kind of Sores, and Shames on my bare-head:
> Steep'd me in povertie to the very lippes,
> Given to Captivitie, me, and my utmost hopes,
> I should have found in some place of my Soule
> A drop of patience. But alas, to make me
> The fixed Figure for the time of Scorne,
> To point his slow and moving finger at.
> Yet could I beare that too, well, very well:
> But there where I have garnerd up my heart,
> Where either I must live, or beare no life,
> The Fountaine from the which my currant runnes,
> Or else dries up: to be discarded thence,
> Or keepe it as a Cesterne, for foule Toades
> To knot and gender in.   (4.2.48–63)

His greatness, Othello tells us, could have sustained anything except the loss of Desdemona's love. He is not just bragging. The Job-like trials that he enumerates in the opening lines he has already undergone and survived intact. Nor is there any evidence in the play that Othello shares Cassio's exaggerated awe of reputation. It is Desdemona's love for him that has come to ratify his identity. Love as defined by these lines is certainly no emotion to attract the carefully rational. Its Euripidean intensity is increased by the physicality which the sexual component of imagery of the last four lines adds to what is primarily a spiritual metaphor. I can only assume, with some awe, that critics who feel that Othello's love is of a low order must be capable of an emotion that I have never felt, observed, or seen described. Unless one wishes to maintain that Shakespeare is here having Othello express an emotion of which he is incapable so that we may be struck by the ironic discrepancy between the words and the man who speaks them. But surely such an artistic tactic would be self-defeating in its complexity.

But if it is difficult to take the lines as unintended irony, it is considerably easier to see them as unintended idolatry. The image of the fountain of life is properly a metaphor for God Himself and its application to a human being, however worthy, is likely to make the pious uneasy:

> This is even that which GOD so greatly complaineth of by his Prophet *Jeremy*, saying, My people have comitted two great offences, they have forsaken mee the fountaine of the waters of life, and have digged to themselves broken pits that can holde no water. Is not that man thinke you unwise that will runne for water to a little brooke, when he may as well goe to the head spring? Even so may his wisedome bee justly suspected, that will flee unto Saints in time of necessity, when hee may boldly and without feare declare his griefe, and direct his prayer unto the Lord himselfe.[19]

The didactically Christian interpretation of *Othello* moralizes the tragedy into an eloquent sermon on the dangers of placing a higher value upon the love of even our saintly fellow humans than upon the love of God. When Desdemona's love seems to fail, Othello cannot seek the divine grace that alone could save him from the consequences of his destructive hatred. By making her the fountain of his life, he cuts himself off from the true source: "For with thee is the fountaine of lyfe: and in thy light shall we see light."[20] In an apocalyptic reversal of the order of creation, Othello forsakes the fountain of life, puts out the light and then puts out the light and chaos comes again.

There is a validity and power to this view of Othello that, I believe, makes a consciousness of it essential to a full understanding of the play. And yet it seems to me too small to be the meaning of the tragedy, though it is, nonetheless, a part of that meaning. It is a possible truth but it should coexist in our minds with other possible truths, and the most important of these is the possibility that in describing Desdemona as the place where he has garnered up his heart and the fountain from which his current runs, Othello is telling the simple (or perhaps double) truth: the lines are a precise expression of what he believes, and what he believes may be true. The *Othello* world may be one in which a man must live in and through his love for at least one other human being or else must bear no life at all. It is possible that the play is telling us that we must love one another or die and that we are incapable of loving one another. If the world is "Pelagian," then man, in his freedom from divine grace, must substitute human love for that grace and that is not possible:

> DES. Nay, we must thinke men are not Gods.
>
> (3.4.148)

No, nor women neither, though the play makes it very clear that women are considerably more capable of sustaining love than men are. Desdemona is not Venus and Othello is not Mars, but the love that Venus embodies is more native to the female than the male. Desdemona's love is human, however, and must lack the force of a divine principle but it is also, I think, insufficiently human in that it is lacking a sufficient admixture of the strife that might preserve it from strife's destructive force. The purer a love is, the more vulnerable it is, the more easily destroyed from the outside. But if love is mixed with strife, there is the danger that the scales of our life will lose their balance and destruction gain the ascendancy as it does with Othello. Men are not gods, but if, as Pico assures us, God has granted man the great and wonderful happiness to have what he chooses and be that which he wills, then man's ability to will and choose correctly must approach the divine or disaster will be the result of freedom and in *Othello* disaster is the result of apparent freedom.

The sense of God's abandonment of man to his own inadequate devices recurs, I think, in the strange play upon the phrase "My Lord" which Shakespeare twice sets up between Desdemona and Emilia in the concluding scenes of the play:

> AEMI. Good Madam,
>   What's the matter with my Lord?
> DES. With who?
> AEMI. Why, with my Lord, Madam?

DES. Who is thy Lord?
AEMI. He that is yours, sweet Lady.
DES. I have none. (4.2.98–101)

There is the same tension here between the possibilities of unintended idolatry and simple truth that is present in Othello's valuation of Desdemona as the fountain of his life. The pious must feel a similar uneasiness with Desdemona's failure to acknowledge that the defection of Othello leaves her and Emilia with a Lord. But, as with Othello, the possibility remains that she is right. Human love has failed her, and it may be that there is no divine grace to replace it.

The confusion between Lord and Lord is repeated (though only in the Quarto) in the macabre stage effect which comes at the end of the murder scene. There Desdemona, denied by Othello the chance to say one prayer, cries out to God while Othello strangles her and her screams are echoed offstage by Emilia crying out to Othello:

DES. O Lord, Lord, Lord.
EMILIA *calls within.* My Lord, my Lord what ho,
my Lord, my Lord. (Q₁.5.2.85–86)

Desdemona's despair and fear produce a cry to God for mercy or justice or something, anything that will alleviate the apparently meaningless horror of what is happening, and, for me at least, these screams evoke the Christian archetype of all such outcries: " *'Eli, Eli, lama sabacthani?'* that is, 'My God, my God, why hast thou forsaken me?' " Like Desdemona's, Emilia's cries are inspired by "foule Murther," but they appeal to man to set right his own world by imposing order and justice upon it. This is Othello's special function as governor and the coinciding of governor and murderer completes the irony begun by the antiphonal "Lord" and "Lord" of Desdemona and Emilia. Men are not gods. But appealing to God appears, in the *Othello* world, to be appealing to a creator who has left man to the wonderful happiness of being what he wills, while in appealing to man for an end to chaos, one is appealing to the very source of chaos.

But the fundamental irony of Desdemona's murder becomes apparent when we realize that Othello's committing it is, in fact, an extraordinary triumph of the human will. That Othello is in immediate danger of psychic disintegration by the end of act 4, scene 1 is perfectly apparent. After a speech of bawdy verbal chaos, he falls in a fit from which he arouses himself to be made a buffoon by Iago and finally, at the end of the scene, he strikes his wife and babbles incoherently in front of the representative of the Venetian Senate, who suspects that he is going mad. The play, I think, invites us to speculate that if Othello had continued to come apart, Lodovico would have moved from suspicion to action and the tragedy might have been averted. But that possibility is prevented by Othello's remarkable assertion of his will, for he imposes upon the chaos of his mind a semblance of order, which makes it possible for him to deal rationally with Lodovico. More important than that, his control allows Desdemona and Emilia to convince themselves that all may be well ("He lookes gentler than he did.") and they assume, tacitly and naturally enough, that his order to Desdemona to go to bed and dismiss Emilia, means that he wants to make love and that the incidents of the afternoon may have been a banal domestic upset that is about to end in a common enough conclusion. Their "foolish minds" know better, however, and the tension between the superficial optimism and their more profound knowledge motivates the "willow scene."

But the greatest achievement of Othello's extraordinary exercise of his will is not the deception of Lodovico or Desdemona or Emilia, but the deception of himself. By bringing his hatred under the control of his will, he is able to convince himself that he has somehow changed the nature of his motive. But the hatred that produced, "I will chop her into Messes: Cuckold me?" also underlies the organ tones of "It is the Cause, it is the Cause (my Soule)." The control of the destructive impulse, obviously an important function of the will for a man of action, entails the control of its expression ("can he be angry?") and thus Othello is able to tell himself that the hatred he can express calmly must be not hatred, but a desire for justice and the satisfaction of honor, and that a murder committed calmly and with dignity is somehow not a murder, but an execution. What Othello seems to demonstrate is that the will cannot bring into being or keep in being either love or hate, but that if the will is strong enough, it can control the forms that the expression of these emotions takes and can thereby aid in the self-deception of their possessor. By having him so deceive himself, Shake-speare runs the risk of having him deceive us too, but he makes such deception difficult to retain by the rapidity with which the planned cere-monial degenerates into a sordid *crime passionnel:*

> O perjur'd woman, thou do'st stone my heart,
> And makes me call, what I intend to do,
> A Murther, which I thought a Sacrifice.
>
> (5.2.63–65)

· · · · · · · · ·

> DES. O banish me, my Lord, but kill me not.
> OTH. Downe strumpet.
> DES. Kill me tomorrow, let me live to night.
> OTH. Nay, if you strive.   (5.2.78–81)

As the self-deceiving, willed facade of the just executioner and sac-rificial priest disintegrates, its collapse hastens the degeneration of the hero, a process which touches its nadir when Othello is tempted by Des-demona's momentary revival and exoneration of him to deny his guilt:

> OTH. Why, how should she be murdred?
> AEMIL. Alas: who knowes?
> OTH. You heare her say her selfe, it was not I.
>
> (5.2.127–128)

But this is as low as Othello gets. The man of action whose self has always been the sum of his actions will not deny what that self has done:

> OTH. She's like a Liar gone to burning hell,
>   'Twas I that kill'd her. (5.2.130–131)

And in his attempt to justify what he has done comes the last image of their love and his hate as an elemental conjunction of opposites:

> OTH. She was false as water.
> AEMIL. Thou art rash as fire, to say
>   That she was false.   (5.2.135–136)

We are reminded that the role of just judge and executioner cannot be Othello's because the verdict he has passed and acted on is false. But it is also essential to remember that the sentence passed was pronounced out of hatred and the punishment meted out was not proper to the supposed offense, as Christ made abundantly clear in passing his sentence upon the woman taken in adultery. It is wrong to kill your wife even if she has slept with somebody else and if *Othello* is a morality play, its moral is a basic one: do not kill your wife.

It is necessary to insist on these absurdly obvious moral principles because of the extreme ease with which one can lose sight of them when trying to understand the play's catastrophe. Lodovico puts clearly and straightforwardly the question we must try to answer:

> Oh thou *Othello*, that was once so good,
> Falne in the practise of a cursed Slave,
> What shall be saide to thee.
>
> (5.2.290–292)

It is a natural tendency of the mind to try to evade the painful answers (or counterquestions) which the play provides to Lodovico's question by denying the validity of the premise on which the question is based. This we can do in one of two ways. We can deny that Othello ever was "good," or we can insist that he still is. The first way out (F. R. Leavis's essay[21] and Olivier's brilliantly perverse interpretation are excellent examples of it) comforts us by maintaining that the causes for the hero's destruction are to be found not in the facts of our shared universal condition, but in the special personal weaknesses of the protagonist. His love for Desdemona, above all, must be shown to be less than perfect love should be and, of course, it is less. But one meaning of the brilliance of Iago's evil is that only such brilliance could destroy a love as strong as Othello's for Desdemona. Othello's love is not good enough but it is as good as man's love gets and that, unhappily, is the point.

The painful significance of Othello's degradation is even more effectively eased if we can convince ourselves that it does not occur, that the noble Moor remains noble to the end, that what he does in no important way results from or affects what he is, that his actions were the result of noble impulses misdirected by the practices of a cursed slave. Unfortunately the main evidence for such a view is in fact evidence against it. Othello himself makes the case in answer to Lodovico's question:

OTH. Why any thing:
 An honourable Murderer, if you will:
 For nought I did in hate, but all in Honour.

(5.2.293–295)

The first and second of these lines might be qualified by self-directed irony, but the last is a statement of what Othello wants to believe, must believe, but can believe only by telling himself lies about why he has done what he has done:

> Looke heere *Iago*,
> All my fond love thus do I blow to Heaven. 'Tis gone.
> Arise blacke vengeance, from the hollow hell,
> Yeeld up (O Love) thy Crowne, and hearted Throne
> To tyrannous Hate.
>
> . . . .
>
> Oh blood, blood, blood.
>
> . . . .
>
oh, I see that nose of yours, but not that dogge, I shall throw it to.
>
> . . . .
>
> I will chop her into Messes: cuckold Me?
>
> . . . .
>
> I tooke you for that cunning Whore of Venice,
> That married with *Othello*.
>
> . . . .
>
> Downe Strumpet.

Hatred has motivated him from the moment he has been convinced that Desdemona has betrayed him and he has realized that his relief must be to loathe her. But if at the end he deceives himself as to his motives, he makes no pretenses about the horror of his actions. What he has done is damnable and he knows it. Indeed, what he has done has damned him, not, so far as we can know, for eternity, but certainly here and now. The knowledge of what he has done has turned his life to hell and he prefers eternal damnation to the hell of that continuing knowledge:

> Whip me ye Divels
> From the possession of this Heavenly sight:
> Blow me about in windes, roast me in Sulphure,
> Wash me in steepe-downe gulfes of Liquid fire.
>
> (5.2.277–280)

Again, there is a pious lesson to be extracted from the concluding incidents of the play. We can see in Othello's attempt at self-damnation a failure of will and nerve. Had he been stronger, we can tell ourselves, he would have sought to repent of his sin. He ought to have made what satisfaction he could for his crime by suffering the punishment imposed on him by the state and he ought, above all, to have turned to God with a contrite heart and sought his forgiveness. All of this is admirable and true, but it is not, in my opinion, quite true enough. There is another possible truth. (No doubt there are many others.) What happens to Othello is what can happen and may happen to any man, even the noblest and greatest, in a world where God has granted man the great and wonderful happiness to have that which he chooses and be that which he wills. If our minds are indeed free of the influence of any other than human and natural forces, if divine grace takes no supernatural form, then *Othello* tells us we may be counted upon to turn our world into a hell that will make the traditional steep-down gulfs of liquid fire a welcome relief by contrast. This will not always happen, but it can always happen and it will happen in spite of our best strength, nobility, and love.

The process of Othello's degradation and destruction is not a gradual revelation of the truth about an only apparently good man. It is a revelation of the potential for degradation and destruction that is inevitably present even in the best of men. In *Othello* Shakespeare takes us on a serial progression through three of Northrop Frye's tragic modes. We begin in the high mimetic, in the presence of what is clearly a protagonist greater than we are—a prince out of our star. We move in act 3 to the low mimetic and watch the painful deception of a man and a brother. In acts 4 and 5 we are in the ironic mode, looking down "upon a scene of bondage [and] frustration."[22] What Shakespeare is showing us, more clearly in this tragedy than in any other, is that a complexly human protagonist is simultaneously every possible sort of protagonist —hero, villain, everyman. At the play's conclusion, in Othello's last long speech, the great man of the play's beginning confronts and destroys the malignant dog he has become and our sense of the role of choice and will in that process of becoming is depressing in the extreme. For the will appears to have served no higher purpose than its own. No divine grace has assisted it. No providential purpose can explain the horrors to which it comes. Othello has freely chosen to believe Iago, to kill Desdemona, and thus to transform himself into what he becomes. So we are left in the end to contemplate the final benefit of our powers of self-creation: we are free to destroy the things we turn ourselves into.

If our chronology is correct, *Othello* was written midway between *Hamlet* and *Lear*. In *Hamlet* we have a strong sense of experiencing the tragic horrors of existence in a world which is providentially ordered; in *Othello*, of the at least equal horrors of a world not providentially ordered. The God of *Hamlet* appears to have willed the justice of Claudius's death and to have chosen Hamlet as the instrument of that justice. Unlike Richard III, Hamlet gives evidence of being the elect scourge and minister of heaven, and though Hamlet's evil impulses serve the purposes of divine justice there are signs, as when Hamlet for evil reasons refrains from the evil of killing the defenseless, praying Claudius, that heaven directs that evil to its peculiar ends in such a way as to preserve its instrument from damnation. Like Othello, Hamlet determines to punish crime, but unlike Othello, he takes the precaution of making certain that the crime has occurred. It is also to his credit that the death he inflicts is appropriate to the crime he is punishing. Again, unlike Othello, he leaves the punishment of adultery to heaven and to the conscience of the sinner. And yet Hamlet is not, surely, a better man than Othello—only less free to follow the evil impulses of his nature. On the other hand, the world of *Hamlet*, providentially ordered though it be, is surely no less terrible than the world of *Othello*. For me at least, the horrors of Desdemona's death and Othello's suicide are no worse than the more intellectual horror of Claudius's inability to repent.

In creating *Hamlet* and *Othello*, Shakespeare has given imaginative life to two ways of conceiving the world that were possible for the men of his time. In neither of these ways has he found much for our comfort. But in addition to seeing these plays as companion pieces (the Augustinian world versus the Pelagian world), one can see them related temporally in the progress of Shakespeare as a tragic artist, with *Othello* as halfway house between the Christian pessimism of *Hamlet* and the pagan pessimism of *King Lear*. It is as if Shakespeare, in reading Montaigne's *Apologie for Raymond Sebonde*, had taken it as a challenge to his art as a writer of tragedy; "Let us now but consider man alone without other help, armed but with his own weapons, and unprovided of the grace and knowledge of God."[23] In *Hamlet* Shakespeare has considered man's tragic situation when provided with the grace and knowledge of God; in *Othello*, when provided with the knowledge but not the grace; in *Lear*, when provided with neither grace nor knowledge. All three conceptions appear to be equally appropriate as settings for the tragic action.

CHAPTER 7
Macbeth

Macduffe was from his Mothers womb
Untimely ript.

SO MUCH OF *Macbeth* is concentrated in this "horrid image" that a tracing of all its metaphoric connections would result in an essay on the whole play. Macbeth, for example, first enters our consciousness when the bleeding captain describes how he ripped the life from merciless Macdonwald by unseaming him from the nave to the chops. To list all the torn bodies that fill the space between that image and the play's end would be almost as tedious as it was for Macbeth to wade through the resulting blood. Fewer and more to our point are the instances of the more specific images of a bloody child. The figure is literally present, an ironic clue to hidden meaning, as one of the apparitions that the juggling fiends use to trap Macbeth. The child's advice to be bloody, bold, and resolute, Macbeth puts into practice by having his murderers stab Macduff's little son to death before his mother's eyes. Early in the play another version of mother and child is suggested to us by Lady Macbeth's claim that she would snatch the nursing baby from her breast and dash its brains out if she had sworn to do so. But perhaps the most meaningful as well as the most enigmatic of these children is Pity, which Macbeth, in the "If 'twere done" soliloquy in act 1, scene 7, describes as a naked, newborn babe. Because the helplessness of the babe inspires pity, the personification is appropriate, but this is an odd infant, for it strides the blast—walking upon the wind, or bestriding it, perhaps, or marching to the trumpet sound of Duncan's pleading virtues. But Pity is also like one of heaven's cherubin, one of God's angelic instruments, because Macbeth's great enemy, and hence a prime servant of divine justice, is decent human emotion—compassion, the horror and pity that will be aroused by the sight of the murdered, virtuous Duncan. So the bloody child is Macbeth's enemy, the innocent inspiration for compassion.

In the beginning the source of such inhibiting compassion is within as well as outside Macbeth, and that is why Lady Macbeth symbolizes its destruction by the murder of life to which she has given birth. The bloody body of Macduff's young son is proof, if we need any, that Macbeth's inhuman cruelty finally achieves the intensity urged on him by his wife. But the blood which covers the body of the child which Lady Macbeth murders in imagination and Macbeth has killed by his murderers in reality is the blood of the child itself. The blood upon the apparition is ambiguous. It may be the child's and it may not and at the moment it does not occur to us to wonder which it is. But the image of the newborn Macduff is unequivocal. This child is covered with the blood of its mother and thus act 5 presents us with a companion piece to the diabolical madonna of act 1. Lady Macbeth imagines a mother who has killed her child. Macduff presents us with a child whose birth has killed its mother.

The pairing of these icons directs us to questions which are central to our concerns. Lady Macbeth's imagined infanticide is the most horrible crime it is possible for her to conceive, and most of us would, I hope, admit the difficulty of going her one better. The murder's special horror derives from its supreme unnaturalness. But what about the horror of the death of Macduff's mother? It is the result of the natural processes of nature in a fallen world. The newborn child, symbol of innocence, cannot, we tell ourselves, be made guilty of the blood with which it is covered. Its life results in death, but there is no element of willed action that could turn that responsibility into guilt. The natural processes of a postlapsarian nature may result in events as cruel and horrible as the crimes of Macbeth, but the events are not therefore crimes, because the element of will is missing. Except, of course, that it isn't. Will is present if the events of nature are conceived of as ultimately caused by divine will. The proper Christian response to such events as deaths in childbirth is, "Thy will be done." Which leads us to ask ourselves if this is also the proper Christian response to the crimes of humanity. All Christian theologies, I think, agree that human crimes are made to serve divine purposes, and most maintain that no such crimes could be committed without divine permission, but the crimes of men are held to be the results of the wills of men and as such, deserving of divine punishment. This conclusion is easily acquiesced in so long as the human will is held to be free. Lutheranism and Calvinism, however, deny the freedom of the will, but continue to insist that the eternal punishment of the reprobate is just. All men justly deserve punishment because all are born corrupted by original sin. This, I presume, is the final significance of the bloody child. Any newborn babe is as guilty and as subject to eternal punishment as Lady Macbeth herself.

The child ripped from its mother's womb grows up to become Macduff and in so doing embodies three times the human condition of simultaneous guilt and innocence. In being born he is guilty and innocent of the death of his mother. But he is also guilty and innocent of the deaths of his wife and children. They die for the courage of his opposition to Macbeth and for the stupidity of his abandonment of his family. Unlike Hamlet, Macduff feels guilt rather than responsibility for these deaths:

> Sinful *Macduff*,
> They were all strooke for thee: Naught that I am,
> Not for their owne demerits, but for mine
> Fell slaughter on their soules. (4.3.224–227)

Finally he kills Macbeth. For that death, quite properly, he feels no guilt at all. Like Hamlet, he kills as the scourge and minister of heaven, and as such he is no more (or less) guilty than the child ripped from his mother's womb. In Hamlet's play the mystery of the antagonist's evil was dramatized by Claudius's inability to repent. In *Macbeth* antagonist has become protagonist and the examination of the mystery is much more complicated as a result.

But if Macduff stands to Macbeth in the relationship of Hamlet to Claudius, he stands more obviously as a symbolically highly complicated version of Richmond in relation to Richard III. In our terms, *Macbeth*, after *Hamlet* and *Othello*, is a return to the concerns of *Richard III*. It is a triumphal return, to be sure. Shakespeare's ability to create characters and to devise symbolic actions, as well as his command of poetic language, are markedly subtler and more powerful than they were fifteen years earlier. It is important to remember that these skills are not merely Shakespeare's means of expressing thought. They are his means of thought, and as his means increase in subtlety and power his thought grows more complex, profound, and difficult to understand. In *Henry VI, Part 3* and *Richard III*, a series of slaughtered innocents brought to our attention the possible presence of a jealous God whose justice visited the sins of guilty fathers upon their children unto the third and fourth generations. In *Macbeth* the image of the bloody child is in the visual and verbal texture of the play, profoundly a part of the way the play exists as a work of art, and the result is to deepen the meaning—or rather the mystery—of this human suffering in a way that makes Shakespeare's previous employment of it seem brutally obvious. Nonetheless, the connection between the early histories and *Macbeth* is clear. The last two plays of the first tetralogy share with *Macbeth* a common pattern and a common problem. Like *Richard III*, *Macbeth* presents us with a story which must be apprehended in two different ways simultaneously—as the providential tragedy or tragicomedy of a society and as the psychological tragedy of a villain protagonist.

The providential tragicomedy opens with a society in revolt—in, that is to say, a state of sin, for the king revolted against is a lawful monarch and a saintly man. The indistinct figures of the merciless Macdonwald, Sweno the Norway's king, and the Thane of Cawdor are important for the sense they give us that Macbeth's murder of Duncan is not, like Claudius's fratricide, a personal crime primarily, but rather one which a sizable proportion of the society is trying to commit and for which the entire society will inevitably suffer. The second scene of *Macbeth* is thematically a condensation of the History plays' narrative of the War of the Roses. The rebels are sinning against God as well as man and the war they wage threatens to "memorize another Golgotha"—except of course that it is Macbeth whom the bloody captain describes as meaning to do so, and it is Macbeth who does so. The murder of Duncan is a hideous blasphemy:

> Most sacrilegious Murther hath broke ope
> The Lords anoynted Temple, and stole thence
> The Life o' th' Building.   (2.3.71–73)

And the death of Duncan, like the death of Christ, is attended with storm and darkness. Rosse has the explanation: "Thou seest the Heav-

ens, as troubled with mans Act, / Threatens his bloody Stage" (2.4.6–7).
Here is the theatrical metaphor of the providential tragedy. God is present as spectator at the theater of his judgments but when necessary he
will intervene as participant. "Man" is both individual and universal.
The "act" is Macbeth's, but it is also man's—witness the recent revolt
—and man must suffer for it. The instrument for man's punishment
will be—with a logic and justice that could only be divine—the specific
man who did the act for which man will be punished. But, of course, in
God's good time, the evil minister of chastisement will be destroyed as
a punishment for his crimes, including those he has committed as the
instrument of chastisement. Grace, in the person of Malcolm, will be
restored to Scotland.

The inadequacy of this design as a description of the action of *Macbeth* is perfectly obvious but it is one of the patterns that make up the
play's complexity. Shakespeare's main interest, as it was in *Richard III*,
is in the nature and meaning of the evil instrument and that is the subject of the other, the psychological tragedy. But Shakespeare has developed (or retained from *Hamlet*) an interest in God's good instruments
as well. A part of the functioning of the tasteless and colorless Richmond of *Richard III* has in *Macbeth* been assigned to Macduff and another part to Malcolm. The interest of these figures is not in the least
psychological. Malcolm and Macduff have not been endowed with minds
in the way that Macbeth, Othello, Iago, Hamlet, Claudius, and Richard
have. Their interest—and particularly Macduff's—lies in their symbolic
complexity, the complexity of their functions in the *Macbeth* world.

In this sense, Malcolm is the less complicated of the two. His function is to be good, a dull proceeding in the theater, however difficult in
life. Shakespeare enlivens his character by following Holinshed and having him, in act 4, scene 3, pretend to be bad in order to try Macduff's
sincerity. The result is a scene in danger of being tedious if regarded
only as a piece of theatrical naturalism, or an "atmospheric" device for
depicting the loss of confidence in human beings that is one result of
tyranny. Its important subject is the mystery of grace. In convincing
Macduff of his insatiable voluptuousness and his staunchless avarice,
Malcolm describes a potential or possible Malcolm, a vessel and instrument of wrath, one who, like Macbeth, exists to

> Poure the sweet Milke of Concord, into Hell,
> Uprore the universall peace, confound
> All unity on earth.   (4.3.98–100)

He then reveals that he is not in fact the villainous Macbeth-equivalent that he has pretended to be. But not being Macbeth does not, of course, make him the opposite of Macbeth. All, and it is rather a good deal, that Malcolm claims for himself is a prior innocence. Up to this point in his life, he has refrained from doing evil. He is not saying "I am good," but "I have been good up to now." Macbeth's true opposite is Edward the Confessor as described by the doctor and by Malcolm. The job of the actor playing Malcolm is to convince us that Edward is his chosen potentiality, the royal possibility that Malcolm wills himself to become. But it is up to us to wonder if it lies within the power of any unaided human will to become what Edward is described as being:

> He hath a heavenly guift of Prophesie,
> And sundry Blessings hang about his Throne,
> That speake him full of Grace.
>
> (4.3.157–159)

The orthodox, Augustinian answer, and one that is clearly supported by Malcolm's speech, is that grace is the unmerited gift of God. This is, of course, an answer that creates a question: is the opposite of Edward equally the result of God's will, of the withholding of grace? This is one of the questions Shakespeare examines by creating the characters of Macbeth and his wife.

Macduff's symbolic function is considerably more complicated than Malcolm's, and one way of understanding it is, I think, to see it in the light of Shakespeare's concerns in *Hamlet*. Like Hamlet—though like him in no other way—Macduff is the elect instrument for the destruction of an evil king. But in *Hamlet* Shakespeare explored the psychological meaning of the concept. In *Macbeth* he limits himself largely to a symbolic exploration through the image of the bloody child. Largely, but not entirely. In depicting Macduff's agony for what he sees as his guilt for the deaths of his wife and children, Shakespeare is dramatizing realistically the horrors of life under tyranny. He is also dramatizing one of the ways in which an instrument of divine justice comes into being. By killing Macduff's innocent family, Macbeth is teaching his enemy bloody instructions, which will return to plague the inventor. Perhaps the most terrible sentence in the play is Macduff's reply to Malcolm's urging of revenge: "He ha's no Children." There is little doubt, however, what their fate would be if they existed and were left to Macduff's mercies. If Macduff does not become guilty of Macbeth's most horrible crimes, it is because he cannot. Malcolm is right in the speech which concludes the scene in England: "the Powres above / Put on their Instruments." But it is not a pretty sight. Macduff's example suggests one meaning for election: the good man will not do the evil that he cannot do.

The primary concern of the play is with the evil man, however, and with the question of the guilt of the evil. The consideration of the theme leads Shakespeare to create a world of double evil—human and superhuman—and to speculate dramatically on their interrelationship. Chronologically, in terms of the succession of scenes, supernatural evil—the witches—is presented as prior to human evil, as the fall of Satan is prior to the fall of man. But man in *Macbeth* is fallen and Macbeth's mind, like all human minds, though to an extraordinary degree, is prepared for the witches before he meets them. His first line "So foule and faire a day I have not seene" (1.3.38) seems to indicate that he is tuned in to the witches in some extrasensory fashion. And yet his variant of the witches' "faire is foule, and foule is faire" is morally neutral: the weather is terrible and the battle is won, a human observation on a banal paradox which is reassuringly different from the witches' diabolical reversal of moral values. Ordinary humanity soon ceases to obtain, however. Macbeth's reaction to the third witch's "All haile *Macbeth*, that shalt be King hereafter" constitutes the first mystery of the play. Banquo asks our question: "why doe you start, and seeme to fear / Things that doe sound so faire?" Macbeth soon tells us, though not Banquo:

> This supernaturall solliciting
> Cannot be ill; cannot be good.
> If ill? why hath it given me earnest of successe,
> Commencing in a Truth? I am *Thane* of Cawdor.

If good? why doe I yeeld to that suggestion,
Whose horrid Image doth unfixe my Heire,
And make my seated Heart knock at my Ribbes,
Against the use of Nature? Present Feares
Are lesse than horrible Imaginings:
My Thought, whose Murther yet is but fantasticall,
Shakes so my single state of Man,
That Function is smother'd in surmise,
And nothing is, but what is not.

(1.3.130–142)

Macbeth fears the contents of his own mind, and well he might. If I were told that I was to be king hereafter my mind would provide me with Malvolian images for contemplation: myself seated in my state, in my branched velvet gown, receiving homage. Macbeth imagines the murdered Duncan. The oddity is rationally inexplicable. Macbeth tries to explain it by seeing his mind as the object of temptation, of "supernaturall solliciting," and the immediate source of the "horrid image" as a "suggestion" to which he has yielded. But there has been no soliciting and no suggestion audible to the audience. The witches have simply presented Macbeth with a morally neutral fact about the future, one which asks nothing whatever of him either in thought or action, and he knows this:

If Chance will have me King,
Why Chance may Crowne me,
Without my stirre.   (1.3.150–152)

The play's word for Macbeth's odd psychological state at this moment in the action is "rapt" and it is used twice, once by Banquo ("Looke how our Partner's rapt") and once, in his letter to Lady Macbeth, by Macbeth himself. The word is suggestive. Clearly both Banquo and Macbeth intend to indicate some such natural condition as that defined by the *O.E.D.:* "Transported with some emotion . . . Deeply engaged or buried in (a feeling, subject of thought, etc.); intent upon." But the word has stronger supernatural meanings as well and "rapt" suggests, I think, the possibility that Macbeth's condition may bear some resemblance to the *"raptus Pauli."* Perhaps Macbeth, on the road to Forres, has an experience similar to Saul's on the road to Damascus. "Trembling and astonyed" he may be possessed and converted by an exterior, super-human force. If so the force is diabolical rather than divine and this possibility—that the forces of evil may have a way into and power over the human mind analogous to that of divine grace—accounts for some measure of the difference in complexity and intensity of the characterization of Macbeth by comparison with his earlier version in *Richard III.*

What "enraptures" Macbeth is not, however, the words of the witches but the image which those words inspire, the horrid image of murder. The problem of the precise origin of that image and of others like it is crucial to our understanding of the protagonist and the play. The origin of any image is, of course, the imaginative faculty of the mind in which it appears, but Shakespeare makes it difficult to dismiss as purely subjective the horrid image by which Macbeth is originally "rapt" by making it the first of a series of four. The other three, the bloody dagger, the voice which cries "Sleep no more," and the ghost of Banquo, form a progression of phenomena whose pure subjectivity is made to seem increasingly doubtful. Macbeth knows that the first image of murder is "but fantasticall." About the second he has doubts. Perhaps it is "a Dagger of the Minde." He thinks he heard a voice cry, "Sleep no more" and knows he may merely have thought it. But he does not doubt the reality of the ghost of Banquo for an instant and we are left to wonder if he is right or if Lady Macbeth is correct in characterizing the ghost as "the very painting" of Macbeth's fear.

But whatever the origin of these phenomena, one thing is clear: Macbeth is obsessed by images of evil. What is less clear is what we mean by "obsessed." Obsession may be an entirely natural process: "The action of any influence, notion or 'fixed idea,' which persistently assails or vexes, esp. so as to discompose the mind" (*O.E.D.*). This is a reasonably precise description of the action upon Macbeth's mind of the notion of bloody, violent murder. But obsession may also be a super-natural process: "The hostile action of the devil or an evil spirit besetting any one; actuation by the devil or an evil spirit from without; the fact of being thus beset or actuated" (*O.E.D.*).

There are then, two opposed possible sources for the causes of Macbeth's raptness and his obsession. The origin of these psychic phenomena may be natural or supernatural. They may be the unaided products of Macbeth's imagination. But they may also be the result of the working of diabolical powers, either through the presentation of exterior stimuli to Macbeth's senses or through the direct working upon Macbeth's imagination of diabolically controlled physiological forces.[1] But if the question of the source of the phenomena that obsess Macbeth admits of two possible answers, so does the question of their control. Is Macbeth's will free to exclude these images of evil from his mind? Again, it seems to me, the play does not give us an answer and as a result of Shakespeare's careful reticence in dealing with both these problems, anyone attempting to understand the play confronts a quadruple Macbeth, a character who may be conceived of in four different ways. Macbeth may be criminal, or insane, or self-damned, or reprobate. If the source of his horrid images is within his own mind and within the control of his will, then he is a morally responsible criminal who freely conceives of and executes his crimes. If the source is within his own mind, but outside the control of his will, then he is a madman whose diseased psyche presents him with hallucinations so powerful that they force him to action. If the source is supernatural but his will is free and strong enough to drive the phenomena from his consciousness, then he is "sufficient to have stood, though free to fall" and he damns himself by choosing to permit the domination of the powers of evil over him. If the source is supernatural and his will is not free, then Macbeth is one of the Calvinist reprobate whom God has damned from eternity and abandoned to the powers of evil.

In the other three Shakespearean tragedies we have looked at, a similar though more limited choice of conceptual versions of the protagonist has been presented to us. But in each case, or so it seems to me, one possibility is emphasized as the most probable explanation of the protagonist's nature. Richard III appears most likely to be the reprobate instrument of divine providence. Hamlet, however mysteriously, seems to be an elect scourge and minister of heaven. Othello most probably is a free agent who through errors of judgment and wrong choice comes to desire damnation. But in the case of Macbeth, I think Shakespeare keeps the possibilities in suspension so that, at the play's end, the mystery is

extraordinarily complex, almost as baffling, despite the strongly emphasized Christian context, as *King Lear* itself.

Our belief in the criminal Macbeth, a free agent freely conceiving
and executing his crimes, is encouraged, particularly in the play's beginning, by the evidence that, despite his proclaimed nobility and courage, Macbeth is by nature a destroyer, a killer. The bloody sergeant's
enthusiastic image of Macbeth's smoking sword unseaming Macdonwald
from the nave to the chops prepares us to accept without surprise his
notion that Macbeth meant to bathe in reeking wounds and memorize
another Golgotha. By evoking his own dramatization of the killing of
Caesar and coupling it with the crucifixion, Shakespeare suggests that,
though he begins as a defender of order, Macbeth (like Banquo, who
is also being described) is potentially an agent of strife and chaos. When
we discover from Lady Macbeth that her husband wanted to kill Duncan
before the supernatural soliciting, when neither time nor place adhered
to make the murder possible, we realize that the identity is more than
potential. Macbeth's moral nature does not require the supernatural as
an explanation for why his mind presents him with strange images of
death—the odd phrase used by Rosse to describe the corpses Macbeth
has left behind him on the battlefield. Macbeth, we begin to suspect, is
an artist in death whose imagination presents him with forms which he
then brings into being, his (and confusion's) masterpiece being the
corpse of the king.

If Macbeth's obsessive images are the creations of his own mind, unaided by supernatural powers, his degree of moral responsibility depends
upon the freedom and strength of his will. If Macbeth's imagination is
free of supernatural influence then his will may be also. If it is, and if
it is not the naturally bound will of a madman, then Macbeth is a
criminal who deserves whatever punishment is visited on him in this
world and the next. The strongest evidence for the freedom and health
of Macbeth's powers of choice is undoubtedly the soliloquy which begins, "If it were done when 'tis done, then 'twere well, / It were done
quickly." The psychomachy there dramatized is won by the forces of
reason, and of political reason in particular. Macbeth sees clearly that,
leaving "the life to come" entirely out of consideration, there is a justice
built into the operation of the political world of here and now. His

murder of Duncan will be an example to the men he wishes to rule, particularly since there is no moral or political justification for the destruction of so good a king. Rational ambition must give way to other claims of reason which indicate so clearly that the fulfillment of ambition must be finally self-destructive.

The decisive clarity of this triumph of the reason can only emphasize the culpability of Macbeth when he capitulates to his wife's scorn of his manhood. Macbeth as criminal dominates our view of him at this point in the play, I think. We see him as freely conceiving and freely executing his crimes.

But our doubts of this identity begin at once. With the next soliloquy we start to suspect that Macbeth is, or is becoming, madder than we thought. The dagger which Macbeth sees and we do not and which he finally decides has no objective existence could be evidence of a sane mind under strain, sane enough, indeed, to recognize hallucination for what it is and to dismiss it at will. And yet this victory for reason does not result in the rule of reason. What replaces hallucination is an indulgence of the imagination in a theatrical self-contemplation which is a dissociation from the true self. Macbeth tries to dignify the sordid reality of a murderer sneaking up on his victim by decorating it with the inflated rhetoric of "wither'd Murder," "his Centinell the wolf," and "Tarquin's ravishing strides." The second half of the dagger soliloquy is Macbeth's equivalent of Othello's "Put out the light," an exalted prelude to the brutality of the crime which ensues. Shakespeare foregoes the dramatization of the crime and of the third of our phenomena, the voice which tells Macbeth that he shall sleep no more. As with the vision of the dagger, our natural assumption is that Macbeth is again hallucinating but the terror with which he describes the event is far more intense than his earlier reaction. Shakespeare, I think, is directing our minds toward two possibilities. The first is to strengthen our previous suspicion that Macbeth is or soon will be insane. Lady Macbeth encourages us:

> These deeds must not be thought
> After these wayes: so, it will make us mad.
>
> . . . .

You doe unbend your Noble strength, to thinke
So braine-sickly of things.

(2.2.33–34, 45–46)

The act of the murder has so taxed Macbeth's will that it no longer has
the strength to control and repress his mind's horrible imaginings or to
distinguish them from what really happens. But the terror which Macbeth communicates in his description of the voice might raise another
possibility and would certainly have done so in the minds of all but the
most skeptical Elizabethans. What if Macbeth is not going mad, but is
being driven mad by supernatural powers intent on his destruction? One
effect of Shakespeare's decision to have the third of our phenomena nar-
rated is that we are free to doubt its purely subjective nature. Perhaps
if we had been present, we would have heard it too.

There is no such doubt about Banquo's ghost. The evidence of the
Folio stage directions, supported by Simon Forman's report of a 1610
production, make it as certain as these things can be that the ghost should
be on stage for us to see.[2] But what is the nature of what we see? Obviously it is not what Macbeth first takes it to be—the animated corpse
of Banquo. No one except Macbeth and the audience can see it. It may
be what Macbeth finally concludes it is—a horrible shadow, an unreal
mockery, an illusion produced by the working of supernatural powers
of evil upon Macbeth's mind. Or it may be a naturally explicable hallucination, the product of a guilty mind that has gone over the brink into
madness. The ghost's visibility to us would then be the result of Shakespeare's decision to make Macbeth's insanity as vivid as the theater can.
Finally there is a third possibility: the ghost may be Banquo's spirit, as
the ghost in *Hamlet* is old Hamlet's spirit but visible only to Macbeth
as old Hamlet is visible only to his son (and us) in the closet scene. In
any case, it is at this point that the criminal Macbeth and the insane
Macbeth become one. The free criminal, if that is what he is, has become the madman as a result of the evil he has done. Whether the fascination of doing evil has been at any time within the control of his will,
Macbeth's doing of it has brought him to the condition of a raving
lunatic. But having arrived at that condition, he does something quite

astounding. By an effort of the will, he ceases to be mad. If we consider Macbeth as the prey to natural hallucination, then what we see and hear is a man issuing orders to his own mind: "Hence horrible shadow, / Unreall mock'ry hence" (3.4.119–120). The ghost disappears, and, although the play is only half over, its disappearance ends the series of puzzling phenomena we have been concerned with. From this point on Macbeth is plagued with no more "horrid images." They are replaced by illusions of a very different kind—the false expectations raised by the visions presented to him by the witches. But the change goes further than that.

It is hard to demonstrate, but I would maintain that the quality of Macbeth's mind is very different after his victory over the ghost of Banquo. In the first part of the play Macbeth is a man of action who thinks associatively, like a poet. His life is apprehended and created through his imagination and Shakespeare, by Macbeth's expression of it, brilliantly suggests the quality of such a life, evil as, in this case, it is: "Light thickens, / And the Crow makes Wing to th' Rookie Wood" (3.2.51–52). But once the ghost is conquered, this odd, cruel lyricism disappears from Macbeth's speech leaving dull brutality and bitterness in its place:

> It will have blood they say:
> Blood will have Blood.
>
> .   .   .   .
>
> I am in blood
> Stept in so farre, that should I wade no more,
> Returning were as tedious as go ore.
>
> (3.4.123–124, 138–140)

If *rapt* is the best word for the Macbeth of the play's first half, "tedious" replaces it in the second half. Not, by any means, tedious to us. He remains fascinating. But tedious to himself. Macbeth has become a bored thug.

The best explanation for this puzzling change is probably to be found in the relationship of Macbeth's will to his imagination. The triumph of Macbeth's will is a Pyrrhic victory. In order to destroy the vision of

Banquo's ghost, Macbeth must destroy its source, his imaginative power. Most imaginations wither slowly. Macbeth kills his. Only by murdering his imagination can Macbeth retain his sanity, but the sanity that remains to him is horrible, a kind of rational madness. The destruction of Macbeth's imagination by his will is an act of self-preservation, but the self preserved turns out to be much like Richard III's, an "I" that has neither pity, love, nor fear.

If Macbeth's obsession is natural, he conquers it by an act of partial self-destruction that leaves him, in a secular and temporal sense, a damned soul, despairing and brutish, whose life is a horror to be waded through. He remains that if his obsession is supernatural, but when we so consider him we see that there may be dimensions to the meaning of his tragedy that would escape us if we neglected the supernatural possibility. Not that we need much change our account of what happens to Macbeth and what he does about it if diabolical forces are responsible for the series of psychic phenomena we have considered. In either case Macbeth's imagination is the immediate source of image, vision, voice, ghost; and in destroying his imaginative powers, Macbeth is destroying the instrument through which the forces of evil exercise their power over him. The irony of this triumph of the will alters its nature, however. Diabolical powers are bent on destroying Macbeth by driving him insane through working upon his imagination. They succeed in destroying Macbeth by forcing him to destroy his imagination in order to preserve his sanity. But this act of self-preservation turns out simultaneously to be an act of spiritual self-destruction. Is the triumph of evil over Macbeth inevitable then? I believe the play suggests that it may be. But it also suggests that it may not be.

If the play is taking place in an Augustinian world, then the power of evil over Macbeth's mind must be permitted by God, but the Augustinian God, though he permits the triumph of evil, ought not to permit its inevitable triumph. The possibility of a saving choice should be open to Macbeth—and perhaps it is. The diabolical temptations and torments to which Macbeth is subjected may also be manifestations of divine grace. When Macbeth has heard the witches' prophecy he yields to the "suggestions" that in order to become king he must murder Duncan. The form of that suggestion is a vision of the murdered king:

> that suggestion,
> Whose horrid Image doth unfixe my Heire,
> And make my seated Heart knock at my Ribbes,
> Against the use of Nature. (1.3.140–143)

A suggestion is a "prompting or incitement to evil . . . a temptation of the evil one" (*O.E.D.*). The paradox of this temptation is obvious: it repels while attracting. Temptations often do. That the horror has a perverse attraction for Macbeth does not however cancel its nature for him as horror. The temptation takes a form that warns the tempted against yielding to it and thus the origin of the horrid image may be as much divine as diabolical. The same can be said for the bloody dagger. Macbeth interprets it as marshaling him the way that he is going but another mind might take it as a barrier in his way and so Macbeth's rejection of it may be a rejection of divine warning. The voice that cries "sleep no more" can even more obviously be the threat of divine justice as well as the triumph of the devil. Finally the ghost of Banquo, which drives Macbeth to the brink of madness, may simultaneously be driving him toward true sanity through the sacrament of penance. Macbeth, as a result of the vision of Banquo's ghost, is brought to something like Claudius's psychological condition after "The Mousetrap." If he were to repent, confess his sin, and suffer its temporal consequences, he would save his soul. Thus the whole series of psychic or supernatural phenomena partake of a possible double nature and reveal that Macbeth's imaginative faculty is potentially as much the instrument of grace for his salvation as the instrument of evil for his temptation and destruction.

But the possible double nature of these phenomena is not the only evidence for the working of grace upon Macbeth through his imagination. Again, in the "If it were done" soliloquy, Macbeth's arrival, for once, at a correct choice is attributable not simply to the action of right reason upon the will, but to the action of the imagination as well. Macbeth's stated purpose in the soliloquy is to confine his thought to a consideration simply of his temporal situation "heere, upon this Banke and Schoole of time," jumping the life to come. He concludes as a result of an eminently rational process of thought that judgment will be visited upon him even here, and that he must therefore refrain from murder.

But throughout this logical consideration of a practical moral and political problem, the imagery in which his thought takes form betrays the presence beneath the conscious surface of his mind of the pressure upon it of his knowledge and fear of eternity and this presence may well be evidence of the working of grace. When, for example, he comes to consider the evenhanded justice that will see to it that the murderer of Duncan will himself become the victim of a murderer whom he has taught to kill, Macbeth's poetic imagination personifies the idea. He embodies the concept, however, not as the usual blindfolded lady with the scales, but as the commender of a chalice to the lips—an image of the evenhanded priest at the sacrament of Communion. The image is a natural result of the fact that Macbeth has just come from what he has proposed shall be the saintly Duncan's last supper, but it is also evidence of the possible existence of forces within his mind, but not of it, that present his consciousness with thoughts that will not let him "jump the life to come." Again, when he considers what effect the saintliness of Duncan may have upon the men who will determine whether to punish his killer, he imagines Duncan's virtues pleading: "like Angels, Trumpet-tongu'd against / The deepe damnation of his taking off" (1.7.19–20). Virtues plead, like angels, against damnation most notably in the highly popular allegory of the Four Daughters of God where Justice and Truth, Mercy and Peace argue the fate of fallen man before their divine Father and are reconciled when Christ agrees to satisfy justice by taking upon himself the punishment which man deserves. The form which Christ's pity for humanity inspires him to assume is that of a naked newborn babe and that is the form which Macbeth imagines for the pity that will inspire men to destroy him if he murders Duncan. Within the confines of this soliloquy then, Shakespeare has Macbeth use imagery that suggests God's decision to save fallen man through Christ's atonement, the Nativity and the Last Supper.

For a modern reader of the play this emergence of images of eternity into a soliloquy ostensibly devoted to the political and moral decisions of here and now is a brilliant example of Shakespeare's ability to convey a sense of the unconscious mind working upon the consciousness. But what for us is evidence of the unconscious is for Shakespeare's time explicable as extrapsychic, as supernatural, so that some of Shakespeare's brilliance as an imitator of the human psyche may have its origin in a desire to suggest that at times the contents and movements of the mind are the result of forces outside the mind itself. Here his verse suggests, I think, how grace may strive to work upon Macbeth's will through the power of his imagination. Reason and imagination combine to bring Macbeth to the rejection of evil. Then Lady Macbeth enters and the work of grace is overthrown. Macbeth's will freely rejects its earlier decision and he continues on the course which leads to his damnation.

If the origin of the psychic phenomena is supernatural and if Macbeth's will is free, then Macbeth is self-damned, for if evil works on him through the power of his imagination, so does grace and his will chooses to obey the promptings of the former. But one last possible Macbeth remains. If Macbeth's mind is subject to the suggestions of the supernatural and if his will is not free, then he is a reprobate sinner as conceived by Calvin, one upon whose damnation God decided in his secret councils before the creation of the world.

In *Macbeth* the evidence for this most frightening of tragic possibilities is found largely in the nature of time and the characters' relationship to it. Shakespeare uses the witches and their prophecies to suggest that the future may be immutable. W. C. Curry explains the witches' power of foreseeing the future as the result of a superhuman version of logical inference from their superior understanding of the causes of things: "In this sense, the demons, having lost nothing of their angelic nature, know the future development of events conjecturally though not absolutely."[3] This is convincing enough so long as the only prophecies in question are those about Macbeth's future glories. But the later misleading revelations are considerably harder to account for. Perhaps the witches might have known that Macduff was born by Caesarean section and that he was likely to kill Macbeth. But how could they foresee Malcolm's sudden development of a talent for camouflage and the precise moment and form of its expression? Or what except supernatural knowledge of what must occur in the future could have informed them that Banquo's descendants would turn out to be the House of Stuart?

The witches necessarily give us the strong sense that what Lady Macbeth calls "this ignorant present" is that instant in which the illusion of possibility can exist, but only because ignorance allows it to. The immutable future seems subject to the exercise of will because we cannot see it in the instant. In fact it exists with the same finality as the past and it is known with the same certainty to supernatural intelligence. But the importance of the relationship of the characters to future time is considerably larger than that suggested by the witches' enigmatic knowledge of what will be hereafter. The significant differences between Macbeth and his wife and the changes that take place in their natures are defined and determined by their different and altering relationships to time. In the first two acts of the play it is obvious enough that each is dominated by a different psychic element. Macbeth embodies imagination. Lady Macbeth embodies will. What each in this way *is* determines the difference in each of the quality of his knowledge of what will be. Macbeth apprehends the future sensually. He knows the murder of Duncan by his experience of the horrid image. He sees the bloody dagger before he has brought it into existence. He experiences the future torture of his mind, the restless ecstasy that lies ahead of him, when he hears the voice cry, "Sleep no more." Lady Macbeth, on the other hand knows what will be because she wills it to be: "Glamys thou art, and Cawdor, and shalt be / What thou art promis'd" (1.5.13–14). Her knowledge of the future is less apprehension than information. Duncan will be killed because she has determined that he will be. If she had sworn to dash her baby's brains out, that would happen too. Macbeth's letter transports her beyond this ignorant present because it instructs her will. All in all she is a frightening demonstration of the stupidity of the will when it is not informed by imagination. Her reason foresees results but not consequences, so she can invite evil to possess her without regarding the invitation as more than a necessary precondition for Duncan's murder. Once done, it will be done, "what's done, is done"—or so she thinks. Macbeth's apprehending, associating, essentially poetic mind knows better: the assassination cannot trammel up the consequence. The truth that Lady Macbeth discovers is very simple: the past does not cease to exist, but it does pass beyond the power of the will to alter it.

Not only that, the existence of the unalterable past saps the power of the will to control the future—or to believe that it can control the future. Macbeth asserts his will to subjugate his imagination and the result is a new Macbeth incapable of fully experiencing either past, present, or future, a Macbeth who is an easy prey to the juggling and paltering of the witches. The vacuum left by the disappearance of his own imaginative vision of the future is easily filled by the misleading, the merely factual information of the witches. His will has lost the game by winning it. And the paradoxical triumph of Macbeth's will is simultaneously the defeat of his will-dominated wife.

Lady Macbeth's relationship to the play's time is oddly stationary. She exercises her will in turn upon future, present, and past. When the future she wills into existence becomes the present, she ceases to have a future, and when it has become the past, she ceases to have a present as well. From the beginning she is locked into the moment of the murder. At first her function is to will the murder into existence and until that moment, her function smothers surmise. When the moment arrives, her will successfully exercises itself by imposing upon that bit of time the order needed to prevent disaster. She can return the daggers because she refuses to allow her imagination to discover the meaning of what she will see when she sees the murdered Duncan:

> . . . the sleeping, and the dead,
> Are but as Pictures: 'tis the Eye of Child-hood,
> That feares a painted Devill. (2.2.55–57)

Life and death are no more meaningful to her than art, and without imagination neither life, death, nor art can have meaning.

But once his wife's will has brought him safely past the moment of Duncan's murder, Macbeth begins to deprive her will of its future-determining function:

> LADY: What's to be done?
> MACB. Be innocent of the knowledge, dearest Chuck,
> Till thou applaud the deed. (3.2.45–47)

He starts to savor the pleasure of the future's imagined crimes:

> Come, seeling Night,
> Skarfe up the tender Eye of pittifull Day,
> And with thy bloodie and invisible Hand

Cancell and teare to pieces that great Bond,
Which keepes me pale.   (3.2.47–51)

But these horrible imaginings must be paid for when they have become
realities and as past crimes they erupt into the present in the form of
Banquo's ghost. Again Lady Macbeth's will must try, this time more
frantically, to preserve the order of the present moment. Desperately
she deploys her familiar arguments. Macbeth is not a man. The ghost is
but a picture, the painting of his fear. But she is powerless against this
strange image of death. Only Macbeth's will can control it, but though
his will succeeds in doing so, the victory comes too late for Lady Macbeth. Macbeth has ruined the party:

> You have displac'd the mirth,
> Broke the good meeting, with most admir'd disorder.
>
>   (3.4.108–109)
>
> .   .   .   .
>
>   at once, goodnight.
> Stand not upon the order of your going,
> But go at once.   (3.4.118–120)

The essentially suburban nature of her evil mind is nowhere more apparent than in the moment of its defeat. But it will not do to overemphasize the merely bourgeois quality of her aspirations. The festivity
which Banquo's ghost has interrupted is an emblem of the measure,
time, and place which was last possible in the banquet that preceded
Duncan's murder and which will become possible again only when the
butcher and his fiendlike queen are dead. The efforts of her will to impose such order upon the present have proved futile and the present has
turned out to be the product of an immutable past which was once a
future that her will apparently determined. The function of her will is
smothered at that moment when Macbeth's will smothers his "surmise."
After the departure of her guests she has barely twenty exhausted words
to speak to her husband before she leaves the play, returning only as a
will-less, imagination-haunted sleepwalker.

   We see her in that scene, caught in her moment, the one she has willed
and which she can now neither escape nor alter. She has become a walk-

ing shadow tormented by shadows, but unlike Richard the Third or her husband, she cannot respond to the unalterable outside herself by altering herself. She can only escape by destroying herself. As with Richard and Macbeth, her death leaves us in doubt about the real power of her apparently determining will. In *Macbeth* the suspicion that the events of the play are preordained is always present and that suspicion is a logical inference from the witches' knowledge of the contents of future time. This possibility is given poetic expression by Macbeth's last great speech. There Macbeth's sense of himself as poised between meaningless yesterdays and meaningless tomorrows comes into focus on the enigmatic phrase "recorded time" with its implication that all time, future as well as past, is history, a matter of eternal record. Man's considerations of possibility, his exercises of will, are predicated on an illusion of possibility. His psychomachies are sciamachies, the struggles of a walking shadow. The literary metaphor that concludes the speech is an answer to and a development of Rosse's early theatrical metaphor for the intervention of divine providence. Man's acts are nothing more than the strutting and fretting of a poor player and the bloody stage is not his, but the idiot's who has invented the tale that is being told upon it. Our sense that in *Macbeth* life may be meaningless arises, however, not from an idiotic lack of logical coherence in the action, but from its opposite, the sense that the form of Macbeth's life, is, to adapt Coleridge's critical distinction, mechanical rather than organic. If the events of Macbeth's tragic existence have been predetermined by divine power, if indeed "Der Herr Gott würfelt nicht," then the bitterness of "Tomorrow and tomorrow and tomorrow" is entirely justified.

The last of our four Macbeths, the predestined reprobate instrument and object of God's wrath, suggests the existence of a world conceived by Calvin and re-created imaginatively by Shakespeare. Each of the other three possible Macbeths similarly suggests a world that would account for his nature. The criminal who freely conceives and executes his crimes embodies evil in a Pelagian universe. The man whose own mind pushes him to the brink of madness and who must destroy his imagination in order to survive inhabits a world ruled by natural determinism. The Macbeth who freely chooses to follow the promptings of supernatural evil rather than those of divine grace inhabits the universe created by

Augustine's God and embodies in it the same mystery that Claudius defines in *Hamlet*. The coexistence of these versions of our reality has characterized the other three plays we have examined. But Richard III appears most likely to be a creature of Calvin's God. Othello seems to inhabit a Pelagian world, though one whose optimism has been tragically qualified by Shakespeare's sense of the ways in which our minds are bound by their very natures. The Augustinian solution to Hamlet's mystery seems more satisfactory than any other, but in his tragedy, as in the other plays, probability is never certainty and the mystery remains a mystery. In *Macbeth*, it seems to me, no possibility predominates. The various suggested causes of the protagonist's tragic destruction coexist in perfect equilbrium.

But, of course, the destruction of the protagonist does not conclude the play's action and Macbeth's last great speech is not the play's final word. The beneficence of providence is reasserted strongly at the end. As a result of his killing of Macbeth, Macduff tells us, "The time is free," suggesting that our previous sense of its enslavement was, though accurate, the result of a special condition—the temporary subjection of the play's world to evil through the capitulation to diabolical forces by Macbeth and his wife. Now, to take up Malcolm's vocabulary, the threat and fact of chaos have given way to "measure, time and place." Thanks to "the grace of grace," justice and mercy have been restored to Scotland and the retributive portion of justice has already begun to operate in the destruction "of this dead Butcher, and his Fiend-like Queene."

The element of the unsatisfactory in this highly satisfactory conclusion needs careful definition. It stems in part from the inadequacy of the words *butcher* and *fiend*. Our experience of Macbeth and his wife has been so complex that this simplicity inevitably calls attention to itself. Not, in my opinion, because we find the terms too harsh. They are as deserved as the fates of the people to whom they apply. For the purposes of Shakespearean temporal justice, a man is what he has done and I cannot see that the play solicits the smallest sympathy for what this butcher and fiend have done. But *Macbeth* is not only a presentation of actions. To an extraordinary degree, even for Shakespeare, the world of the play is the cause and the result of the protagonist's mind. That world contains forces—divine grace and supernatural evil—that are not of Macbeth's mind yet cause that mind to be what it is. And Macbeth's mind, in turn, causes his world to be what it is, not only because of the impact of his crimes upon the world, but because the quality of that world is communicated to us as it is apprehended by Macbeth's mind. His subjective world becomes the world of our dramatic experience. Shakespeare has made us know what it is like to live within the associative, obsessed mind of a man like Macbeth, and we must, I think, admit that Macbeth's last great speech evaluates our knowledge of Macbeth's world accurately. Life in the world as Macbeth knows it signifies nothing.

We can, of course, take that knowledge to be the knowledge of an illusion. The play permits us to choose to believe that Macbeth's life is a tale told by an idiot only to Macbeth and only because Macbeth has willfully destroyed his ability to see the measure, time, and place that Malcolm and Macduff can see. But does the text insist that the subjective vision is illusion and the objective is reality? I do not think so. I have said that *Macbeth* should be apprehended simultaneously as the providential tragicomedy of a society and as the psychological tragedy of a villain protagonist. I have also maintained that there are at least four different and equally valid ways of understanding that protagonist. Two of these ways, by seeing the protagonist of the psychological tragedy as a creature without free will, call into doubt the meaningfulness of the providential pattern. And this, surely, is what Macbeth does at the end of the play by maintaining that he is a poor player in a tale told by an idiot. If he is without free will, then he is trapped in recorded time and his life signifies nothing. What the play shows us is that, experienced from within, by its victim and instrument, the providential pattern signifies nothing.

CHAPTER 8

Conclusion—*King Lear*

EDGAR AND his blind father are on stage at line 90 of act 4, scene 6 of *King Lear* when Lear enters, mad and talking to himself: "No, they cannot touch me for coyning.[1] I am the King himselfe." Edgar is moved to exclaim, "O, thou side-piercing sight" and the king says "Nature's above Art, in that respect." Lear's second sentence has, I believe, always been taken as spoken by the king to himself and it is usually para-phrased "A born king can never lose his natural rights."[2] This is a per-fectly possible reading but surely there is another. The rest of Lear's speech is addressed to Edgar and there seems no reason why its opening sentence should not be too. If it is, its meaning is clear: Lear comments on Edgar's exclamation by observing that nature is above art when it comes to the production of side-piercing sights.

It seems to me that what Edgar says is also considerably more signifi-cant than the commentators have allowed. John Dover Wilson points out that the side-piercing sight is a "Gospel echo"[3]—an evocation of John 19: "and one of the souldiers with a speare perced his side, and forthewith came there out blood and water." Edgar's exclamation is ap-propriate to what he sees: a tormented, mock king, who is yet a true king, the king himself, but who is now crowned, if not with thorns, then with:

> . . . ranke Fenitar, and furrow weeds,
> With Hardokes, Hemlocke, Nettles, Cuckoo flowres,
> Darnell, and all the idle weedes that grow
> In our sustaining Corne.   (4.3.3–6)

An analogy between Christ's passion and Lear's is suggested by Ed-gar's brief phrase. But it is important to notice that Edgar's phrase de-scribes not Lear, but Edgar's reaction to the sight of Lear: the behold-er's side is pierced. Edgar's manner of expressing himself brings to mind not only Christ's passion, but a whole tradition or technique of Chris-

183

tian worship, the *unio passionalis*, in which the meditator upon the passion attempts to participate in Christ's sufferings on the cross.[4] The idea of the necessity for such an effort appears to have originated with Saint Bernard of Clairvaux in his Sermons on the Song of Songs. By the fourteenth century the theme was being treated with a passionate intensity that was clearly still very much alive for the mystics of the sixteenth (one thinks of Bernini's representation of Saint Theresa in ecstasy). For more ordinary Christians, however, the tradition was available in forms distinctly more rational and sedate. The recusants in Shakespeare's audience would have known such treatises as those on the art of meditation, the use of the rosary, and so on, that abounded in Elizabethan England, some of them printed clandestinely, others smuggled in from the Continent.[5] Most such works are concerned with Christ's passion and they usually draw their inspiration from the spiritual exercises of Saint Ignatius of Loyola, which instruct the exercitant to pray for "grief, tears and pain in union with Christ suffering."

Elizabethan Protestant preachers insist equally on the necessity for contemplating Christ's passion. *The Book of Homilies* urges that the "image of Christ crucified, bee alwayes printed in our heartes."[6] Particularly brilliant considerations of the topic are those produced by Lancelot Andrewes in his three Good-Friday Sermons on the Passion.[7] In the first of these, preached at court on 25 March 1597, Andrewes takes as his text the line from Zechariah (12:10) which Saint John cites as a prophecy of the thrusting of the spear into Christ's side: "And they shall looke upon Me, whom they have pierced." Andrewes presents the text as a command to look at the sufferings of Christ with total compassion, in such a way as to inspire within the beholder a full range of emotional and intellectual response, from pain and self-reproach through love to hope. In fact, Andrewes is asking us to see feelingly, like Gloucester, so that what is "to *flesh and blood* . . . but a dull and *heavy spectacle*" may "grow into a delight of this *looking*"—a process that begins, if the beholder is capable of it, with the physical *unio passionalis:* "*Looke upon Him that is pierced*; and with *looking upon Him,* be *pierced* thyself: *Respice & transfigere.*"[8] For Andrewes this sense of Christ pierced is the epitome of Christian knowledge:

the perfection of our knowledge, is Christ: The perfection of our knowledge in, or touching Christ, is the knowledge of *Christ's piercing*. This is the chiefe *Sight; Nay* . . . in this sight, are all sights: so that, know this and know all.[9]

Edgar's gospel allusion expands when contemplated. So does what I take to be Lear's reply to it. Nature is art's superior in the production of objects for our compassion. The image of Christ crucified is an artifact—obviously so to the Catholic who prays before a crucifix but just as much so to the iconoclastic Protestant who calls the "dull and heavy sight" into existence within his mind. Shakespeare is having Lear tell us that if we wish to see Christ crucified we should look around us. In so doing he is demanding from us what he demands throughout the play—that we look. Lear's dying words ("Do you see this? Looke on her? looke her lips, / Looke there, looke there.") have, since Bradley, generally been taken to mean that Lear, under the illusion that Cordelia is still breathing, dies of joy. It may be so, but surely the lines are also Shakespeare's imperative to his audience. We are being told to look at this pieta, the body of Cordelia in Lear's arms, which Shakespeare has devised for our contemplation. What we see, it is generally agreed, is the most painfully side-piercing sight in art. And yet, its creator has told us, the spectacles of human suffering produced by nature surpass it in intensity.

What I take to be the exchange between Edgar and Lear then is a paradox which can be restated as follows: Edgar's words equate the effect of the sight of Lear's suffering upon the beholder to that of the image of Christ's crucifixion upon the Christian meditant. Lear's reply points out that suffering in nature should inspire a more intense compassion than suffering imagined by art. But of course, Christ's suffering was originally in nature and Lear's suffering is presently in art, so that Shakespeare, in asking us to respond to Lear with the compassion which we would give to Christ, is also deprecating his art with respect to nature, the great source and original of tragic suffering. But beyond this paradox are two others of particular interest to this study. Edgar's complex gospel allusion is, of course, anachronistic. It is supposed to have been spoken some centuries before the birth of Christ. But it is not a real anachronism—that is, the exclamation can be taken as spoken without intention of allusion by the character. Shakespeare has not violated the proclaimed paganism of the tragedy, but the existence of the allusion raises a question crucial to our concerns: what is the nature of Christ's presence in *King Lear?* Lear's reply also raises such a question, an even more complex one, in fact. What is the relationship of the nature in this art to the nature outside art which Lear's line invites us to contemplate?

In the other plays we have looked at, the nature imitated by Shakespeare's art is assumed to be, I think, the art of God and Shakespeare's stage is an artistic version of the theater of God's judgments. One of the primary sources of the tragic power of these plays is to be found in the questions raised and the doubts inspired about the nature of the God who has created the great original of the nature Shakespeare imitates. The meaning of every Shakespearean tragedy is interrogative. Its significance derives from the questions it asks and from the context of the doubts which it inspires. *Richard III, Hamlet, Othello,* and *Macbeth* ask religious questions in a Christian context, thus directing our minds toward the mysteries and paradoxes of Christian theology. *Julius Caesar, Antony and Cleopatra, Timon of Athens,* and *Coriolanus* ask secular questions in a pagan context, thus directing our minds toward problems of psychology and political morality. *King Lear,* uniquely among the tragedies, I believe, considers religious questions in a pagan context. In this play Shakespeare confronts his characters with questions about the meaning of nature, and the existence of divine justice, but he has deprived the characters he so confronts of the Christian answers of his original audience.

The potential results of this strategy are at least double. In *King Lear* Shakespeare's conceptual "given" is Christianity—his audience's and, perhaps, his own. The Christian way of understanding nature is Shakespeare's starting place and remains a fixed constant—one point of view from which the action of the tragedy may always be contemplated and understood, one pole in the conceptual structure which Shakespeare proceeds to build. From the Christian vantage point, the nature which Shakespeare creates through his art is and remains an imitation of its original, of nature outside that art, as nature appears to men without a knowledge of God. The nature of *Lear* is thus nature seen, in Luther's phrase, by the light of nature. The resulting vision is (or can be) very bleak indeed and in the unlikely event that Shakespeare needed to have this bleakness pointed out to him, Montaigne had done so, most persausively, in the *Apology for Raymond Sebonde*. For the convinced Christian, Shakespearean art in *Lear* is the imitation of an illusion, an imitation of the way things seem. The Christian beholder may correct that illusion by turning on the light of grace. The result of that illumination is, however, not necessarily a rosy glow. The mysteries remain, just as they remain in the overtly Christian tragedies we have looked at, and primary among them is the mystery of God's judgments, for it would surely take at least the light of glory to reveal the justice of Cordelia's death. Seen even from a Christian perspective, the tragedy of *Lear*, like *Hamlet*, is incomprehensible though not meaningless.

There is, however, a large and essential difference between Christianity's mode of existence in *Hamlet* and in *Lear*. In *Hamlet* Christianity is integral to the work of art. It is the point at which the hero at last arrives and from which he recognizes and accepts the incomprehensibility of his condition. Christianity is entirely foreign to *Lear* as a self-contained artifact. Christ exists only as a buried allusion, an occasional reminder of the revelation which has intervened in time between the ostensible date of the tragic action and its living human audience. Nonetheless, any alert Christian can make theological sense of *Lear*. He can make similar sense of Auschwitz and Buchenwald. It is one of the purposes of theology to make sense of such things. My point is that *Lear* does not make such sense of itself. Any Christian meaning must be an imposition from the outside, though it differs from other imposed interpretations—Marxist, existential, psychoanalytical—in that it is the interpretation that was most available for imposition to the play's author and first audience. It is the exterior interpretation of which the play, so to speak, is conscious.

Which leads us to the question, "What sense does *Lear* make of itself?" Within the play, the characters—especially the good ones—try constantly to make sense of what is happening to them. In the second scene of the play, Edmund characterizes one such attempt—his father's belief in astrology—as "an admirable evasion of Whore-master-man." The phrase is useful. Edmund is thinking of whoremaster man's attempts to evade responsibility for the consequences of his own actions, which is precisely what Edmund himself ends up doing in the practice of his own evasion, the worship of nature. ("I should have bin that I am, had the maidenlest Starre in the Firmament twinkled on my bastardizing.") But the admirable evasions of these characters have, it seems to me, a profounder motive than self-justification. What they are doing, particularly when they look for meaning to the concept of divine justice, is seeking to evade the apparent meaninglessness of their own condition.

Albany, the play's master of cliché, is practicing such evasion when, on hearing of Cornwall's death, he says:

> This shewes you are above
> You Justicers,[10] that these our neather crimes
> So speedily can venge.   (4.2.54–56)

But we know, and Albany has been told, that "this" shows nothing of the kind. The justice of Cornwall's death is the result of the self-sacrificing and very human heroism of Cornwall's servant. Albany is evading the senseless horror of Gloucester's blinding by imposing meaning upon it. But, of course, Edgar finds far more memorable and disturbing meaning in his father's sufferings:

> The Gods are just, and of our pleasant vices
> Make instruments to plague us:
> The dark and vitious place where thee he got,
> Cost him his eyes.   (5.3.176–179)

This grim assertion has the advantage over Albany's of characterizing accurately the justice that appears to be operating in the play, and surely one if its effects is to make us wonder if it might not be less disturbing ultimately to abandon the notion of divine judgment altogether. But Gloucester himself appears not to think so. His famous claim that the gods kill us for their sport (itself an attempt to evade or repress the unbearable knowledge of his mistreatment of Edgar) again is a desperate refusal to admit that what has happened to him cannot be referred to some higher will, however idiotic. More humane is his acceptance of his suffering on the grounds that it has benefited those more wretched than himself:

> Heavens deale so still:
> Let the superfluous, and Lust-dieted man,
> That slaves your ordinance, that will not see
> Because he do's not feele, feele your powre quickly:
> So distribution should undoo excesse,
> And each man have enough.   (4.1.65–70)

Gloucester sees distributive justice as having its origin in divine retribution, but Lear's great companion piece to Gloucester's speech qualifies it importantly, I think:

> Take Physicke, Pompe,
> Expose thy selfe to feel what wretches feele,
> That thou maist shake the superflux to them,
> And shew the Heavens more just.
>
> (3.4.33–36)

More just, presumably, than they are.

Lear proposes that "Divine justice" is, in fact, man's doing. Edgar proceeds to extend Lear's meaning through the salutary deception of his father. By convincing Gloucester that he has fallen from the cliffs of Dover without getting hurt, Edgar makes endurance possible for the old man by persuading him that he is the creature of powers that are not only righteous, but beneficent: "Thinke that the cleerest Gods, who make them Honors / Of mens Impossibilities, have preserved thee" (4.6.79–80). Think it, although it is not true. The play at this point could not make it clearer that a sense of meaning is a human necessity. For *Lear*'s first audience, a man's life was given meaning by being at least observed and preferably judged by a supernatural consciousness. To subtract divinity from the universe was to render it meaningless. Gloucester's despair has no such radical cause. He believes in the gods, but the incomprehensibility of their "great opposelesse willes" drives him to attempt self-destruction. Edgar then convinces him that the incomprehensibility conceals benevolence and that life is therefore endurable. But the play insists that the only evidence of this belief is illusion, an essential life-illusion in Gloucester's case, the admirable evasion of a desperate man.

At the play's conclusion, the necessary belief in meaning is subjected to the severest test that Shakespeare can devise for it. By the light of nature the side-piercing sight of the dead Cordelia in Lear's arms is a nihilist pieta. But Albany, Edgar, and Kent combine forces in an attempt to sustain meaning in the face of it. Their success is ambiguous:

> KENT. Is this the promis'd end?
> EDG. Or image of that horror.
> ALB. Fall and cease.   (5.3.264–266)

The promised end is apocalypse, but will that horror be the horror of justice, or the horror of the revelation that when the heavens fall and things cease nothing remains? If the body in Lear's arms is an image of the divine justice of the latter day, then we cannot understand it. If it is not, then there is nothing to understand. By the light of nature *King Lear* is either incomprehensible or meaningless, or both. That is, it is certainly incomprehensible and may also be meaningless. It may be incomprehensible because it is meaningless, or because its meaning is concealed by a mystery which is beyond the power of man's mind to solve.

The natural tendency of the critical intelligence is to treat such an artistic statement as a choice to be made, an ambiguity to be resolved. If the critic plumps for "simple" incomprehensibility, he is often quick to discern that what we cannot understand may be transcendentally glorious and that *Lear* can therefore be taken as, for example, "like the *Paradiso*, a vast poem on the victory of true love."[11] The critic who experiences the meaninglessness will tell us that the play tells us "that we inhabit an imbecile universe."[12] In fact, I suspect, what the plays tells us is different from and rather worse even than that. It tells us nothing. It shows us that in a state of nature, without the knowledge or the grace of God, we are nothing—O's without a figure. And it suggests that perhaps we *are* in a state of nature. It suggests but does not say that our knowledge may be illusion, that the faith and theology of the original audience, may, by analogy with the evasions within the play, be one more admirable evasion of whoremaster man. Indeed, any attempt to deal with the play's either/or statement of incomprehensibility and meaninglessness by resolving it in favor of one or the other is to evade the play's demonstration of our incertitude.

The play, then, brings us to an imaginative experience of what it is like to be nothing. Needless to say, we cannot stand the knowledge and the play does not ask that we should. It comes to an end. But it does not dismiss us, I think, with peace, consolation, and calm of mind. The *Lear* experience must be dealt with, either by forgetting it as efficiently as possible or by some process of critical analysis. But when I attempt such analysis, I inevitably find, as I am afraid I have made it very clear, that there is no rational way to deal with *King Lear*. Or rather there are two—Lear's own. Lear, faced with the knowledge of his nothingness, goes mad. He is restored to sanity by the irrationality of Cordelia's love and when that is taken from him, he goes mad again and dies. Surely we have long known that there are two rational courses to take in response to *Lear:* we can go mad or die, or both. Most of us would prefer to do neither and fortunately the play does not insist that we must or even should.

What the play brings us to finally is the necessity for evading the experience of nothingness. We must believe something or at least do something: faith, hope, or gardening; politics, drink, scholarship, chemistry, lechery, or interior decoration. The play does not assign a superior intellectual value to any belief or course of action. In proclaiming our ignorance the play proclaims its totality. We cannot even be sure that we do not know the truth and what are unquestionably our evasions may simultaneously be discoveries. Though most surely we do not understand anything, it is quite possible that we know something—and equally possible that we do not.

Obviously the play's inability to assign intellectual value to our beliefs does not apply to the moral and ethical value of our actions. *Lear* does not propose that we respond to nothingness by tossing old gentlemen out of railway carriages. Love is presented as the proper and perhaps as the only possible ratification of identity. Compassion, above all, is the only possible human replacement for divine justice. If there are no powers above, or if they do not choose to send down their visible spirits to protect and punish us, then only the ability to share the pain of our fellow men prevents us from preying upon ourselves like monsters of the deep. But I cannot discover that the play assigns transcendent value to love and compassion. Cordelia's love is dependent upon Cordelia's life, and her death destroys Lear. Edgar's compassion does much, but in the end it can do nothing. At the play's end Edgar, Kent, and Albany intensely share Lear's suffering but they can do no more to alleviate it than we in the audience can. The final scene imitates with horrible effect that moment in nature when human suffering resembles art in that the intensity of its pain places it beyond communication with those who see and share it. Schlegel said that in *King Lear*, "the science of compassion is exhausted."[13] I am not sure that I understand what that means, but it if means that the play shows us how much and how little compassion can achieve, then I would agree.

What only compassion can achieve is, of course, a proper experience of the tragedy of *King Lear*. At a performance of the play, the Gonerils and Regans of the world would be bored. Whatever cause in nature makes these hard hearts, it effectively prevents the art of tragedy from succeeding. What the play proposes as the human quality essential to the proper functioning of nature is also essential to the proper functioning of the play as art. We must be affected by the spectacle of *Lear* as Edgar is. Our sides must be pierced, but the play reminds us that the nature which the play imitates is above art in that respect.

But if the play makes Edgars of us by piercing our sides, it also makes Lears of us by cutting us to the brains. Our participation in Lear's discovery of his nothingness demonstrates that, by the light of nature, we too are O's without a figure. Our observation of the characters' attempts to substitute sense for apparent meaninglessness may lead us to recognize that the sense we make may be no more than an admirable evasion of the knowledge that meaninglessness is not apparent but real.

It seems to me that *King Lear* brings its audience to something like that point at which Pascal arrives just before he urges upon us the necessity of taking his famous bet:

Parlons maintenant selon les lumières naturelles. S'il y a un Dieu, il est infiniment incompréhensible, puisque, n'ayant ni parties ni bornes, il n'a nul rapport à nous. Nous sommes donc incapables de connaître ni ce qu'il est, ni s'il est. Cela étant, qui osera entreprendre de résoudre cette question? Ce n'est pas nous qui n'avons aucun rapport à lui.[14]

Shakespeare's art has arrived at this point partly as a result of the imaginative contemplation in tragedy of the mystery of God's judgments. His progress, I would maintain, is cultural as well as individual. The medieval dramatist disregarded that mystery and presented his audience with a world in which man is free to determine his own eternal fate. The movement of the will to contrition was presented as an act of free choice and its necessary motivation, according to orthodox theology, by God's prevenient grace was disregarded in the drama. The result was a semi-Pelagian dramatic world and that world survived in the Elizabethan drama as an appropriate context for comedy, and particularly for those plays which I have elsewhere called comedies of forgiveness. But the Reformation was founded intellectually on a revival of the Augustinian tradition—a revival that went beyond the doctrines of its originator to an insistence that man's will is not free and could not be free given the absolute nature of predestination. This "solution" of the mystery of God's judgments was, of course, a restatement and deepening of it. Luther and Calvin presented their contemporaries with a tragic image of the human condition and that image had its effect on dramatic art. For the theologically trained Marlowe, the story of *Dr. Faustus* had a "moral" that was not apparent in its earlier versions: the God who sends Faustus to hell is a monster. But one mustn't say so. One mustn't, perhaps, even think so. Yet the rumor or fact of Marlowe's atheism is easy to understand. *Faustus* is the story of a man who did not repent. Marlowe's version of that story suggests that perhaps Faustus did not because he would not, but it also suggests that perhaps he could not and it then goes on to wonder what he could not do. Accept God's proffered grace? Because he did not receive the prevenient grace which is a necessity for the acceptance of that grace? Or could he not accept it because, in fact, it was never proffered? The scene of Faustus's damnation can inspire more than fear and pity. It can inspire revulsion with the God it imagines. It is all very well for Pascal and all the theologians to maintain that "la justice envers les réprouvés est moins énorme et doit moins choquer que la miséricorde envers les élus,"[15] and it is no doubt possible to believe this as an intellectual proposition, but art transforms such propositions into imagined experience. One possible effect of the shock of vicariously experiencing God's justice in *Faustus* is the desire not to believe in God at all.

The subtler and more profoundly moving art of Shakespeare sometimes derives its power from the mysteries that give intensity to *Dr. Faustus*. The mystery of *Richard III* is that of the vessel and the reprobate instrument of God's wrath. The paradoxical figure of Claudius in *Hamlet* also evokes that mystery and, in the prayer scene, adds the *Faustus* mystery to it. The mystery of Claudius's apparent reprobation is balanced by the mystery of Hamlet's apparent election and the acting out of their mutually destructive tragedy leaves us with the knowledge that the Christian revelation gives meaning to the world *Hamlet* imitates, but does not make it comprehensible. In *Othello*, I think, Shakespeare tests the possibility that comprehensibility might be found in a conceiving of the will as free in a Pelagian sense—free, that is, of supernatural control. The result is comprehensibility of a sort, for the play is all too horribly clear in its demonstration that the human mind, left to its own devices, not dominated by grace or directed by providence, will turn its world to hell.

If our chronology is correct, *Lear* follows *Othello* and if my reading of these plays is correct, in *Lear* Shakespeare dramatizes the final possibility: there is no God. Shakespeare communicates this sense of cosmic emptiness by making palpable the ignorance of an imagined paganism and then by making the attempts of the characters to evade the knowledge of that ignorance analogous to the Christian discoveries of "truth." *King Lear* does not maintain anything nor do the other plays we have examined. Rather it and they imagine possible worlds, possible versions of the human condition. *Lear* makes us see feelingly what Pascal informs us of: "selon les lumières naturelles . . . Nous sommes . . . incapable de connaître ni ce qu'il [Dieu] est, ni s'il est."

For Pascal the necessary next step after this knowledge of ignorance is to decide whether God exists or not: "il faut parier." Shakespeare's art next moves back to its starting point in terms of its examination of the mystery of God's judgments. *Macbeth* reexamines the mystery of *Richard III*: the creation and destruction of a vessel of God's wrath. The intensity and complexity of that examination is far too great to permit a single intellectual resolution. The victory of grace and providence is more mysterious than ever. *Macbeth* is Shakespeare's last overtly Christian tragedy—his last overtly Christian play with the exception of *Henry VIII*. With the great Plutarchan tragedies he returns to an imagined paganism, but in *Antony and Cleopatra* the experience of meaninglessness, of nothingness, that gives *Lear* its terrifying power is remarkably replaced by the sense that if human life is lived thoroughly enough, even by human beings as ridiculous as Antony and Cleopatra—which is to say by characters as ridiculous as human beings are—then human life itself fills up the void and means itself without the aid of divine definition. But this counterstatement to *Lear* is then followed by the grimmer and deepening ironies of *Coriolanus* and *Timon of Athens*.

The late Romances combine the paganism of *Lear* with the Pelagianism of *Othello*, but they add to both a sense of a mysteriously beneficent providence that prevents the ultimate cruelty and horror of the tragic worlds. And this version of providence is so manipulated that it does not raise the questions which the providence of *Richard III*, *Hamlet*, and *Macbeth* forces upon our consciousness. In *Pericles*, *The Winter's Tale*, *The Tempest*, in *Cymbeline* above all, Shakespeare has reconstructed the semi-Pelagian world of *Théophile* and *Robert le Dyable*. The horrors of human life are not neglected by either the medieval or the Renaissance plays but they end with hymns of praise: "Disons: *Te deum laudamus*." "Laud we the Gods, / And let our crooked Smoakes climbe to their Nostrils / From our blest Altars." Does this mean that Shakespeare has to his own satisfaction solved the mystery of God's judgments, decided to take both Pascal's bet and his advice? Of course not. Shakespeare can achieve the Christian confidence of the medieval art only by paganizing it. In an overtly Christian world too many problems arise to permit such serenity.

Shakespeare, if I may proclaim the obvious, is not Luther nor Calvin nor Pascal. He did not write *The Bondage of the Will* or the *Institutes* or the *Pensées*, nor did he write their didactic artistic equivalents. His art is given form—tragic form—by the problems with which Luther, Calvin, and Pascal struggled. But unlike them he is under no necessity to come to conclusions, not, at least as an artist. As a man he may well have felt under the same necessity as Pascal for making his decisions, "*croix ou pile*," heads or tails. But his art does not insist on that necessity. *King Lear* does not preclude *The Tempest*. One need not choose between *Othello* or *The Winter's Tale*. They can coexist as possible versions of our condition. Pascal's imagined interlocutor objects to the notion that choice is necessary and says of those who have made the Christian choice, "je les blâmerai d'avoir fait, non ce choix, mais un choix; car, encore que celui qui prend croix et l'autre soient en pareille faute, ils sont tous deux en faute: le juste est de ne point parier." Pascal agrees and disagrees: "Oui; mais il faut parier."[16]

For the philosopher, the theologian, this may be the case, but it is not so for the artist:

> it struck me, what quality went to form a Man of Achievement especially in Literature & which Shakespeare possessed so enormously —I mean *Negative Capability*, that is when man is capable of being in uncertainties, Mysteries, doubts, without any irritable reaching after fact and reason.[17]

When negative capability is asked to sustain the knowledge of meaninglessness, of nothingness, however, the strain is likely to prove insupportable and the mind to take refuge in faith or distraction. Of all the distractions tragedy is the most nearly capable of confronting mystery without denying it. It can cope without evading and can take as its motto "le juste est de ne point parier." Art is above nature in that respect.

Notes

INTRODUCTION

1. Since I began working on this study, the following books which deal directly with some portion of my subject have appeared: Wilbur Sanders, *The Playwright and the Received Idea;* Eleanor Prosser, *Hamlet and Revenge;* R. H. West, *Shakespeare and the Outer Mystery;* Roger Cox, *Between Earth and Heaven;* Roy Battenhouse, *Shakespearean Tragedy;* Henry A. Kelly, *Divine Providence in the England of Shakespeare's Histories;* George C. Herndl, *The High Design;* Ivor Morris, *Shakespeare's God;* W. R. Elton, *King Lear and the Gods.*

From these in particular and from the body of Shakespearean criticism in general I have learned most of the things that this book contains, though, needless to say, I am of the opinion that I have something of my own to add. As for my primary sources, I have quoted from the original texts and I have used Elizabethan translations of the theologians whenever possible. Quotations from Shakespeare are from the First Folio, unless otherwise identified. I have modernized the Elizabethan usage of *i* and *j, u* and *v,* and the long *s.*

CHAPTER 1: *ROBERT LE DYABLE*

1. Graham A. Runnalls, "The Manuscript of the *Miracles de Nostre Dame par Personnages,*" *Romance Philology,* August 1968, pp. 15–22, and "The *Miracles de Nostre Dame par personnages:* Erasures in the MS, and the Dates of the Plays and the 'Serventois,' " *Philological Quarterly,* January 1970, pp. 19–29.

2. *Miracles de Nostre Dame par Personnages,* ed. G. Paris and U. Robert, Paris, 1876–1893, vol. 6.

3. Dorothy Penn, *The Staging of the "Miracles de Nostre Dame par personnages" of ms. Cangé,* New York, 1933.

4. The universality of Robert's evil propensities, which the play's original audience would have seen as evidence in support of the doctrine of original sin, is nicely demonstrated for the twentieth-century sensibility by an incident from the legend which had necessarily to be left out of the dramatic version. In Wynkyn de Worde's prose version (ca. 1510) the infant Robert "had longe teeth wherwith he bote the norshes pappes in such wyse, that there was no woman durste gyve gim souke, for he bote off the hedes of theyr brestes." This bizarre detail, according to psychoanalytical studies of infancy, is in fact

the statement of a universal destructive impulse: "In his destructive phantasies, he [i.e., every infant] bites and tears up the breast, devours it, annihilates it" Melanie Klein, *Developments in Psychoanalysis*, ed. J. Rivière, London, 1952.

Robert the Devil and Richard the Third are literally born with teeth. Most of the rest of us are not, but in infancy at least we wish we were and if we were, we would know what to do with them.

5. Henri Bergson, *Le Rire*, Paris, 1900, p. 35.

6. A. Vacant, E. Mangenot, etc., *Dictionnaire de Théologie Catholique*, Paris, 1899–1950, vol. 6², col. 1558. Hereafter cited as *D.T.C.*

7. *Ibid.* "la grâce . . . est *externe* ou *interne*. *Externe* est tout don surnaturel qui est en lui-même et reste extrinsèque à l'homme. . . . La grace *interne* est tout don surnaturel qui se trouve dans le sujet qui le reçoit."

8. *Ibid.*, cols. 1574–1575. "Ces décisions (of the Council of Carthage, 418) proclament donc la necessite absolue de la grâce interne (considérée en général), pour obtenir la justification et pour ne pas la perdre par le péché."

9. Saint Augustine, *Grace and Free Will*, tr. R. P. Russell, Washington, D.C., 1968, chap. 9.

10. Ibid., chap. 5.

11. *D.T.C.*, 14², cols. 1849–1850.

CHAPTER 2: *THE CONFLICT OF CONSCIENCE*

1. Rutebeuf, *Le Miracle de Théophile*, ed. G. Frank, Paris, 1925.

2. Meyer Schapiro points out that "the church satisfies through this legend the popular demands, so crucial to the protestants of the twelfth and later centuries, for an individual, unmediated relation to God and for an inexpensive piety. But it encloses them within the physical framework of the organized orthodox religion." See Meyer Schapiro, "The Sculptures of Souillac," in *Medieval Studies in Honor of A. K. Porter*, ed. W. R. W. Koehler, New York, 1939, vol. 2, p. 379.

3. Saint Thomas Aquinas, *The "Summa Theologica,"* tr. Fathers of the English Dominican Province, New York, 1917–1927, 2.2.q.14, pp. 173–174.

4. Ibid., p. 180.

5. Ibid., pp. 180–181.

6. John Calvin, *The Institution of Christian Religion*, tr. T. Norton, London, 1582, 3.3.22. Hereafter cited as Calvin, *Institutes*.

7. Nathaniel Woodes, *The Conflict of Conscience*, ed. H. Davis and F. P. Wilson, Oxford, 1952.

8. For a discussion of the Spira story and its possible relationship to *Dr. Faustus*, see Lily B. Campbell, "*Dr. Faustus:* A Case of Conscience," *PMLA* 67 (1952): 219–239.

9. Matteo Gribaldi, *A notable and marveilous epistle* . . ., tr. E. Aglionby, London [1570].

10. Martin Luther, *The Bondage of the Will*, tr. J. I. Packer and O. R. Johnston, London, 1957, p. 319.

11. *D.T.C.*, vol. 4^2, col. 2241.

12. *D.T.C.*, vol. 12^2, col. 2996.

13. Calvin, *Institutes*, 3.23.7.

14. John Calvin, "Articles concerning Predestination" in *Calvin: Theological Treatises*, tr. and ed. J. K. S. Reid, Philadelphia, 1954, p. 179.

15. Luther, p. 317.

16. Calvin, *Institutes*, 1.18.4.

17. Here and in my other references to the Articles of Religion I have used the version printed in E. J. Bicknell, *A Theological Introduction to the Thirty-Nine Articles of The Church of England*, 3rd ed., rev. H. J. Carpenter, London, 1955. Hereafter cited as *Articles of Religion*.

CHAPTER 3: *DR. FAUSTUS*

1. *Articles of Religion*, X.

2. Ibid., XI.

3. "Of the salvation of all mankinde," *Certaine Sermons or Homilies*, London, 1623 (Facsimile, ed. M. E. Rickey and T. B. Stroup, Gainesville, Fla., 1968), pp. 13, 14, 20. Hereafter cited as *Homilies*.

4. *Articles of Religion*, XVII.

5. S. L. Ollard, G. Crosse, and M. F. Bond, *A Dictionary of English Church History*, London, 1948, p. 82.

6. H. C. Porter, *Reformation and Reaction in Tudor Cambridge*, Cambridge, 1958, p. 373.

7. Christopher Marlowe, *Doctor Faustus, 1604–1616*, parallel texts edited by W. W. Greg, Oxford, 1950. For my purposes the use of both the A and B texts is essential. I will indicate which I am referring to at the end of each specific quotation.

8. A. Ward cited by J. D. Jump in the Revels edition of *Dr. Faustus*, London, 1962, p. 5.

9. Unless otherwise indicated, biblical citations in this chapter and in those on Shakespeare will be to *The Geneva Bible, A facsimile of the 1560 edition*, ed. L. Berry, Madison, Wis., 1969.

10. Saint Augustine, *Admonition and Grace*, tr. J. C. Murray, New York, 1947, chap. 14.

11. Calvin, *Institutes*, 3.24.15.

12. William Perkins, *A Golden Chaine*, London, 1591, U_3 verso, V_1 verso.

13. Blaise Pascal, *Oeuvres Complètes*, ed. H. Gouhier and L. Lafuma, Paris, 1963, p. 348.

14. Perkins, V_2 verso.

15. *The English Faust-Book of 1592*, ed. H. Logeman, Ghent, Belgium, 1900, p. 37.

16. Ibid., p. 22.

17. Calvin, *Institutes*, 1.18.2.

18. William Perkins, "A Treatise Tending Unto a Declaration, Whether a Man Be in the Estate of Damnation, or in the Estate of Grace . . .," in *Workes*, London, 1612, p. 415.

19. Calvin, *Institutes*, 3.23.8.

CHAPTER 4: *RICHARD III*

1. Northrop Frye, "New Directions from Old," in *Myth and Myth Making*, ed. H. Murray, Boston, 1968, p. 117.

2. Richard Hooker, *Works*, ed. Keble, rev. Church and Paget, Oxford, 1888, vol. 2, p. 563.

3. $F_1 =$ hop'st.

4. "The Catechism" in *Liturgies and Occasional Forms of Prayer Set Forth in the Reign of Queen Elizabeth*, ed. W. K. Clay, Cambridge, 1897, p. 212.

5. See Fredson Bowers, "Hamlet as Minister and Scourge," *PMLA*, 1955, pp. 740–749.

6. See above pp. 32–33.

7. Ibid.

8. See Harry Levin, "The Heights and the Depths: A Scene from *King Lear*," in *More Talking of Shakespeare*, ed. J. Garrett, London, 1959.

9. J. P. Brockbank, "The Frame of Disorder—*Henry VI*," in *Early Shakespeare* (Stratford-upon-Avon Studies #3), London, 1961, pp. 97–98.

10. Andrew S. Cairncross, ed., *The Arden Shakespeare: Henry VI, Part III*, London, 1964, p. 78.

11. Ibid., p. 138.

12. *D.T.C.* vol. 13^1, col. 965.

13. "An Homilie against disobedience and wilfull rebellion," *Homilies*, pp. 278ff.

14. Calvin, *Institutes*, 1.18.4. The quotation from Augustine is from *Grace and Free Will*, chap. 20.

CHAPTER 5: *HAMLET*

1. All quotations are from the Folio except as noted. I have attempted to call the reader's attention to all substantive variants in Q_2.

2. Eleanor Prosser, *Hamlet and Revenge*, Stanford, Calif., 1971, pp. 118ff.

3. Calvin, *Institutes*, 1.18.2.

4. Roy Battenhouse, *Shakespearean Tragedy*, Bloomington, Ind., 1969, pp. 378–379.

5. Saint Augustine, *Against Two Letters of the Pelagians*, in *Works*, vol. 12, ed. M. Dods, Edinburgh, 1871–1934; 2.22.

6. Saint Augustine, *On the Spirit and the Letter*, tr. P. Holmes, in *Basic Writings of St. Augustine*, ed. W. J. Oates, New York, 1948; chap. 60.

7. Calvin, *Institutes*, 3.2.11.

8. Ibid. 2.5.5.

9. F_1: Court = Count. This passage is not in Q_2.

10. brother = Q_2; F_1 = Mother.

11. Folio omits owne.

12. This passage is not in F_1.

13. defeat = Q_2; F_1 = debate. Q_2 omits line 61.

14. Q_2 omits this passage.

15. . . . , since no man of ought he leaves, knowes what ist to leave betimes, let be = Q_2; F_1 = . . . , since no man ha's ought of what he leaves. What is't to leave betimes?

16. Richard Hooker, p. 584.

17. Calvin, *Institutes*, 3.23.7.

CHAPTER 6: *OTHELLO*

1. See above p. 93.

2. "An Homilie for Rogation weeke," *Homilies*, p. 221.

3. Ibid.

4. William Baldwin, etc., *The Mirror for Magistrates*, ed. Lily B. Campbell, Cambridge, 1938, p. 346. This passage is from the prose bridge at the end of Sackville's "Henry, Duke of Buckingham."

5. reprobation = Q_1; F = Reprobance.

6. ballance = Q_1; F = braine.

7. Roy Battenhouse, *Shakespearean Tragedy*, Bloomington, 1969, pp. 380ff and W. R. Elton, *King Lear and the Gods*, San Marino, Calif., 1966, p. 137.

8. Freud was highly conscious of the resemblance of his theory of the two basic instinctual drives to the thought of Empedocles: "the theory of Empedocles which especially deserves our interest is one which approximates so closely to the psychoanalytic theory of the instincts that we should be tempted to maintain that the two are identical, if it were not for the difference that the Greek philosopher's theory is a cosmic phantasy while ours is content to claim biological validity." *Analysis Terminable and Interminable* in *The Complete Psychological Works of Sigmund Freud*, ed. J. Strachey, London, 1964, vol. 23, p. 245.

9. Norman Holland, *Psychoanalysis and Shakespeare*, New York, 1966, pp. 249–250.

10. Q_1 = "Does beare all excellency"—an easier reading, but not a better

one. The "Ingeniuer" is the artist who is exhausted by his attempt to capture the beauty of Desdemona with his blazoning pen.

11. M. R. Riley, ed., *The Arden Shakespeare: Othello*, London, 1959, p. 51.

12. Edgar Wind, *Pagan Mysteries in the Renaissance*, New York, 1968, pp. 85ff.

13. Titus Lucretius Carus, *On the Nature of Things*, tr. T. Jackson, Oxford, 1929, p. 2.

14. Wind, p. 89.

15. Ernst Cassirer, *The Platonic Renaissance in England*, tr. J. P. Pettegrove, London, 1953, pp. 95–96.

16. Pico della Mirandola, *On the Dignity of Man*, tr. Charles Glenn Wallace, New York, 1940, p. 5.

17. Wind, *loc. cit.*

18. Randle Cotgrave, *A Dictionarie of the French and English Tongues*, reproduced from the first edition, London, 1611, Columbia, S.C., 1950.

19. "An Homilie of Prayer," *Homilies*, p. 115.

20. Psalms 36:9. Bishop's Bible version. The verbal parallel with Jeremiah 2:13, as cited in the *Homilies*, is considerably more striking in the King James Version, where "pits" is translated "cisterns."

21. F. R. Leavis, *The Common Pursuit*, New York, 1952, pp. 136–159.

22. Northrop Frye, *Anatomy of Criticism*, Princeton, N.J., 1957, pp. 33–34.

23. Michel de Montaigne, *The Essayes*, tr. John Florio, London, 1891, p. 225.

CHAPTER 7: *MACBETH*

1. See R. H. West, *The Invisible World*, Athens, Ga., 1939, p. 29.

2. Kenneth Muir, ed., *The Arden Shakespeare: Macbeth*, p. xvii.

3. W. C. Curry, *Shakespeare's Philosophical Patterns*, Baton Rouge, La., 1937, p. 48.

CHAPTER 8: CONCLUSION—*KING LEAR*

1. Coyning = Q; F = crying.

2. This is Schmidt's reading as cited by Muir in the Arden edition, London, 1952, p. 163.

3. *King Lear*, ed. G. I. Duthie and J. D. Wilson, Cambridge, England, 1962, p. 246.

4. See Erich Auerbach, *Literary Language and Its Public in Late Latin Antiquity and in the Middle Ages*, New York, 1965, pp. 75, 77.

5. See John R. Roberts, *A Critical Anthology of English Recusant Devotional Prose*, Louvain, Belgium, 1966.

6. "Of the Passion for good Friday," *Homilies*, p. 184.

7. Lancelot Andrewes, *Ninety-six Sermons*, London, 1629, pp. 333ff.

8. Ibid., p. 342.

9. Ibid., p. 335.

10. Justicers = Q; F = Justices.

11. R. W. Chambers, 'King Lear,' *W. P. Ker Memorial Lecture*, Glasgow, 1940, p. 49.

12. J. Stampfer, "The Catharsis of *King Lear*," *Shakespeare Survey 13* (1960): 10.

13. A. W. Schlegel, *Lectures on Dramatic Art*, tr. J. Black, London, 1815. Cited in *King Lear, A New Variorum Edition*, ed. H. H. Furness, Philadelphia, 1880, p. 449.

14. Blaise Pascal, p. 550.

15. Ibid.

16. Ibid.

17. John Keats, *Letters*, ed. H. E. Rollins, Cambridge, Mass., 1958, vol. I, p. 193.

Index

INDEX

Donne, John, 65

Election, 18, 31–34, 39: Anglican Church on, 41–42; Augustine on, 47; Calvin on, 32, 47, 125; in *Dr. Faustus*, 63; in *Hamlet*, 114, 116, 117–18, 121, 125, 157, 194; in *Macbeth*, 165; William Perkins on, 47; Protestantism on, 31; semi-Pelagian view of, 31
Elton, William, 132
Erasmus, 30
Eros, Othello's bondage to, 143
Evil, supernatural, in *Macbeth*, 181–82

Faith, Luther on, 40–41
Fatalism, in *Hamlet*, 124–25
Faust Book, 57
Forman, Simon, 171
Fortune, 69, 72
Free Will *see* Will, Free
Frye, Northrop, 67, 156

Ghosts, function of, 104–7, 171–72, 174
God: Augustine on, 112; Calvinistic conception of, 43–44, 112; in *Dr. Faustus*, 64–66; in *Hamlet*, 105, 111, 124, 125–26; man's rejection of, 20; in *Othello*, 127; in Richard III plays, 69, 71–72, 73–75, 79, 80, 81, 162
  See also justice, divine; providence, divine; vengeance, divine; will, divine; and wrath, divine
Good and evil: semi-Pelagian view of, 133; Augustine on, 18, 33, 110, 140; in *Conflict of Conscience*, 30, 35–37; and contrition, 39; in *Dr. Faustus*, 52, 62–63, 193; in *Hamlet*, 110–11, 116, 128, 158; and human love, 128; in *King Lear*, 158, 190; Luther on, 30–31, 80; in *Macbeth*, 163–64, 173–76, 181–82; as manifested in Desdemona, 127, 130–31, 136; in *Othello*, 127, 128, 130–31, 136, 149, 150–51, 156, 158;
  prevenient: Augustine on, 110, 140; in *Conflict of Conscience*, 30;

in *Dr. Faustus*, 52, 193; and free will, 16–17, 39; in medieval drama, 193; in *Othello*, 130–31; in *Théophile*, 30; in *Robert le Dyable*, 9, 11–12, 13;
  psychology of, 18–19; sacramental, 12; in Richard III plays, 98–99, 128; in *Robert le Dyable*, 9, 11–12, 13; in *Romeo and Juliet*, 101; in *Théophile*, 23, 30; varieties of, 12, 15–17, 18
Greg, W. W., 59
Gribaldi, Matteo, 26
Guilt: of Claudius, 126; of Hamlet, 119–21, 121–23; in *Macbeth*, 165; and responsibility, 121; of Rosencrantz and Guildenstern, 121–23

Hatred, 134–35, 144
History, artists' use of, 67–68
Holy Ghost: sin against the, 23–26; Aquinas on, 23–25, 30; Calvin on, 25; Christ on, 23; Faustus, 50–51; Philologus', 29
Hooker, Richard, 65, 74
Hubris, in *Hamlet*, 113
Humanism, of *Othello*, 147
Humor, black, in *Robert le Dyable*, 13

Icarus emblem, 44–45, 83–84, 86
Ignatius of Loyola, Saint, 184
Imagination, embodied by Macbeth, 177
Insanity: of Hamlet, 119–20; of Macbeth, 168, 170–71

Justice: divine, 17; Calvin on, 32, 33; in *Dr. Faustus*, 194; in *Hamlet*, 106, 112, 113–14, 115–16; in *Lear*, 186, 188–90, 191; Luther on, 32–33; in *Richard II*, 101–2; in Richard III plays, 70, 77–79, 80–81
Justification by faith, Luther on, 40–41

Knowledge, 65–66, 70, 190–91

Lambeth Articles, 41–42, 43

INDEX